Second Clement

Second Clement

An Introductory Commentary

WILLIAM VARNER

FOREWORD BY
JAMES A. KELHOFFER

Apostolic Fathers Commentary Series

PAUL A. HARTOG AND SHAWN J. WILHITE
Series Editors

CASCADE *Books* · Eugene, Oregon

SECOND CLEMENT
An Introductory Commentary

Apostolic Fathers Commentary Series

Copyright © 2020 William Varner. All rights reserved. Except for brief quotations in critical publications or reviews, no part of this book may be reproduced in any manner without prior written permission from the publisher. Write: Permissions, Wipf and Stock Publishers, 199 W. 8th Ave., Suite 3, Eugene, OR 97401.

Cascade Books
An Imprint of Wipf and Stock Publishers
199 W. 8th Ave., Suite 3
Eugene, OR 97401

www.wipfandstock.com

PAPERBACK ISBN: 978-1-5326-6146-4
HARDCOVER ISBN: 978-1-5326-6147-1
EBOOK ISBN: 978-1-5326-6148-8

Cataloguing-in-Publication data:

Names: Varner, William C. (William Clayton), 1947–, author. | Kelhoffer, James A., foreword.

Title: Second Clement : an introductory commentary / by William Varner ; foreword by James A. Kelhoffer.

Description: Eugene, OR: Cascade Books, 2020. | Apostolic Fathers Commentary Series. | Includes bibliographical references and index.

Identifiers: ISBN 978-1-5326-6146-4 (paperback). | ISBN 978-1-5326-6147-1 (hardcover). | ISBN 978-1-5326-6148-8 (ebook).

Subjects: LCSH: Second epistle of Clement to the Corinthians. | Christian literature, Early—Greek authors.

Classification: BR65 V37 2020 (print). | BR65 (ebook).

Unless otherwise noted, canonical scriptures cited in this translation and commentary are the author's translations.

Scripture quotations marked (ESV) are taken from the ESV® Bible (The Holy Bible, English Standard Version®), copyright © 2001 by Crossway, a publishing ministry of Good News Publishers. Used by permission. All rights reserved.

Scripture quotations marked (NIV) are taken from the Holy Bible, NEW INTERNATIONAL VERSION®, NIV® Copyright © 1973, 1978, 1984, 2011 by Biblica, Inc.® Used by permission. All rights reserved worldwide.

Quotations marked (NETS) are taken from *A New English Translation of the Septuagint*,© 2007 by the International Organization for Septuagint and Cognate Studies, Inc. Used by permission of Oxford University Press. All rights reserved.

Manufactured in the U.S.A.   09/03/20

To
Daniel B. Wallace,
who appreciates tradition

Contents

Series Foreword | ix
Foreword | James A. Kelhoffer | xv
Preface | xvii
Abbreviations | xix
Translation of 2 Clement | xxiv

Part I: Introductory Articles

1. Introduction to 2 Clement | 3
2. Reception and Use of Sacred Tradition in 2 Clement | 29
3. Theology of 2 Clement | 36

Part II: Commentary

Theological Section (2 Clem. 1.1—2.7) | 49
Ethical Section (2 Clem. 3.1—14.5) | 61
Eschatological Section (2 Clem. 15.1—20.5) | 122
Conclusion | 142

Bibliography | 155
Author Index | 163

Series Foreword

Introduction to the Apostolic Fathers
Commentary Series

Who Are the Apostolic Fathers?

THE LABEL "APOSTOLIC FATHERS" reflects a narrow collection of early Christian texts that generally date from the first and second centuries CE.[1] The works of the Apostolic Fathers offer a remarkable window into early (especially second-century) Christianity, as communities forged their religious and social identities within the broader Graeco-Roman culture.[2] As these early authors defined themselves and their readers in relationship to pagan culture, Jewish religiosity, and internal rivals, they ultimately influenced Christian movements for generations to come. Each book within the collection sheds unique light on the diversity of theology, worship, and life within nascent Christian communities.

The collection of Apostolic Fathers is an "artificial corpus" and a "modern construct."[3] Authors in antiquity did not use the label to describe such a collection.[4] Some of the Apostolic Fathers appear in the fourth-century Codex Sinaiticus (Barnabas and Hermas) and the fifth-century Codex Alexandrinus (1 Clement and 2 Clement).[5] Some were read in public worship,

---

1. Jefford, *Reading the Apostolic Fathers*, xvii. Some scholars have dated the Letter to Diognetus or the Martyrdom of Polycarp into the third century. See Moss, "On the Dating of Polycarp."

2. Jefford, *Apostolic Fathers*.

3. Foster, Preface to *Writings of the Apostolic Fathers*, vii.

4. According to Robert Grant, the term "Apostolic Fathers" was employed by the Monophysite Severus of Antioch in the sixth century, but not of a collection of writings as now recognized. See Grant, "Apostolic Fathers' First Thousand Years," 421, 428.

5. Batovici, "Apostolic Fathers in Codex Sinaiticus and Codex Alexandrinus."

were cited as "scripture," or were mentioned in the context of early canonical discussions.⁶ Codex Hierosolymitanus (1056 CE), which was discovered in 1873, contains the Didache, Barnabas, 1 Clement, 2 Clement, and a long recension of the Ignatian epistles.

Jean-Baptiste Cotelier produced the first printed edition of a collection akin to the Apostolic Fathers in 1672.⁷ Cotelier's Latin collection was titled *SS. patrum qui temporibus apostolicis floruerunt; Barnabae, Clementis, Hermae, Ignatii, Polycarpi*.⁸ Inclusion within the collection was thus associated with an assumed historical connection to the times of the apostles (*temporibus apostolicis*). Within the text of his work, Cotelier spoke of an *Apostolicorum Patrum Collectio*.⁹ In 1693, William Wake put forth an English edition of the Apostolic Fathers: *The Genuine Epistles of the Apostolical Fathers: S. Barnabas, S. Ignatius, S. Clement, S. Polycarp, the Shepherd of Hermas, and the Martyrdoms of St. Ignatius and St. Polycarp*.¹⁰ In 1699, Thomas Ittig abbreviated Cotelier's Latin title to *Bibliotheca patrum apostolicorum Graeco-Latina*.¹¹ Early commentators continued to insist that at least some of the apostolic fathers had contact with the original apostles.¹²

Andreas Gallandi added the Letter to Diognetus, extant material from the Apology of Quadratus, and the Papias fragments to the corpus of the Apostolic Fathers in 1765.¹³ The Didache, since its rediscovery in the nineteenth century, has regularly accompanied the collection as well.¹⁴ The scholarly work of J. B. Lightfoot, Theodore Zahn, and others elevated the "middle recension" of Ignatius's epistles as the preferred form of the Ignatian correspondence.¹⁵

In the Anglophone world, the "most readily available" and "widely used" editions of the Apostolic Fathers are Bart Ehrman's entry in the Loeb

---

6. See Bingham, "Senses of Scripture in the Second Century"; Steenberg, "Irenaeus on Scripture, *Graphe*, and the Status of *Hermas*."

7. Lincicum, "Paratextual Invention of the Term 'Apostolic Fathers.'"

8. Cotelier, *Patrum qui temporibus apostolicis floruerunt*.

9. For this and related history, see Fischer, *Die ältesten Ausgaben der Patres Apostolici*.

10. Wake, *Genuine Epistles of the Apostolical Fathers*.

11. Rothschild, "On the Invention of *Patres Apostolici*," 9. See Ittig, *Bibliotheca Patrum Apostolicorum Graeco-Latina*.

12. Jefford, *Reading the Apostolic Fathers*, xvii.

13. Gallandi, *Bibliotheca veterum partum antiquorumque scriptorium ecclesiasticorum* (1765).

14. Jefford, *Reading the Apostolic Fathers*, xix.

15. Lightfoot, *Apostolic Fathers*, I.1 and I.2; Zahn, *Ignatius von Antiochien*. For a history of this debate, see Hartog, "Multifaceted Jewel."

Classical Library (2003) and Michael Holmes's thorough revision of Lightfoot and Harmer's work, now in its third edition (2007).[16] Both Ehrman and Holmes include the Didache, 1 Clement, the fragment of Quadratus, the seven letters of the middle recension of the Ignatian correspondence, Polycarp's *Epistle to the Philippians*, the fragments of Papias, the Epistle of Barnabas, 2 Clement, the Shepherd of Hermas, the Martyrdom of Polycarp, and the Epistle to Diognetus. This list of eleven has attained somewhat of a quasi-canonical status within Apostolic Fathers studies, though a few works float in and out of the boundaries of investigations within the field.[17] Although early modern scholars tended to insist upon the direct contact of the apostolic fathers with the apostles, contemporary scholars recognize the phenomenon of pseudepigraphal attribution within the corpus, and they acknowledge a diverse notion of "apostolicity" within the primary source texts themselves.[18]

Why Are the Apostolic Fathers Important?

The works of the Apostolic Fathers represent a spectrum of literary genres, including a church manual (Didache), occasional letters (1 Clement, the Ignatian correspondence, Polycarp's *Epistle to the Philippians*), a theological tractate in epistolary form (Barnabas), apocalyptic and visionary materials (Hermas), a martyr narrative in epistolary form (Martyrdom of Polycarp), a homily (2 Clement), an apology with appended homiletic material (Diognetus), and fragments of both expositional and apologetic works (Papias and Quadratus).[19] The Apostolic Fathers also represent a wide range of geographical provenance and intended audience, pointing interpreters to early Christian communities in locations scattered throughout the Roman Empire, such as Corinth, Philippi, Rome, Asia Minor, Egypt, and Syria.[20]

The Apostolic Fathers reflect variegated facets of early church life and organization, theological and liturgical development, spirituality and prayer, moral instruction and identity formation.[21] The Apostolic Fathers

---

16. Jefford, *Reading the Apostolic Fathers*, xiii. See Ehrman, ed., *Apostolic Fathers*; and Holmes, *Apostolic Fathers*.

17. See Pratscher, "Corpus of the Apostolic Fathers."

18. Khomych, "Diversity of the Notion of Apostolicity in the Apostolic Fathers."

19. Tugwell, *Apostolic Fathers* (2002); Jefford, *Reading the Apostolic Fathers*.

20. See Trevett, *Christian Women and the Time of the Apostolic Fathers*.

21. Koester, "Apostolic Fathers and the Struggle for Christian Identity"; Kenneth Berding, "'Gifts' and Ministries in the Apostolic Fathers"; Jefford, "Prophecy and Prophetism in the Apostolic Fathers"; Borchardt, "Spirituality of the Apostolic Fathers."

are important witnesses to the transmission and consolidation of earlier traditions, including the reception of the scriptures (both the Hebrew Scriptures and works now found in the New Testament).[22] A number of the apostolic fathers draw from Jesus traditions and especially the Pauline letters.[23] For example, Papias hands on traditions concerning the origins of the Gospels, and Polycarp seemingly provides evidence of the reception of 1 Timothy, 1 Peter, and 1 John.[24] The Apostolic Fathers provide insights into biblical interpretation, as well as valuable assistance with linguistic and philological investigations.[25]

The Apostolic Fathers do not delve deeply into philosophical theology but rather address specific pastoral concerns in particular contexts.[26] They reflect a diversity of theological perspectives and emphases, although sharing a common yet malleable core kerygma. The works assume the role of the one God as Creator and Ruler, and they proclaim Jesus Christ as the crucified, risen, and exalted Lord.[27] Relatively fewer texts discuss the Holy Spirit's continuing work in the *ekklesia*, while some warn of the continuing threats of satanic opposition.[28] The Apostolic Fathers underscore future resurrection and judgment. They center salvation in the person and work of Christ, although differing in their explanations of grace and human response.[29]

The Apostolic Fathers serve as a window into theological trajectories and themes that emerged in early Christianity. Specific developments include the incorporation of the "Two Ways" literary tradition (Didache, Barnabas), apostolic succession (1 Clement), the Eucharist as sacrifice and medicine (Didache, Ignatius), a threefold ministry resembling monoepiscopacy

---

22. Pratscher, "Die Rezeption des Neuen Testament bei den Apostolischen Vätern"; Jefford, *Apostolic Fathers and the New Testament* (Peabody, MA: Hendrickson, 2006); Gregory and Tuckett, eds., *Reception of the New Testament in the Apostolic Fathers*; Norris, "Apostolic and Sub-Apostolic Writings"; Oxford Society of Historical Theology, *The New Testament in the Apostolic Fathers*.

23. Young, *Jesus Tradition in the Apostolic Fathers*; Lindemann, "Apostolic Fathers and the Synoptic Problem"; Still and Wilhite, eds., *Apostolic Fathers and Paul*.

24. Lookadoo, "Polycarp, Paul, and the Letters to Timothy"; Hartog, "Opponents in Polycarp, *Philippians*, and 1 John."

25. Trigg, "The Apostolic Fathers and Apologists." A valuable linguistic tool is Wallace et al., eds., *Reader's Lexicon of the Apostolic Fathers*.

26. Lawson, *Theological and Historical Introduction to the Apostolic Fathers*.

27. Stark, *Christology in the Apostolic Fathers*; McGuckin, "Christ: The Apostolic Fathers to the Third Century."

28. Marshall, "Holy Spirit in the Apostolic Fathers"; Burke, "Satan and Demons in the Apostolic Fathers"; Farrar, "Satanology and Demonology in the Apostolic Fathers."

29. Bounds, "Understanding of Grace in Selected Apostolic Fathers"; Whitenton, "After ΠΙΣΤΙΣ ΧΡΙΣΤΟΥ"; Bounds, "Doctrine of Christian Perfection in the Apostolic Fathers." See also the influential but now dated work by Thomas F. Torrance, *The Doctrine of Grace in the Apostolic Fathers*.

(Ignatius), emphatic Sunday observance (Didache, Ignatius, Barnabas), baptism as a seal (2 Clement), stipulations concerning postbaptismal sin and repentance (Hermas), the metaphor of the church as the "soul" within the world (Diognetus), references to the "catholic church" (Ignatius, Martyrdom of Polycarp), and an incipient veneration of martyrs (Martyrdom of Polycarp). The apostolic fathers confronted so-called docetic and judaizing opponents (Ignatius, Polycarp), as well as pagan critics (Quadratus, Diognetus). The Apostolic Fathers illuminate differing courses of the "parting of the ways" between Judaism and Christianity.[30]

What Is the Apostolic Fathers Commentary Series?

The Apostolic Fathers Commentary Series (AFCS) proposes to offer a literary and theological reading of individual works among the Apostolic Fathers corpus. Although the compositional development and textual history of some of the texts are quite complex, the series offers a literary and theological reading of the final form text in an intelligible fashion for a broad audience.

Each volume in the series will offer a similar, two-part structure. Part 1 will include introductory essays, and part 2 will consist of exegetical, theological, and historical commentary on the final-form text in a section-by-section format. In the first part, each volume will include an essay on preliminary matters, such as historical placement, provenance, and social setting; an essay on the use of scripture; and an essay on themes and theology. All volumes will offer a fresh and readable translation of the text, along with brief textual notes.

The AFCS is designed to engage historical-critical scholarship and to synthesize such material for a wide range of readers. The series will make use of international scholarship, ancient languages (with English cotranslations), and primary research, aiming to elucidate the literary form of the text for students and scholars of earliest Christianity. The exegesis of AFCS will engage grammatical, rhetorical, and discourse features within the given work. In particular, the series will expansively discuss the elements relevant to theological interpretation of the texts. The AFCS thus seeks to fill a niche by offering a theological and literary reading of the Apostolic Fathers in both an economical and accessible form for a wide readership.

Paul A. Hartog
Shawn J. Wilhite
AFCS Series Editors

---

30. Robinson, *Ignatius of Antioch and the Parting of the Ways*; Lanfranchi, "Attitudes to the Sabbath."

Foreword

THE ANONYMOUS WRITING WHICH came to be called the Second Letter of Clement may be that work of the Apostolic Fathers which you read decades ago in seminary or graduate school but subsequently forgot. The writing's relative neglect in both earlier and recent scholarship is regrettable for several reasons. For one thing, 2 Clement may be the earliest work that cites and interprets sayings of Jesus that stem, either directly or indirectly, from the Gospels of Matthew and Luke. Additionally, its sometimes surprising interpretations and extensions of those sayings illustrate the creativity that often underlay early Christian biblical interpretation. Second Clement also contains several unusual sayings of Jesus, such as the quasi-androgynous prediction that, prior to the kingdom's arrival, the "two" must become "one" and there will be "neither male nor female" (2 Clem. 12.2).

In addition to the import of the work's sources, its message is significant since it represents a distinctive—and, in several respects, a unique—voice among the second-century Jesus movements which were competing for influence. One example of that distinctive message is the explanation of the first "person" (ἄνθρωπος) in Gen 1:27: the male is identified as Christ, rather than Adam, and the female is not Eve but the preexistent "church" (ἐκκλησία, 2 Clem. 14.2). Another noteworthy contention is that believers, by virtue of having received God's grace, are obligated to render "repayment" (ἀντιμισθία, 2 Clem. 1.3, 5; 9.7; 15.2) to God in order to receive a "repayment" from God (11.6) and, ultimately, to withstand the final judgment and be saved. If we interpret a need for "repayment" in the light of the reciprocal giving and receiving which characterized ancient patron-client relationships, the obligation signaled by ἀντιμισθία would be an integral means of both fostering and preserving believers' relationship with God (or Christ), their divine patron.

As historians and theologians, we make the most of the oftentimes anecdotal sources which happened to survive, pondering the light they could shed on the early church and its development. Given that 2 Clement cites several enigmatic sources, and that the work advocates for some possibly controversial theological positions, it is somewhat surprising that it is preserved in not one but three manuscripts. One reason for its preservation could be that it appears directly after 1 Clement in an early manuscript, Codex Alexandrinus (ca. 450–500 CE): although the two Clementine writings clearly stem from different authors (and, as many argue, address different communities), the notion that 2 Clement was somehow connected to a subapostolic leader (i.e., Clement of Rome) may have enhanced the work's stature and secured its preservation. Additionally, the placement of 1 and 2 Clement in Codex Alexandrinus directly after the twenty-seven New Testament writings could have attributed to the Clementine writings a canonical status, leading some Christ-believers to transmit them and, quite possibly, to use them in liturgical and catechetical contexts.

Those who have devoted themselves to the study of 2 Clement belong to a modest, albeit by no means an exclusive, club and tend to engage in detail with one another's views. This volume by William Varner is only the second English-language commentary on 2 Clement to appear since the 1960s, and invites us to take a closer look at a writing that all too often has been ignored or misunderstood. The strengths of Varner's study include the lucid discussion of isagogical questions (e.g., the work's genre, sources, and theological tendencies), which makes up around one-third of the volume; a fresh new translation; the attention to semantics; and the discussions of the work's structure. The commentary will inform, intrigue, and even challenge not only its primary audience of evangelical Protestants but also those who stem from other religious and hermeneutical traditions. The volume will also spur others, myself included, to continue work on this fascinating text.

James A. Kelhoffer
Pentecost 2020
Uppsala, Sweden

Preface

I DEVELOPED AN ACADEMIC interest in the Apostolic Fathers by exposure to the Greek texts of the Didache and Polycarp's *Epistle to the Philippians* during courses that I taught on translating various Koine Greek texts. This interest eventually developed into a commentary on the Didache that was published in 2007.[1] Because of my special interest in texts that are often overlooked, my initial interest in 2 Clement was based on the fact that far more attention has been given to its larger "sister," 1 Clement, in the scholarly literature. A significant amount of secondary literature has developed on many of the other individual works that are styled "Apostolic Fathers," especially the Didache and 1 Clement. This is not the situation with 2 Clement. This commentary addresses this lack of attention and hopefully provides an introduction to 2 Clement that will help rescue it from its shadows of neglect. I have sought to interact with everything to my knowledge that has been written in English on 2 Clement, and I have consulted a representative selection of secondary literature written in German.

I would like to thank those classes that worked through the Greek text of 2 Clement with me in the last few years. My thanks are also to The Master's University for a sabbatical in the spring of 2019, when most of the writing of this commentary took place. Further gratitude is offered to the staff of the library for offering a quiet place to research and write and for providing the resources to finish such a project. Students Jeremiah Seidman and Brent Niedergall also provided valuable proofreading of the manuscript. I have cited the magisterial commentary on 2 Clement by Christopher Tuckett more than any other work, and he has been a fruitful dialogue-partner on every chapter, even when we disagreed! Finally, Professor James A. Kelhoffer took time from his own research on 2 Clement to share with me his articles on the book. He has greatly influenced my approach while writing this commentary.

1. Varner, *Way of the Didache*.

I come from an ecclesial tradition that has not always shown a deep interest in early Christian literature beyond those works that came to be included in the New Testament. I offer my thanks to the editors of this series of commentaries for seeing the importance of such literature and for their patience and diligence in walking me through the editing process. I extend my special thanks to Professor Daniel Wallace also, whose interest in preserving the written texts of the New Testament and Christian literature has always provided me with encouragement likewise to study and to preserve this great literary heritage of early Christianity. My wife, Helen, has supported my interest in the Didache and 2 Clement with patience beyond what I could expect.

William Varner
Santa Clarita, California
Pentecost, 2020

Abbreviations

Ancient Works

1 Apol.	Justin, *1 Apology*
1 Clem.	1 Clement
2 Clem.	2 Clement
A	Codex Alexandrinus
Acts Paul	Acts of Paul
Agr.	Philo, *On Agriculture*
Ant.	Josephus, *Antiquities of the Jews*
Apoc. Pet.	Apocalypse of Peter
Apos. Can.	Apostolic Canons
Apos. Con.	Apostolic Constitutions
Bibl.	Photius, *Bibliotheca*
Barn.	Barnabas
Biblio.	Photius, *Bibliotheca*
Comm. Jo.	Origen, *Commentary on John*
Dial.	Justin, *Dialogue with Trypho*
Diatr.	Epictetus, *Diatribes*
Did.	Didache
DSS	Dead Sea Scrolls
Fr.	Aristophanes, *Frogs*
Gos. Eg.	Gospel of the Egyptians
Gos. Naz.	Gospel of the Nazarenes
Gos. Pet.	Gospel of Peter

Gos. Thom.	Gospel of Thomas
H	Codex Hierosolymitanus
Haer.	Irenaeus, *Adversus haereses*
Herm. *Mand.*	Shepherd of Hermas, *Mandates*
Herm. *Sim.*	Shepherd of Hermas, *Similitudes*
Herm. *Vis.*	Shepherd of Hermas, *Visions*
Hist.	Herodotus, *Historiae*
Hist. eccl.	Eusebius, *Historia ecclesiastica*
Ign. *Eph.*	Ignatius, *To the Ephesians*
Ign. *Phld.*	Ignatius, *To the Philadelphians*
Ign. *Pol.*	Ignatius, *To Polycarp*
Ign. *Rom.*	Ignatius, *To the Romans*
Ign. *Trall.*	Ignatus, *To the Trallians*
Isth.	Pindar, *Isthmionikai*
Leg.	Philo, *On Allegorical Interpretation*
Mut.	Philo, *De mutatione nominum*
NT	New Testament
OT	Old Testament
Phaed.	Plato, *Phaedo*
Plant.	Philo, *On Planting*
Pol. *Phil.*	Polycarp, *To the Philippians*
Sir	Sirach
Sobr.	Philo, *On Sobriety*
Spec.	Philo, *On the Special Laws*
Spect.	Tertullian, *De Spectaculis*
Tob	Tobit
Vir. Ill.	Jerome, *Illustrious Men*

Modern

AB	Anchor Bible
ABD	Anchor Bible Dictionary
AF	Apostolic Fathers

AFCS	Apostolic Fathers Commentary Series
AJEC	Ancient Judaism and Early Christianity
AST	*Ashland Theological Journal*
ANRW	*Aufstieg und Niedergang der römischen Welt*
AV	Die Apostolischen Väter
BDAG	Frederick W. Danker, Walter Bauer, William F. Arndt, and F. Wilbur Gingrich. *Greek-English Lexicon of the New Testament and Other Early Christian Literature*. 3rd ed. Chicago: University of Chicago Press, 2000
BDF	Friedrich Blass, Albert Debrunner, and Robert W. Funk. *A Greek Grammar of the New Testament and Other Early Christian Literature*. Chicago: University of Chicago Press, 1961
BETL	Bibliotheca Ephemeridum Theologicarum Lovaniensium
Bib	*Biblica*
BibAC	Bible in Ancient Christianity
BSac	*Bibliotheca Sacra*
BTB	*Biblical Theology Bulletin*
BZAW	Beihefte zur Zeitschrift für die alttestamentliche Wissenschaft
BZAW	Beihefte zur Zeitschrift für die neutestamentliche Wissenschaft
CBQ	*Catholic Biblical Quarterly*
CH	*Church History*
ConBNT	Coniectanea Biblica: New Testament Series
EC	*Early Christianity*
ECHC	Early Christianity in Its Hellenistic Context
ECL	Early Christianity and Its Literature
ECS	Early Christian Studies
ExpTim	*Expository Times*
GE	Franco Montanari, *The Brill Dictionary of Ancient Greek*. English ed. Edited by Madeleine Goh and Chad Schroeder. Leiden: Brill, 2015
HNT	Handbuch zum Neuen Testament
HTR	*Harvard Theological Review*

JBL	*Journal of Biblical Literature*
JECS	*Journal of Early Christian Studies*
JR	*Journal of Religion*
JTS	*Journal of Theological Studies*
KAV	Kommentar zu den Apostolischen Väter
Lampe	G. W. H. Lampe, *A Patristic Greek Lexicon*. Oxford: Clarendon, 1961
LCL	Loeb Classical Library
LEC	Library of Early Christianity
LSJ	Henry George Liddell, Robert Scott, Henry Stuart Jones. *A Greek-English Lexicon*. 9th ed. with revised supplement. Oxford: Clarendon, 1996
Neot	*Neotestamentica: Journal of the New Testament Society of South Africa*
NETS	New English Translation of the Septuagint
NIDNTTE	Moises Silva, ed. *New International Dictionary of New Testament Theology and Exegesis*. 5 vols. Grand Rapids: Zondervan, 2014
NovT	*Novum Testamentum*
NovTSup	Novum Testamentum Supplements
NTAF	The New Testament and the Apostolic Fathers
NTS	*New Testament Studies*
OAF	Oxford Apostolic Fathers
PAST	Pauline Studies
RB	*Revue Biblique*
RJFTC	The Reception of Jesus in the First Three Centuries
SEÅ	*Svensk exegetisk årsbok*
SecCent	*The Second Century: A Journal of Early Christian Studies*
ST	*Studia Theologica*
StPatr	Studia Patristica
SU	Schriften des Urchristentums
SVTQ	*St. Vladimir's Theological Quarterly*
TDNT	*Theological Dictionary of the New Testament*. Edited by Gerhard Kittel and Gerhard Friedrich. Translated by

	Geoffrey W. Bromiley. 10 vols. Grand Rapids: Eerdmans, 1969–1976
TLZ	*Theologische Literaturzeitung*
TS	*Theological Studies*
VC	*Vigiliae Christianae*
VCSup	Vigiliae Christianae Supplements
WesTJ	*Wesleyan Theological Journal*
WTJ	*Westminster Theological Journal*
WUNT	Wissenschaftliche Untersuchungen zum Neuen Testament
ZNW	*Zeitschrift für die neutestamentliche Wissenschaft*

Translation of 2 Clement

Chapter 1

1. Brothers,[1] we must think of Jesus Christ as of God, as of "the Judge of the living and the dead." And we ought not to undervalue our salvation,

2. for when we undervalue him, we also hope to receive little. And those who listen as if it is a little matter are sinning, and we also are sinning if we do not recognize from where and by whom and to what place we were called, and what great suffering Jesus Christ endured for our sake.

3. What repayment, then, should we give to him, or what fruit should we offer that is worthy of what he has given us? And what holy deeds do we owe him?

4. For he gave us the light, as a Father he called us "sons," he saved us when we were perishing.

5. What praise, then, will we give him, or what repayment for what we received?

6. We were maimed in our understanding, worshiping stones and wooden objects and gold and silver and copper, the products of men, and our whole life was nothing else than death. We were thus covered with darkness, and our sight was filled with mist, but we have received our sight, and by his will we have cast off the cloud that covered us.

7. For he had pity on us and saved us by his mercy, even though he had seen in us great error and destruction, when we had no hope of salvation except what comes from him.

---

1. I have preferred the translation "brothers" even though ἀδελφοί generically includes "and sisters." This decision provides clarity to an authorial conscious choice in 19.1 and 20.2. There the author switches to "brothers and sisters."

8. For he called us when we did not exist, and out of nothing he willed us into existence.

Chapter 2

1. "Rejoice, O barren woman, who bears no children. Break forth and cry, you who have no labor pains, because the deserted woman has more children than the one who has a husband."[2] In saying, "Rejoice, O barren woman, who bears no children," he spoke about us, for our church was barren before children were given to her.

2. And when he said, "cry, you who have no labor pains," he means this: that we should offer our prayers sincerely to God, and not grow weary like women who are giving birth.

3. And when he said, "the deserted woman has more children than the one who has a husband," he meant that our people seemed to be deserted by God, but now we who have believed have become more than those who seem to have God.

4. And another scripture also says, "I came not to call righteous ones, but sinners."[3]

5. He means that those who are perishing must be saved,

6. for that is a great and marvelous thing, namely, to support not those things that are standing but those that are falling.

7. So Christ also desired to save the perishing, and he saved many by coming and calling us who were already perishing.

Chapter 3

1. Seeing, then, because he has shown mercy towards us—first that we who are living do not sacrifice to the dead gods and do not worship them, but through him we have come to know the Father of Truth—what is the true knowledge about him if it is not refusing to deny him through whom we have come to know him?

---

2. Isa 54:1; cf. Gal 4:27. Unless otherwise noted, canonical scriptures cited in this translation and commentary are the author's translations.

3. Matt 9:13; Mark 2:17; Luke 5:32.

2. And he himself also says, "Whoever acknowledges me before men, I will acknowledge him before my Father."[4]

3. This, therefore, is our reward, if we acknowledge him through whom we were saved.

4. But how do we acknowledge him? By doing what he says, and not disobeying his commandments, and honoring him not only with our lips, but "from all our heart and all our mind."[5]

5. And he also says in Isaiah, "This people honors me with their lips, but their heart is far away from me."[6]

Chapter 4

1. Let us, therefore, not just call him "Lord," for this will not save us.

2. For he says, "Not everyone who says to me, 'Lord, Lord,' will be saved, but only the one who does righteousness."[7]

3. So then, brothers, let us acknowledge him in our deeds by loving one another, by not committing adultery nor slandering one another nor being jealous, but by being self-controlled, compassionate, and good. And we ought to sympathize with one another, and not love money. By these actions we should acknowledge him and not by their opposites.

4. And we must not fear men but rather God.

5. Because of this, you who do these things, the Lord said, "If you have gathered with me in my breast but do not obey my commandments, I will throw you out, and I will say to you: 'Depart from me; I do not know where you are from, you who commit iniquity.'"[8]

Chapter 5

1. For which reason, brothers, let us turn away from our temporary sojourn in this world, and do the will of him who called us, and let us not fear to depart from this world.

---

4. Matt 10:32; Luke 12:8.
5. Mark 12:30.
6. Isa 29:13.
7. Matt 7:21.
8. Source unknown; cf. Matt 25:41–43.

2. For the Lord says, "You will be like lambs among wolves."[9]
3. But Peter answered and said to him, "What if the wolves tear apart the lambs?"
4. Jesus said to Peter, "Let the lambs have no fear of the wolves after their death, and have no fear of those who kill you and can do nothing more to you, but fear him who after your death has power to cast body and soul into the flames of hell."[10]
5. And be assured, brothers, that our temporary stay in this world of the flesh is a little thing and lasts a short time, but the promise of Christ is great and wonderful, and brings us rest in the coming kingdom and eternal life.
6. What then will we do to secure these things except to live a holy and righteous life, and to regard these worldly things as not our own, and not desire them?
7. For when we desire to acquire these things, we fall away from the right way.

Chapter 6

1. Now the Lord says: "No servant can serve two masters."[11] If we desire to serve both God and Mammon, it is harmful to us.
2. "For what is the advantage if someone gains the whole world but loses his soul?"[12]
3. Now this age and the coming one are two enemies.
4. This age speaks of adultery and corruption and love of money and deceit, but that age renounces these things.
5. Therefore, we cannot be the friends of both, but we must renounce this age in order to make the most of that one.
6. We think that it is better to hate the things that are here, because they are insignificant and short-lived and corruptible, but to love those things that are good and incorruptible.

---

9. Cf. Matt 10:16.
10. Source unknown; cf. Matt 10:28.
11. Matt 6:24; Luke 16:13.
12. Matt 16:26; Mark 8:36; Luke 9:25.

7. For if we do the will of Christ, we will find rest; on the other hand nothing will rescue us from eternal punishment if we disobey his commandments.

8. And the scripture also says in Ezekiel, "Even if Noah and Job and Daniel arise, they will not rescue their children in the captivity."[13]

9. Now if even such righteous men as these are not able to save their children by their own righteous deeds, with what confidence will we enter the kingdom of God if we do not keep our baptism pure and undefiled? Or who will be our advocate if we are not found to have holy and righteous deeds?

Chapter 7

1. So then, my brothers, let us compete, knowing that the competition is at hand, and that many are arriving by boat for corruptible prizes, but not all are crowned, except those who have trained hard and competed well.

2. Let us therefore compete that we may all be crowned.

3. Let us run the straight course, the incorruptible competition, and let many of us sail to it and compete, that we may also be crowned. And if we all cannot receive the crown, let us at least come close to it.

4. We must remember that if someone taking part in the contest for a corruptible prize is found cheating, he is flogged, disqualified, and thrown out of the stadium.

5. What do you think? What will he suffer who cheats in the contest for what is incorruptible?

6. Concerning those who have not kept the seal he says: "Their worm will not die, and their fire will not be quenched, and they will be a spectacle for all flesh."[14]

Chapter 8

1. Therefore, while we are still on earth, let us repent.

---

13. Ezek 14:14–20.
14. Isa 66:24; cf. Mark 9:44, 46, 48.

2. For we are clay in the hand of the craftsman. For in the same way as the potter, if he makes a vessel, and it becomes misshapen or breaks while it is in his hand, he reshapes it; but if he has put it into the kiln, he no longer is able to mend it. So also, as long as we are in this world, let us repent from all our heart from the wicked things we have done in the flesh, so that we may be saved by the Lord while we still have time to repent.

3. For after we have departed the world, we are no longer able there to confess or to repent anymore.

4. So, brothers, if we have done the will of the Father and have kept the flesh pure and have obeyed the commandments of the Lord, we will receive eternal life.

5. For the Lord says in the Gospel, "If you have not observed what is small, who will give you what is great? For I tell you that whoever is faithful in what is little is faithful also in what is much."[15]

6. He means this then: keep the flesh pure and the seal unstained so that we may receive life.

Chapter 9

1. And let none of you say that this flesh is not judged nor rises again.

2. Understand this. In what condition were you saved? In what condition did you receive your sight, if not while you were in this flesh?

3. We must therefore guard the flesh as a temple of God.

4. For just as you were called in the flesh, you will also come in the flesh.

5. If Christ the Lord who saved us, although he was originally spirit, became flesh and called us, so we will also receive our reward in this flesh.

6. Therefore, let us love one another, so that we all may come into the kingdom of God.

7. While we have time to be healed, let us give ourselves to God, who heals us, making a payback to him.

8. What sort? Repentance from a sincere heart.

---

15. Luke 16:10–12.

9. For he is the one who knows all things beforehand and knows what is in our heart.

10. Therefore, let us then give him eternal praise, not only from the mouth, but also from the heart, so that he may receive us as sons.

11. For the Lord also said: "My brothers are these who do the will of my Father."[16]

Chapter 10

1. So, my brothers, let us do the will of the Father who called us, that we may live, and let us rather pursue virtue, and let us give up malice as the forerunner of our sins, and let us flee ungodliness so that evil things not overtake us.

2. For if we are eager to do good, peace will pursue us.

3. For this reason it is not possible for a person to find peace when they bring in human fears and prefer the present pleasure to the coming promise.

4. For they do not know what great torment the present pleasure brings, and what delight the coming promise brings.

5. And if they alone were doing these things it could be endured, but now they continue teaching evil to innocent souls, not realizing that both themselves and their hearers will receive a double punishment.

Chapter 11

1. Let us therefore serve God with a pure heart, and we will be righteous; but if we do not serve him because we do not believe the promise of God, we will be miserable.

2. For the prophetic word also says: "Miserable are the double-minded who doubt in their heart, saying, 'We heard all these things long ago and in the time of our fathers, but waiting day to day, we have seen none of them.'"

---

16. Matt 12:59; Mark 3:35; Luke 8:21.

female."²³ The male is Christ, the female is the Church. Also the scrolls and the apostles say that the church belongs not to the present, but has existed from the beginning. For she was spiritual, as was also our Jesus, but he was manifested in the last days so that he might save us.

3. And the church, which is spiritual, was manifested in the flesh of Christ, showing us that if any of us guard her in the flesh without corruption, he will receive her back again in the Holy Spirit. For this flesh is a copy of the Spirit. Therefore no one who has corrupted the copy will partake in the original. So, then, he means this, brothers: guard the flesh, so that you may partake of the Spirit.²⁴

4. And if we say that the flesh is the church and the Spirit is Christ, then the one who abused the flesh has abused the church. Such a person, therefore, will not partake of the Spirit, who is Christ.

5. So great is the life and immortality this flesh is able to partake of, if the Holy Spirit is joined with it, that no one is able to express or to speak of the things "which the Lord has prepared" for his chosen ones.

Chapter 15

1. Now I think that I have not given unimportant advice about self-control, which if anyone follows he will have no regret, but will save both himself and me, his advisor. For it is no small reward to turn to salvation a wandering and perishing soul.

2. For this is the return which we can pay back to God who created us: if the one who speaks and hears both speaks and hears with faith and love.

3. Let us, therefore, remain righteous and holy in our faith, that we may boldly ask God, who says, "While you are speaking, I will say, 'Behold, I am here.'"²⁵

4. For this saying is the sign of a great promise, for the Lord says that he is more ready to give than we are to ask.

5. Let us then share in such great kindness, and not begrudge ourselves the gaining of such good things, for as great is the pleasure that these

---

23. Gen 1:27.
24. Possibly a quotation from an unknown source.
25. Isa 58:9.

words bring to those who do them so severe is the condemnation they bring to those who disobey.

Chapter 16

1. So, brothers, as we have received no small opportunity to repent, while we have time, let us turn to the God who calls us, while we still have the one who accepts us.

2. For if we renounce these pleasures and conquer our soul by not doing its evil desires, we will receive Jesus' mercy.

3. But you know that the day of judgment is already approaching like a burning oven, and some of the heavens will melt, and the whole earth will be like lead melting in a fire, and then both the hidden and the open deeds of people will be made visible.

4. Charitable giving is, therefore, as good as repentance from sin. Fasting is better than prayer, but charitable giving is better than both; and love "covers a multitude of sins,"[26] but prayer from a good conscience rescues from death. Blessed is everyone who is found to be full of these things, for charitable giving lightens the burden of sin.

Chapter 17

1. Therefore, let us repent with our whole heart, so that none of us perish. For since we have commands that we should do this, to tear men away from idols and to instruct them, how much more must we save from perishing a soul who already knows God?

2. Let us then help one another, and restore those who are weak in goodness, so that we may all be saved, and turn each other around and admonish each other.

3. And let us not only appear to believe and pay attention now, while we are being admonished by the elders; but also when we have returned home, let us remember the commandments of the Lord, and let us not be dragged off by worldly desires. Rather by coming here more frequently, let us attempt to progress in the commands of the Lord, so that we may all think the same way and be gathered together for life.

---

26. 1 Pet 4:8; cf. Prov 10:12.

4. For the Lord said, "I am coming to gather together all the nations, tribes, and languages."²⁷ Now by this he means the day of his appearance, when he will come and rescue us, each one according to his deeds.

5. And the unbelievers will see his glory and power, and they will be astonished when they see the sovereignty of the world given to Jesus; and they will say, "Woe unto us, because it was you, and we did not know it or believe it, and we did not obey the elders who proclaimed to us about our salvation." "And their worm will not die and their fire will not be quenched, and they will be a spectacle for all flesh."²⁸

6. He means the day of judgment, when they will see those who were ungodly among us and who perverted the commands of Jesus Christ.

7. But the righteous who have done good, who endured torture, and who hated the pleasures of the soul, when they see those who have gone astray and denied Jesus by words or deeds punished with terrible torment in unquenchable fire, will give glory to their God, saying that there will be hope for the one who served God from his whole heart.

Chapter 18

1. Let us then also be among those who give thanks, who have served God, and not among the ungodly, who are judged.

2. For I myself am also completely sinful, and I have not yet fled from temptation, but while still in the midst of the devil's tools, I am endeavoring to pursue righteousness, so that I may have the strength at least to come near to it, while in fear of the coming judgment.

Chapter 19

1. So then brothers and sisters, following the God of Truth, I am reading you an appeal to pay attention to what is written, so that you may both save yourselves and the one who is the reader among you. For as a compensation I ask you to repent from all your heart, giving yourselves salvation and life. For when we do this, we will set a goal for

---

27. Isa 66:18.
28. Isa 66:24; cf. Mark 9:48.

all the younger ones who wish to devote themselves to piety and the goodness of God.

2. And we should not be displeased or be indignant in our foolishness when anyone admonishes us and attempts to turn us away from unrighteousness to righteousness. For sometimes, when we do evil, we do not realize it because of the double-mindedness and faithlessness that is in our breasts, and we are darkened in our understanding by useless desires.

3. Let us then do righteousness, so we may be saved at the end. Blessed are those who obey these instructions; although they may suffer evil for a short time in this world, they will reap the immortal fruit of the resurrection.

4. So then, the godly person should not grieve if he endures misery at this present time; a blessed time awaits him. He will live again with the fathers above and will rejoice in an age when there is no sorrow.

Chapter 20

1. But neither let it disturb your mind that we see the unrighteous being wealthy and God's servants being oppressed.

2. Let us then have faith, brothers and sisters. We are competing in the contest of the living God and being trained in the present life, so that we may be crowned in the coming one.

3. None of the righteous has received fruit quickly but waits for it.

4. For if God paid the wages of the righteous quickly, we would immediately be engaged in commerce and not in godliness, for we would appear to be righteous when we were pursuing not piety but gain. And because of this, divine judgment punishes a spirit that is not righteous and burdens it with chains.

5. To the only invisible God, the Father of Truth, who sent forth to us the Savior and Founder of immortality, through whom he revealed to us the truth and the heavenly life, to him be the glory forever and ever. Amen.

Part I

Introductory Articles

1

Introduction to 2 Clement

IN 1627 A GIFT from the Patriarch of Constantinople, Cyril Lucaris, for the monarch, James I, arrived in England. The gift was a codex copied in the fifth century CE that contained the entire Old and New Testaments with the texts of 1 Clement and 2 Clement at the end of the New Testament books. The manuscript without explanation broke off at 2 Clem. 12.5, the rest of the contents being lost. Subsequently these two books appeared in what was the first collection of books that went by the name Apostolic Fathers, published by the French scholar J. B. Cotelier in 1672. Included in his collection were the recently rediscovered writings attributed to such early Christian figures as Barnabas, Hermas, Ignatius of Antioch, Polycarp of Smyrna, and the above two works attributed to Clement of Rome. The lengthy Latin title was *S.S. Patrum qui temporibus apostolicis floruerunt: Barnabae, Clementis, Hermae, Ignatii, Polycarpi. Opera edita et inedita, vera et suppositicia. Una cum Clementis, Ignatiis, Polycarpi, Acts atque Martyriis.*[1] Subsequent editions of these so-called Apostolic Fathers continued to include the above two works attributed to Clement of Rome.[2] The role of 2 Clement in that corpus of writings was greatly strengthened by its inclusion in a codex of early church writings discovered by Philotheus Bryennios in Constantinople around 1873.[3] To the delight of scholars, this codex included the eight chapters of 2 Clement that were missing in Codex A. A common opening sentence in

---

1. Ehrman is careful to point out that although the title Apostolic Fathers is not in the title, Cotelier does refer to the books as a "collection of the Apostolic Fathers" (*Apostolicorum Patrum collectio*) in his preface. Ehrman, ed., *Apostolic Fathers*, I, 8–9.

2. In subsequent years, writings such as the rediscovered Didache, the Letter to Diognetus, and the Fragments of Papias have been included, and occasionally the Apology of Quadratus.

3. The text critical siglum of the codex is H54, but this commentary will refer to it simply as H, a practice also followed in Ehrman, ed., *Apostolic Fathers*, I, 161. Some scholars also refer to the manuscript as C, a practice followed in Holmes, ed., *Apostolic Fathers*, 136. The siglum H54 is also used in Wilhite, *Didache*, xxv.

many popular and academic treatments of the "Second Letter of Clement" goes something as follows, "This work is neither written by Clement, nor is it a letter."[4] Such a comment is often followed by a statement that the work is in fact the earliest Christian sermon outside the New Testament.[5] Each of these very important issues will be addressed at its proper location in the commentary. Another remark about 2 Clement by Bart Ehrman expresses an opinion shared also by the current author after years of research on the book. "Second Clement is probably the most overlooked and least appreciated of the writings of the Apostolic Fathers."[6] Overshadowed by its "Big Sister" (1 Clement) in many discussions, this shorter document appears in all editions of the Apostolic Fathers. Yet, many writers rarely cite or give attention to 2 Clement, when compared to the much greater attention given to other works in the Apostolic Fathers corpus.

While it has not received the degree of attention given to many other works among the Apostolic Fathers, scholars have not totally neglected 2 Clement. German scholarship has produced some excellent commentaries, in addition to briefer treatments.[7] The two commentaries by Lindemann and Pratscher reflect a model of scholarship, and references to Lindemann's commentary will often show up in my own comments.[8] English-language commentaries as part of a series include the magisterial work of J. B. Lightfoot in his multivolume set on the Apostolic Fathers.[9] Holt Graham, in a series edited by Robert Grant, has offered a brief but still helpful commentary.[10] To this writer's knowledge, the only one-volume commentary in English is by Christopher Tuckett in the Oxford Apostolic Fathers series.[11] The published dissertation by Karl Paul Donfried is an excellent monograph on 2 Clement that offers many comments on the text.[12]

    4. Examples of this type of comment abound, but only two will be mentioned. "Besides the authentic letter by Clement . . . tradition knows of another 'letter,' 2 *Clement*, though it is neither a letter nor written by Clement" (Drobner, *Fathers of the Church*, 57); "The so-called second letter of Clement is not a letter, nor is it by Clement" (Holmes, ed., *Apostolic Fathers*, 132).

    5. See, for example, the excellent contribution by Paul Parvis: "2 Clement and the Meaning of the Christian Homily."

    6. Ehrman, ed., *Apostolic Fathers*, I, 154. Ehrman adds: "This is somewhat to be regretted, as it is in some ways a historically significant work."

    7. One of the better survey treatments by a German author is the English translation of Pratscher, *Apostolic Fathers*, 71–90.

    8. Lindemann, *Apostolischen Väter*, 183–261.

    9. Lightfoot, trans., *Apostolic Fathers*, I.2, 189–316.

    10. Grant and Graham, *First and Second Clement*, 107–38.

    11. Tuckett, *2 Clement*.

    12. Donfried, *Setting*. Donfried's volume is not technically a commentary but a

Students of 2 Clement await the major commentary in the Hermeneia series by James A. Kelhoffer. Kelhoffer's recent articles are noted in many footnotes and the bibliography, since he offers some fresh ideas on issues surrounding the book. Later in this Introduction, I will address the issues of the authorship and provenance of 2 Clement. Because we do not know the identity of the author, this commentary often refers to the "author" or "speaker." On some occasions, even the name "Clement" will be mentioned as writing something in the text. This practice does not imply any claim about authorship and is simply done for convenience.

Manuscript Tradition of 2 Clement

Direct Manuscript Witnesses

Two Greek manuscripts preserve what we call 2 Clement along with 1 Clement. The Alexandrian (A) codex dates from the fifth century CE while the Hierosolymitanus 54 (H54) codex was copied in 1056 CE. Second Clement also appears, again with 1 Clement, in a Syriac manuscript (c. 1170).

Codex Alexandrinus

Codex Alexandrinus (A), housed in the British Library in London (MS Reg. 1 D VIII), was a gift from the Patriarch of Constantinople Cyril Lucaris to King James I of England in 1624. Many agree that A was copied in Alexandria in the fifth century CE, and the codex includes the entire Old and New Testaments along with 1 Clement and 2 Clement appended at the end of the codex. Unfortunately, the manuscript breaks off at 2 Clem. 12.5 in the last word of the expression, οὔτε ἄρσεν οὔτε θῆλυ τοῦτο, the rest of the contents being lost. The text of 2 Clement commences at the top of column 2 on folio 168a, immediately following the text of 1 Clement and its colophon. Full titles normally appear before each book, with the superscription for 1 Clement being "ς κορινθιους α." No title, however, appears before 2 Clement. A separate table of contents includes the titles of both books under the heading Η ΚΑΙΝΗ ΔΙΑΘΗΚΗ ("The New Testament"). Following the entry ΑΠΟΚΑΛΥΨΙΣ ΙΩΑΝΝΟΥ are the entries ΚΛΗΜΕΝΤΟΣ ΕΠΙΣΤΟΛΗ Α and ΚΛΗΜΕΝΤΟΣ ΕΠΙΣΤΟΛΗ Β. Scholars agree that this hand was from a scribe of the seventh or eighth century.[13] It appears that both books

---

monograph, although he does attempt to discern the "intention" of 2 Clement by working through the text of most chapters.

13. See the interesting information about this secondary hand supplied by Donfried

were regarded by the scribe as part of the NT. The lack of a superscription following 1 Clement combined with the entry in the table of contents indicates that the scribe(s) believed that the book was either by Clement or at least closely associated with Clement.

Codex Hierosolymitanus

Codex Hierosolymitanus (Latin for "Jerusalem"), sometimes referred to as Codex H or the Constantinople Codex (so also called Codex C), is now housed in the Library of the Monastery of the Holy Sepulcher in the Old City of Jerusalem (MS 54). Philotheos Bryennios discovered the MS in a sister monastery in Constantinople around 1873, and the MS was transferred soon afterward to Jerusalem. The codex contains no canonical NT books but a number of Apostolic Fathers such as the Clements, Barnabas, the longer recension of the Ignatius letters, and the only surviving Greek manuscript of the Didache. A colophon provides a precise date for the manuscript's completion as 1056 CE and even the name of the self-effacing scribe who described himself as "Leon scribe and sinner."[14] For our purposes, this manuscript provides the remaining text of 2 Clement 12 that is missing in the Alexandrian manuscript. Our text in question has the superscription Κλήμεντος προς Κορινθίους Β'.[15] While generally confirming the text of A in the first eleven and a half chapters, the consensus of scholars is that Codex H (also called Codex C) is not as reliable as the earlier manuscript.

Codex S

A Syriac manuscript (S) dated 1170 CE and housed in the Cambridge University Library (MS 1700) contains the Syriac New Testament with the texts of 1 Clement and 2 Clement placed immediately after the Catholic Epistles and before the Pauline Epistles. The two works are titled epistles of "Clement the disciple of Peter the Apostle to the Church of the Corinthians."[16] The placement of the two works and their titles indicate that as far as the scribe is concerned, these works apparently receive canonical status beside

---

(*Setting*, 20n3).

14. Photographic reproductions of the manuscript's leaves containing both Clements appear in Lightfoot, trans., *Apostolic Fathers*, I.1, 425–74.

15. For a thorough treatment of the circumstances surrounding the discovery and purchase of this codex and its peculiar features, see Lightfoot, trans., *Apostolic Fathers*, I.1, 121–29.

16. Translation provided in Lightfoot, trans., *Apostolic Fathers*, I.1, 131–32.

the canonical writings of the NT. Regarding the translation itself, Tuckett observes that S "shows a greater degree of paraphrase and wordiness by comparison" with the Greek texts of A and H.[17] The value of the manuscript called Codex S lies more in its textual than in its translational characteristics. S most frequently agrees with Codex A when A differs from Codex H (also called Codex C). At a few points in the latter chapters of 2 Clement, the Syriac may actually preserve the original that is also preserved in Codex H, also called C (for example, 2 Clem. 14.2 and 19.1). Lightfoot, however, provides evidence when the Syriac text most often agrees with Codex A over against Codex H, also called C.[18]

Did the author of 2 Clement leave any further footprints among the surviving manuscripts?[19] The answer is none that we *certainly* know about. Lightfoot, however, offers the following information from the *Bibliotheca*, a ninth-century description of various literary works read by Photius, the Patriarch of Constantinople. "Photius (*Bibl.* 126) found these two epistles of Clement bound up in one small volume (βιβλιδάριον) with the Epistle of Polycarp to the Philippians."[20] Unfortunately, as in the case with so many of these works described by Photius, this small codex has not survived. A general observation supported by 2 Clement scholars is that of the three surviving manuscripts that we currently possess, Codex A serves as most trustworthy in regard to preserving the earliest form of the text.[21] Of the three surviving textual sources, A is considered the most trustworthy due to its greater antiquity and its often being in agreement with Codex S over against the later Codex H, also called C.[22] At the appropriate locations in the commentary, the most significant variant readings in these witnesses (A, H—or C—and S) will be considered on a case-by-case basis. The Greek text of 2 Clement that has been utilized for well over a century has been the one published by Lightfoot in a number of subsequent editions.[23] Two recent critical editions of the Greek text have been edited by Ehrman[24]

---

17. Tuckett, *2 Clement*, 5.
18. Lightfoot, trans., *Apostolic Fathers*, I.1, 138–39.
19. P.Oxy. 4009 relates an agraphon similar to 2 Clem. 5.2–4, but it instead reads as if from the perspective of Peter. For treatments of this papyrus and its possible relevance to 2 Clement, see Brannan, *Greek Apocryphal Gospels*, 24–25, 67–68, 78–79; and Brummel and Wayment, eds., *Christian Oxyrhynchus*, 201–5.
20. Lightfoot, trans., *Apostolic Fathers*, I.1, 146.
21. Lightfoot, trans., *Apostolic Fathers*, I.1, 120.
22. Tuckett, *2 Clement*, 4–5.
23. See the edition by Lightfoot and Harmer, trans., 43–53.
24. Ehrman, ed., *Apostolic Fathers*, I, 164–99.

and Holmes.[25] The Greek text by Holmes will be utilized in this volume, although attention will also be given to the Ehrman edition at a few locations in the text.[26] Ehrman discusses various readings in 2 Clement and their implications for NT textual criticism in an important volume on the reception of the NT in the Apostolic Fathers.[27] No Latin manuscript witnesses to 2 Clement survive from antiquity through the Middle Ages. This absence in the West should not be surprising since all the surviving witnesses had their origins in the eastern Mediterranean. "Latin versions have not been found. And it seems not to have been known in the West."[28] While Lightfoot's work on the text of 2 Clement has formed the basis of its study until recent years, one critic has raised problems with a few of his textual choices. William Petersen charged Lightfoot with a poor methodology that led to his "wrong" choices of readings in 2 Clem. 3.2; 3.4; and 6.2 (twice).[29] The details of the controversy are not pertinent at this point but will be mentioned at the appropriate locations in the commentary. Christopher Tuckett, in a response to Petersen, concluded that Lightfoot's methodology "does not perhaps merit the strong criticism levelled by Petersen."[30]

Use of 2 Clement in Antiquity

In addition to the small number of 2 Clement manuscripts, a few ancient Christian writers either allude to or cite it. These examples, however, are much fewer than the many attestations by ancient writers to 1 Clement. We will limit these examples to some of the clearer instances.[31]

---

25. Holmes, ed., *Apostolic Fathers*, 138–64.

26. This includes an interesting conjectural reading at 9.5 (Ehrman, ed., *Apostolic Fathers*, I, 178).

27. Ehrman, "Textual Traditions Compared."

28. Crafer, *Second Epistle of Clement to the Corinthians*, x.

29. Petersen, "Patristic Biblical Quotations and Method." See also Petersen's incisive observations about the relevance of the Apostolic Fathers in establishing the NT text in the previously cited volume: Gregory and Tuckett, *Reception of the New Testament in the Apostolic Fathers*, 29–46.

30. Tuckett, "Lightfoot's Text of 2 Clement." See also Tuckett, *2 Clement*, 149–50, 160–61, 180–81.

31. Lightfoot mentions other Syriac and Latin authors (Lightfoot, trans., *Apostolic Fathers*, I.1, 129–38); see also a few possible ones in Tuckett, *2 Clement*, 7–13.

Irenaeus

Irenaeus (*Haer.* 3.3.3) in the late second century provides what might be called an indirect allusion to a teaching found in 2 Clement. In a summary of the teaching in 1 Clement, Irenaeus refers to some material that is clearly found in that work but offers also a description of the fiery judgment that is not found in 1 Clement. The language, however, is quite similar to such a description in 2 Clement (e.g., 2 Clem. 7.6; 16.3; 17.5). It is also possible that he simply confounded the two sources as one. While not a certain citation, it remains at least a possible early testimony to some of the contents in 2 Clement.

Origen

In his commentary on John (*Comm. Jo.* 2.34.207), Origen, writing sometime before 250 CE, utilizes language quite similar to the famous expression in 2 Clem. 1.1: "what we should think about the son of God."[32] The language, however, is not exact, and the allusion remains illusory at best.

Eusebius

Eusebius provides the earliest clear attestation to 2 Clement: "a second letter is ascribed to Clement, but we do not have the same knowledge of its recognition as the former" (that is, 1 Clement), "because we do not know if the ancient writers used it."[33] He wrongly refers to it as an "epistle," which may betray a personal unfamiliarity with the actual text. Eusebius does not classify 2 Clement as belonging to any of the four categories in which he placed Christian literature: (1) recognized books, (2) disputed books, (3) rejected books, and (4) heretical books.[34]

Apostolic Canons

Towards the end of the fourth century, the authors of the *Apostolic Canons* (8.47.85) mention both Clements. This extensive work includes a series of eighty-four or eighty-five canons and is appended to the *Apostolic*

---

32. δεῖ φρονεῖν περὶ τοῦ υἱοῦ τοῦ θεοῦ.

33. *Hist. eccl.* 3.38.4 (personal translation). Jerome's brief mention of 2 Clement (*Vir. Ill.* 15) appears to be wholly dependent on Eusebius.

34. *Hist. eccl.* 3.25.1–7.

Constitutions as book 8, chapter 47. The *Canons* describe a list of what it calls "our books, that is the books of the New Testament" which includes "two epistles of Clement."[35] Thus around the same time that Codex A apparently included the Clements in its canon, another contemporary canon list, the *Apostolic Canons*, knew about 2 Clement and accepted it as canonical.

Severus of Antioch

Severus of Antioch (c. 513–518) in a polemical work (*Adv. Joannem*) cites verbatim the opening verses of 2 Clement (1.1–2) and credits them as follows: "From Clement, the third bishop of Rome after the Apostles, from the Second Epistle to the Corinthians." By the sixth century, therefore, the hesitance of Eusebius and Jerome about its Clementine authorship had evidently begun to disappear.[36]

Photius

Photius, the ninth-century Patriarch of Constantinople, in his "encyclopedia" of literary works that he had read, the *Bibliotheca*, has one of the most extensive descriptions of 2 Clement.

> The second letter, containing advice and exhortation to a better life, at the beginning proclaims Christ as God, although certain foreign expressions, from which even the first letter is not altogether free, are introduced as if from Holy Writ. Certain passages are strangely interpreted. The sentiments are somewhat poor and at times inconsistent.[37]

While Photius appreciated the high Christology of the book, he was concerned about its use of noncanonical writings in its exposition. Photius's reference is the earliest surviving attestation to this concern about 2 Clement—a concern about what has emerged as one of the most controversial aspects of the book's methodology. The manuscript evidence, although relatively small, does attest to a high value given to 2 Clement in various corners of the growing Christian world; some even view it as part of the NT canon.

---

35. "The NT canon list contains the four Gospels, the fourteen letters of Paul, the seven Catholic Epistles, and Acts. It also contains the two letters of Clement" (Gallagher and Meade, *Biblical Canon Lists from Early Christianity*, 137).

36. Lightfoot credits "Cureton" for the English translation of this Syriac text (*Apostolic Fathers*, I, 192).

37. Freese, *Library of Photius*, 213.

The scant but clear attestation by writers mentioned above makes it difficult to understand the reservation expressed by one writer on the Apostolic Fathers: "Apart from the three copies of the text, no other citations of 2 Clement survive among the important theologians and historians of the early church."[38] While attestation by individual writers may go back to the second century, some "citations" may be only hopeful at best. On the other hand, certainly by the fourth century and later the work was well-known, although not appreciated highly by all. The work came to be viewed as a *letter* written by *Clement*, both suppositions that are now widely questioned. The conclusion by Tuckett provides a fair summary for this "history" of the book during its first thousand years. "In general terms, the relatively low level of (explicit) interest shown in the text by patristic writers matches the relatively low amount of extant manuscript evidence for the text."[39]

Authorship and Provenance of 2 Clement

The issues of the authorship of 2 Clement and its original setting will be examined together. Despite the evidence of Codex Alexandrinus and the traditional attribution to Clement from Eusebius and later, no one today seriously identifies the author of 2 Clement with Clement of Rome, the reputed author of 1 Clement. While one may detect some intriguing linguistic connections between the two documents (which will be mentioned), the differences in style and argument are such that their arising from different authors is undoubtedly an accurate assessment. "For example, the author of 1 Clement is heavily dependent on Paul and makes very little use of Jesus traditions; the author of 2 Clement shows little evidence of knowing Paul but makes extensive use of a range of Jesus traditions."[40] This difference in style does not imply, however, that there was no possible early connection between the documents. It is that possible connection between the two works that will be one of the main concerns in this section. There have been a few efforts to identify *by name* the author of 2 Clement. Von Harnack proposed that the author was Soter, a Roman bishop who flourished around 165–75 CE. This Soter was mentioned by Eusebius, *Eccl. hist.* (4.23.9–11). In a letter written by Dionysius of Corinth, Dionysius referred to another letter from Soter while he also mentioned the letter known as 1 Clement.[41] As creative as this

---

38. Jefford, *Reading the Apostolic Fathers*, 124.
39. Tuckett, *2 Clement*, 13.
40. Tuckett, *2 Clement*, 14.
41. Von Harnack, "Zum Ursprung des sog. 2. Clemensbriefs." See also Goodspeed, *Apostolic Fathers*, 83.

possible connection might be, the problems with the suggestion are that (1) it places 2 Clement at quite a late date, and (2) it refers to the document as a letter while 2 Clement has no epistolary features.

J. Rendell Harris, who pioneered a number of creative ideas, suggested that the expression in 2 Clem. 15.1, "concerning self-control" (περὶ ἐγκρατείας), indicates that Julius Cassianus was the author.[42] Cassianus was an Encratite or ascetic who (according to Clement of Alexandria) wrote a book by that name. Harris thought that 2 Clement was that same book. As will be seen later, our author does not really exhibit the gnostic tendencies associated with the ascetic Encratites, mentioned first by name in Irenaeus. Furthermore, the reference to the word in 15.1 certainly does not imply that self-control is the entire theme of the book, since that is the only occurrence of the word. Encratite practice does not compose the main theme of 1 Clement either, although the same noun appears four times in that work (1 Clem. 35.2; 38.2; 62.2; 64.1).

It should be obvious that one cannot isolate the author of 2 Clement from the place of its origin. But the question of origin has produced even more disagreement and uncertainty. There have been advocates for a Rome origination,[43] but the ruling out of Bishop Soter's letter (see above) due to 2 Clement's not being a letter, raises serious problems for a Roman provenance. The problems are mostly due to the possible use of the lost *Gospel of the Egyptians* in 12.2. Both Pratscher and Tuckett advocate Egypt, but with some careful caution that we simply cannot be certain. "An Egyptian origin of the text (probably the most widely held view in current scholarship) is possible, though the lack of firm positive evidence makes it difficult to be certain."[44] Some have occasionally advocated for a Middle Eastern origin, primarily based on its presence in the Syriac manuscript mentioned above.[45]

An almost universal consensus exists today suggesting that we cannot know the personal identity of the author of 2 Clement.[46] But that does not

---

42. Harris, "Authorship of the So-Called Second Epistle of Clement."

43. Both Pratscher (*Apostolic Fathers*, 87) and Tuckett (*2 Clement*, 58–60) mention that this was the view of "earlier scholarship." For a rare recent advocate for an early date in Rome, see Frend, *Rise of Christianity*, 121, 146. See also Ehrman, ed., *Apostolic Fathers*, I, 157–58; and Holmes, ed., *Apostolic Fathers*, 133–35 for a survey of the various views and their concluding openness about the place of origin.

44. Tuckett, *2 Clement*, 62.

45. For a recent scholar advocating a Syrian provenance, see Lindemann, *Clemensbriefe*, 195, but he advocates this position carefully and only as a possibility beside Egypt.

46. Lightfoot mentions that Bryennios, the 1873 discoverer of the codex in which the entire work is located, did affirm Clementine authorship. "In the first place

mean that we should be completely agnostic about the person or persons closely associated with its origin and setting. To be bold enough to venture a suggestion about the original setting demands that another option be presented for the original location of the book. J. B. Lightfoot argued that the original setting of the "sermon"—as he called it—was in Corinth, although he did not suggest the name of an author. Lightfoot based his argument on the athletic language used in 7.1-2.

> So then, my brothers, let us compete, knowing that the competition is at hand, and that many are arriving by boat (καταπλέουσιν) for corruptible prizes, but not all are crowned, except those who have trained hard and competed well. Let us therefore compete that we may all be crowned.

The importance of the verb καταπλέουσιν is crucial to this claim. Lightfoot's extended comments in his Introduction compose the beginning of his argument, which is concluded in his later commentary on chapter 7.

> As regards the audience addressed by the preacher Corinth has highest claims. If the homily were delivered in that city, we have an explanation of two facts which are not so easily explained on any other hypothesis. *First*. The allusion to the athletic games, and presumably to the Isthmian festival, is couched in language which is quite natural if addressed to Corinthians, but not so if spoken elsewhere. When the preacher refers to the crowds that 'land' to take part in the games (εἰς τοὺς φθαρτοὺς ἀγῶνας καταπλέουσιν, §7) without any mention of the port, we are naturally led to suppose that the homily was delivered in the neighbourhood of the place where these combatants landed. Otherwise we should expect εἰς τὸν Ἰσθμόν, or εἰς Κόρινθον, or some explanatory addition of the kind. *Secondly*. This hypothesis alone satisfactorily explains the dissemination and reputed authorship of the document. It was early attached to the Epistle of Clement in the mss and came ultimately to be attributed to the same author. How did this happen? The First Epistle was read from time to time in the Church of Corinth, as we know. This homily was first preached, if my view be correct, to these same Corinthians; it was not an *extempore* address, but was delivered from a manuscript; it was considered of sufficient value to be carefully preserved; and (as we may venture to suppose) it

---

Bryennios (p. ρνθ') maintains that the homily is the work of none other than the famous Clement whose name it bears, the bishop of Rome. This view however has nothing to recommend it, and has found no favour with others" (Lightfoot, trans., *Apostolic Fathers*, I.2, 204).

was read publicly to the Christian congregation at Corinth from time to time, like the genuine Epistle of Clement.⁴⁷

One does not need to affirm Lightfoot's reference to 2 Clement as a "homily" to consider the force of his argument for a Corinthian setting. His key argument is the use of the verb καταπλέω. An exposition of this text will be given in the commentary on chapter 7, but a few comments are appropriate at this point. Critics of Lightfoot's argument center on the metaphorical nature of the analogy in chapter 7.⁴⁸ "Clement" is obviously making an analogy with the athletic games, something that Paul also does in 1 Cor 9. The analogy draws from actual events and the specific use of the verb καταπλέω, which is not used by Paul. The use of the verb contains a vivid message to Clement's original hearers, who would be very aware of their location relative to the Isthmian games.⁴⁹

While not being alone in this idea, Lightfoot discerns the importance of the verb speaking to a Corinthian *Sitz in Leben*. Donfried offers a sustained argument (4–7) for viewing this verb and the overall passage as indicating a Corinthian locale.

> Lightfoot's argument makes sense: for 2 Clement καταπλέω is used to mean a coming to shore and the reason it is unnecessary to name the city is because the persons addressed by 2 Clement are in that city . . . It is most probable that the congregation in Corinth clearly understood the reference in question as referring to the Isthmian games in their city and that it was so intended by the author of 2 Clement.⁵⁰

The verb καταπλέω is not simply understood as "sail" but as "***sail down*** fr. the 'high seas' toward the coast, *sail toward* w. εἰς," with a number of

---

47. Lightfoot, trans., *Apostolic Fathers*, I.2, 197–98.

48. Tuckett, *2 Clement*, 60, 189.

49. "Compounds of πλεῖν are sometimes used metaphorically, as ἐκπλεῖν (Herod. iii. 155 ἐξέπλωσας τῶν φρενῶν), ἀποπλεῖν (Aristoph. Fr. ii. p. 907 Meineke ἀποπλευστέ οὖν ἐπὶ τὸν νυμφίον), διαπλεῖν (Plato Phaed. 85 d διαπλεῦσαι τὸν βίον). But καταπλεῖν can hardly be so explained here; and we must therefore suppose that the allusion is to the ἁλιερκὴς Ἰσθμοῦ δειράς (Pind. *Isthm.* i. 10), which would naturally be approached by sea. In these later days of Greece they seem to have surpassed even the Olympian in importance, or at least in popularity: comp. Aristid. *Isthm.* p. 45. If this homily was addressed to the Corinthians, there would be singular propriety in this image, as in S. Paul's contrast of the perishable and imperishable crown likewise addressed to them" (Lightfoot, trans., *Apostolic Fathers*, I.2, 224).

50. Donfried, *Setting*, 6, who provides additional classical references (e.g., Strabo) illustrating the importance of the Isthmian games in the first and second centuries CE.

examples from Xenophon to Josephus.⁵¹ This passage is the only use of this verb in the Apostolic Fathers, and its only use in the NT is in Luke 8:26 (κατέπλευσαν εἰς τὴν χώραν τῶν Γερασηνῶν). These literal examples of the verb argue for an initial literal meaning in chapter 7 with the following analogy used for Christians metaphorically "sailing toward the port" of the games. Clare Rothschild suggests that the verb and the passage recall the sailing home of the mythical hero Aeneas.⁵² Just as Paul referred to literal running and then bridged to a metaphorical meaning in his analogy, so Clement does the same in a very vivid manner that would have been rhetorically effective with his immediate hearers.⁵³

The argument for a Corinthian origin of 2 Clement suggests a possible setting of the work. An appeal to the tradition is the first point to consider. Why was it preserved with the document we call 1 Clement? A common answer given by many writers is that it was also in the archives of the church there and was read by the church on various occasions. But *why* was it in the archives, and *why* was it preserved with its larger "sister?" I suggest that it was closely associated with 1 Clement from the beginning because it had a vital connection with the issue in Corinth that originally prompted Clement to write.

Karl Paul Donfried's argument is worth reconsidering, although it has not encountered wide acceptance in subsequent scholarship.

> 1 Clement was written from Rome about 96–98 A.D. to the Corinthian church in the hope of ending a schism which had developed there after some persons had succeeded in removing the presbyters from office. The intervention of 1 Clement was successful and these presbyters who had been removed from office were in probability reinstated. It is our thesis that shortly after their reinstatement these presbyters wrote a hortatory discourse, known to us as 2 Clement, which one of them read to the Corinthian congregation assembled for worship. Because both 1 and 2 Clement had together averted a severe

---

51. BDAG, s.v. καταπλέω, 524.

52. Rothschild, "Sailing Past the Competition," 143–57. Further attention will be given to her analysis in the commentary on chapter seven. Her two additional chapters in this volume: "'Belittling' or 'Undervaluing' in 2 Clem. 1.1–2?" (111–24), and "Two *dispositiones* in 2 Clement 2" (125–42) will be considered in the commentary on chapters 1–2.

53. Livy describes the location of the Isthmian games as "between the two opposite seas and furnishing mankind with abundance of all wares, the market was a meeting-place for Asia and Greece" (Livy, *History of Rome, Books 31–34*, LCL 295, Book 33, 365). Lightfoot calls attention to this Latin quotation (Lightfoot, trans., *Apostolic Fathers*, II.1, 224).

crisis in the life of this congregation they were preserved together by the Corinthians.[54]

Donfried's argument has been described as creative and at least worthy of mention and interaction.[55] Donfried does not argue that the "author" of 2 Clement is identical with the proposed Clement's authorship of the first letter. His proposal of course makes such an identity impossible. But that there exists a plausible connection between the two not only arises from their close association in the tradition but is supported by the following additional factors. Assuming Corinth as the origin of the work, the evidence for his view is now summarized.[56]

Since 1 Clement was valued and preserved in the Corinthian church and 2 Clement was preserved with it, it is logical that 2 Clement was held in prominence by the Corinthians. Why? References in 1 Clement indicate that it is an appeal to bring back elders who had been removed, and this is not really disputed by anyone (see, for example, 1 Clem. 2.1; 37; 42–44). The argument is that 2 Clement is a hortatory address originating with elders who had been removed and now reinstated. Second Clement 19.1 asks that the congregation repent as a reward ($\mu\iota\sigma\theta\acute{o}\nu$) in light of God's grace to them: "For as a compensation I ask you to repent from all your heart, giving yourselves salvation and life. For when we do this, we will set a goal for all the younger ones who wish to devote themselves to piety and the goodness of God." He asks for compensation because he has been wrongly removed from office. That compensation is not a monetary one but one that consists of a heartfelt repentance.

The issue of disobeying the presbyters appears in 2 Clem. 17.5-6. Describing the unrepentant at the judgment, he writes: "Woe to us, because it was you, and we did not realize it, nor did we believe; and we did not obey the elders (presbyters) who proclaimed to us about our salvation." The rebellious ones not only failed to recognize Jesus but had failed to obey the presbyters. Donfried believes that both opponents in the two books deny God's eschatological promises and this is reflected in similar themes in 1 Clem. 23 and 2 Clem. 9. First Clement 57.1 says that his readers "must submit to the presbyters . . . and repent." The following commentary will argue that one of the main admonitions of 2 Clement is a thoroughgoing call to repentance. What 1 Clement asked for in general terms, because the

---

54. Donfried, *Setting*, 1.

55. Pratscher, *Apostolic Fathers*, 87n42; Ehrman, ed., *Apostolic Fathers*, I, 158; Holmes, ed., "argued well," *Apostolic Fathers*, 135.

56. Adapted from Donfried, *Setting*, 1–15.

Roman church had only heard about the problem, 2 Clement carries out specifically because the presbyters were very aware of the sin.

Each author (1 Clem. 63.2; 2 Clem. 19.1) actually refers to his own writing as an "appeal" (ἔντευξιν) to obey "what has been written." With this expression 1 Clement describes his own previous words, while it is unclear if 2 Clement is doing the same or making a reference to the Scriptures. What is the connection? "This can be explained easily: 2 Clement is an ἔντευξις from the Corinth presbyters to their congregation. That which enabled the presbyters to make their ἔντευξις was the prior ἔντευξις from the Roman congregation and, because of it, the presbyters were able to urge their fellow believers 'to heed what was written.'"[57]

Has Donfried finally solved the *Sitz im Leben* of 2 Clement? If airtight logic is demanded, the answer must be no. Tuckett concludes that the common use of ἔντευξις "may be no more than coincidental," and that Donfried's arguments about the original setting simply "fail to convince."[58] I would again say that convincing proof is not really possible, given the evidence that we possess. But in this writer's opinion, Donfried has offered the best explanation for why 2 Clement was preserved in the manuscript tradition with 1 Clement.[59] All other explanations also, in my opinion, fail to convince. Some may still in the end fall back on the agnostic position, that we cannot really know. Perhaps Donfried, however, has offered the best possible explanation for the title of his book: *The Setting of Second Clement in Early Christianity*. If Donfried's theory is accepted, and if 1 Clement is dated to the mid-90s (which is also debated), then 2 Clement would be dated near the turn of the century. Most scholars date the work well into the second century (i.e., between 130 and 150).[60]

The Genre of 2 Clement

What type of document is 2 Clement? The words *letter* and epistle in connection with 2 Clement do not arise from any feature of the document itself. Eusebius of Caesarea first referred to 2 Clement as a letter.[61] Many authors

---

57. Donfried, *Setting*, 15. Donfried's view that "what was written" refers back to Clement's letter is possible, but not essential to his overall argument.

58. Tuckett, *2 Clement*, 16, 17.

59. See this approach also in the unpublished dissertation by Stegemann, "Herkunft und Entstehung des sogenannten zweiten Klemensbriefes."

60. See, for example, Tuckett, *2 Clement*, 64; Jefford, *Reading the Apostolic Fathers*, 128; Ehrman, ed., *Apostolic Fathers*, I, 159–60.

61. *Hist. eccl.*, III, 38.4.

have noted that it lacks all the features of the epistolary genre such as salutations and postscripts and also never refers to itself in the terms of a letter.[62] Pratscher sums up well the prevailing opinion about its genre. "The scholarly consensus is that 2Clem, all told, is a sermon."[63] Sometimes authors will use the term *homily*. "It is in fact the earliest surviving Christian homily, apart from the polished and literary sermons which Luke includes in Acts."[64] This is the general scholarly assessment as Pratscher and a host of other scholars make abundantly clear.[65] Some authors are more careful about 2 Clement's label as a sermon or homily. "Instead, the shape of 2 Clement suggests that it was written to serve as a tractate that was designed for presentation to a specific early Christian community."[66] It is clear that 2 Clement was originally delivered orally (19.1) to a gathered congregation who in some way were involved with presbyters as their leaders (17.3, 5).[67] Early in the document (2.1) is a quotation of an extended text from Isaiah which has often been assumed to be the text of the sermon. Finally, the fervent exhortations throughout certainly would seem to embody the exhortation that we have come to expect in a sermon.[68]

On the other hand, a few scholars are not convinced that 2 Clement fits the sermon genre. Consider the following two voices of dissent from the majority view. After correctly concluding that it is not a letter, Tugwell writes:

> The modern practice of calling it a 'homily' is, however, not entirely accurate either. His appeal is distinguished from the exhortations given by the presbyters, in a way which strongly

---

62. For the features of the epistolary genre in antiquity, see: White, *Light from Ancient Letters*; Stowers, *Letter Writing in Greco-Roman Antiquity*; Klauck, *Ancient Letters and the New Testament*; Porter and Adams, eds., *Paul and the Ancient Letter Form*; Weima, *Paul the Ancient Letter Writer*.

63. Pratscher, *Apostolic Fathers*, 74.

64. Parvis, "2 Clement," 34. See also Lightfoot: "The so-called Second Epistle is the first example of a Christian homily" (*Apostolic Fathers*, I, 194–95). While maintaining the term "homily," some reject the designation "sermon" since it does not go verse by verse over a text (Pratscher, *Apostolic Fathers*, 74).

65. See the classic work by Lightfoot, trans., who calls it "an ancient homily" (*Apostolic Fathers*, I, 191). The two most widely used Greek texts with English translations of the Apostolic Fathers also agree. Ehrman, ed., calls it a "homily" (*Apostolic Fathers*, I, 154), while Holmes, ed., prefers the term "sermon" (*Apostolic Fathers*, 132).

66. Jefford, *Reading the Apostolic Fathers*, 125.

67. This of course assumes that the last two chapters were part of the original delivery, a position for which we will argue later.

68. For another extended treatment of 2 Clement as a "homily," see Stewart-Sykes, *From Prophecy to Preaching*, 174–87.

suggests that its author is not himself a presbyter (17.3). Is he perhaps an official reader (lector)? Yet we cannot suppose that the 'reader' of 2 Clement is merely reading out someone else's homily, as his use of the first-person singular shows the author and reader to be identical. The speaker identifies himself in 15.1 as giving the congregation counsel, and as hoping to gain salvation for himself hereby, must be the author. The only parallel I can suggest is the message Hermas presents himself as having received by divine revelation, which he is charged to read to the congregation in Rome (Hermas, *Vis.* 2.4, 8.3), and indeed to read repeatedly (*Vis.* 5, 25.5–7). Hermas too nowhere presents himself as being a presbyter, and he speaks of presbyters as if they are a class to which he does not belong (*Vis.* 2.4). Conceivably the 'preacher' of 2 *Clement* was in a similar position.[69]

More recently Tuckett also raised problems with the homily genre for 2 Clement. He asserts that we simply do not have enough information at this point in church history to adequately define a homily, and "if it is indeed the earliest such (Christian) 'sermon' we possess, it is potentially without analogy."[70] For example, in the description of the Christian gathering by Justin, after the writings of the prophets and the apostles are read, "then, when the reader finishes, the leader verbally instructs and admonishes to imitate these good things."[71] The brief citation of Isa 54:1 in 2 Clem. 2.1 is followed by only two verses of exposition, and then that text is never mentioned again. Tuckett's conclusion does suggest a difference between a sermon and homily. He concludes that "2 Clement may then be a sermon, but it is not a homily in the stricter sense of being a sermon in the form of detailed interpretation of a specific scriptural text."[72]

In a NT description of an address that could be called a homily, the previous chapters of Hebrews 1–12 are referred to in 13:22 as a "message of exhortation" (λόγος τῆς παρακλήσεως) This same expression is also used by the synagogue leaders in Acts 13:15 to describe the expected homily to follow the reading of the Law and the Prophets. That expression is nowhere used as a self-description in 2 Clement. While exhortation is certainly present in 2 Clement, the way the reader describes his address is by an entirely different set of terms. In 2 Clem. 15.1 the speaker says that "I think that I have not given unimportant advice (συμβούλια) I have given about self-control." This noun, which appears only here and in Barn. 21.2, means "advice, counsel"

69. Tugwell, *Apostolic Fathers*, 136–37.
70. Tuckett, *2 Clement*, 19–20.
71. Justin Martyr, *1 Apol.* 67. Author's translation.
72. Tuckett, *2 Clement*, 22.

and in both places appears to be a self-description of each work.⁷³ The word συμβούλια probably refers to the advice contained within the address, and is not intended as a description of the work as a whole. Another descriptive term is used by the speaker in 19.1: "I am reading you an appeal (ἔντευξιν) to pay attention to what is written . . ." This noun means "petition, request," and seems to be a general description of the appeal that has been made in chapters 1–18.⁷⁴ The word is also used in 1 Clem. 63.2 to describe Clement's nonsermonic "appeal" to the church in Corinth.⁷⁵

James A. Kelhoffer has thoroughly extended the argumentation, as previously found in Tugwell and Tuckett, against 2 Clement being a homily.⁷⁶ Kelhoffer suggests that faulty logic has been at work in these discussions. "(1) Second Clement is not a letter; (2) therefore, it is a sermon."⁷⁷ He charges that the unquestioning adoption of the sermon label for 2 Clement stems from the false choice for 2 Clement's genre between sermon or homily on the one hand and letter on the other. He then delivers a critique against utilizing sermon (or homily) as an apt designation for the work and questions if this designation helps to interpret the writing or to define its *Sitz im Leben*. Kelhoffer does cite Donfried as an ally in questioning the sermon genre assigned for 2 Clement. Donfried had earlier concluded that "the term 'homily' is so vague and ambiguous that it should be withdrawn until its literarily generic legitimacy has been demonstrated."⁷⁸ Kelhoffer also bemoans the fact that Donfried's concerns have largely fallen on deaf ears.⁷⁹ Unfortunately to Kelhoffer, however, Donfried offers no alternative genre than simply a "hortatory address." Finally, Kelhoffer criticizes the effort to take the expression "what is written" in 19.1 (τοῖς γεγραμμένοις) as referring to an imagined scripture reading that preceded his "sermon." Kelhoffer compares the participial expression with its identical use in 1 Clem. 63.2 where it refers not to a scripture reading but to the scriptural

---

73. BDAG, s.v. συμβούλια, 957.

74. BDAG, s.v. ἔντευξις, 339.

75. There will be a later opportunity to call attention again to the common use of this word between the two "Clements." The noun is also used over a dozen times in Hermas, another similar idea among many shared between the two works.

76. Kelhoffer, "If Second Clement Really Were a 'Sermon,'" 83–108.

77. Kelhoffer, "If Second Clement Really Were a 'Sermon,'" 84.

78. Donfried, *Setting*, 26.

79. Kelhoffer thinks that this neglect is because "few, if any, scholars have been persuaded by his constructive—and creative—proposal that Second Clement was a 'hortatory discourse' composed by one of the recently reinstated Corinthian elders ca. 98–100 CE as a follow up to First Clement and read to the church in Corinth" ("If Second Clement Really Were a 'Sermon,'" 94–95).

arguments offered previously in that letter.[80] He also notes that "the *Shepherd of Hermas* uses τὰ γεγραμμένα in reference to the instructions on fasting that the author had just given."[81]

In conclusion, I also suggest that we discard the terms *sermon* and *homily* as descriptors for the genre of 2 Clement and look rather to rhetoric for guidance. In that well-trodden ancient field, one of the three types of speeches was *deliberative* in its rhetorical goal.[82] This suggestion is supported by the self-designation of the address as a συμβούλια (15.1), a term that has rhetorical connections.[83] As was previously mentioned, the self-designation of the "speech" as an ἔντευξις also reflects a rhetorical usage.[84] Another transliterated term, *paraenesis*, has been applied to this type of address.[85] This term has occasionally been applied to NT texts such as the Letter of James by scholars including Johnson and Dibelius.[86] Even with his helpful criticism in this regard, Tuckett still maintains that one could use the word *sermon* in a rhetorically confined manner.[87] In the end, it is evident that scholars have failed to identify 2 Clement with an identifiable class of writings that we call sermons. Therefore, the use of the term to describe 2 Clement should be abandoned. What should we then call 2 Clement? Perhaps it is simply a hortatory address delivered in a particular *Sitz im Leben*, namely a Christian congregational setting.

---

80. Kelhoffer, "If Second Clement Really Were a 'Sermon,'" 102–3. It is interesting that both appeals to τοῖς γεγραμμένοις appear toward the end of each work as a review of the scriptural arguments that have previously been offered.

81. Kelhoffer, "If Second Clement Really Were a 'Sermon,'" 103. The Hermas reference is Herm. *Sim.* 5.3.7.

82. Aristotle's threefold division of rhetorical "speeches" were deliberative (συμβουλευτικόν), forensic, and epideictic (*Rhetorica*, I.3.1).

83. The word group surrounding the verb makes this clear. Especially to be noted is the adjective συμβουλευτικός defined as "hortatory, advising." GE further defines the word: "rhet. deliberative, of a speech ... Aristotle, *Rhetorica* 1358b" et al. (2000).

84. GE, s.v. ἔντευξις. 704, and the reference there to its usage in Aristotle's *Rhet.* 1355a 29.

85. The Greek word παραίνεσις, which is not used in Clement or other Apostolic Fathers, was not used as extensively in rhetoric as the other two. See GE, 1549, for the definition as "exhortation, counsel, advice."

86. See Johnson, *Letter of James*, 18–20 for a discussion of how Dibelius applied the term *paraenesis* to the ethical instruction in James. See also Starr and Engberg-Pedersen, eds., *Early Christian Paraenesis in Context*.

87. Tuckett, *2 Clement*, 25.

The Opponents in 2 Clement

"There is a scholarly consensus that the presumed opponents were Gnostics."[88] That bold assertion about the consensus appears to be fairly accurate, especially within German scholarship.[89] Even Pratscher tempers later that bold statement. "It is at best questionable to what degree the preacher consciously takes an anti-Gnostic line" (in Christology). "He clearly does not engage them [Gnostics] directly, but still purposely."[90] That qualified assertion has proven quite justified, especially in recent years. First, what evidence exists that gnostics were the chief opponents exposed in this writing? Many writers are dependent on Irenaeus's *Against Heresies* as the source for their information on Gnosticism and the verbal associations with 2 Clement.

The idea of Christ preexistent with the church (2 Clem. 14.1-2) is to some "an imaging of the Valentinian aeons."[91] The concept of a spiritual church is "close to that of the recently found *Tripartite Tractate* at Nag Hammadi."[92] Pertaining to the topics of fasting and prayer in 2 Clem. 16, Clement refutes "conceptions similar to those found in the Gospel of Thomas."[93] The emphasis on the good value of the "flesh" (σάρξ) as a prerequisite for receiving the eschatological blessing of the "spirit" (πνεῦμα) "also shows an anti-Gnostic orientation."[94] The use of such technical terms as "rest" (ἀνάπαυσις) in 5.5; "Father of Truth" (πατήρ τῆς ἀληθείας) in 3.1; and "the first church, the spiritual one" (ἐκκλησίας τῆς πρώτης τῆς πνευματικῆς) in 14.1 "must at least include the Valentinians."[95]

While this is a very brief survey of possible gnostic opponents addressed in 2 Clement, it represents many observations by commentators on the book. A traditional view of the role of Gnosticism in second-century Christianity is expounded in the important work, *Gnosis: The Nature and History of Gnosticism*, by Kurt Rudolph.[96] Rudolph, along with other writers, interprets Gnosticism as a religion that originated in Simon Magus (echoing

---

88. Pratscher, *Apostolic Fathers*, 85.

89. Only a sample will be mentioned. Warns, "Untersuchungen zum 2. Clemensbrief." 76-90; Donfried, *Setting*, 112 (written in a German university, Heidelberg); Koester, *Introduction to the New Testament*, II, 235-36.

90. Pratscher, *Apostolic Fathers*, 85-86.

91. Pratscher, *Apostolic Fathers*, 85; Donfried, *Setting*, 160.

92. Donfried, *Setting*, 160.

93. Donfried, *Setting*, 171.

94. Pratscher, *Apostolic Fathers*, 86.

95. Pratscher, *Apostolic Fathers*, 86.

96. Rudolph, *Gnosis*.

Irenaeus), then diversified to include Basilides, Valentinus, Marcion, and the Gospel according to Thomas. Eventually it developed into Manichaeism and Mandaeism. This religion was marked by dualism, negativity about the world, and deliverance through "insight." As Gnosticism became a religion, it became evident that its adherents were dualists who believed in a lower creator god, who hated the world and society, who did not believe that Christ was truly human, and whose disdain for the material body led to asceticism or even libertinism.[97] Some of the qualified assertions, like the ones mentioned above by Pratscher, do raise the possibility that the allusions to gnostics may not be as evident as assumed.

In recent years, scholars have questioned the confident assumption that gnostics are in view or assert that the similarities between early Christian literature and gnosticism are greatly overdrawn. Michael Williams offered a severe critique of the category Gnosticism.[98] He exposed the idea that writers like Ptolemy the Valentinian and Marcion all belonged to any movement that could be labeled Gnosticism, and demonstrated that these and others so accused were never either sexually licentious or extremely ascetic.

David Brakke exposes many of the widely accepted ideas about Gnosticism.[99] In only one sample of his critique, he reminds us that the Christian author of 1 Clement rejoiced that Jesus Christ had brought "immortal *gnosis*" (36.2), and he prayed that the blessed person would have "the ability to declare *gnosis*" (48.5; see also 40.1; 41.4).[100] The Letter of Barnabas also refers to Christian teaching as "the gnosis that has been given to us" (19.1; see also 5.4, 9). "Neither of these works contains doctrines that either ancient heresiologists or modern scholars would attribute to Gnostics or Gnosticism (rather, they are seen to represent proto-orthodoxy)."[101]

Recent commentators on 2 Clement also reflect Brakke's hesitance about the accepted view of ancient Gnosticism. In his comments on the text "choosing present enjoyment rather than the promise to come" (10.3), Simon Tugwell observed: "Similar comfortable claims recur in certain forms of Gnosticism, but there is no sign in our text of any of the distinctive tenets of Gnosticism or of the typically Gnostic sophism used to justify evading the challenge of martyrdom."[102] Tuckett has even questioned

---

97. Rudolph, *Gnosis*, 53–67; Brakke, *Gnostics*, 19–21.
98. Williams, *Rethinking "Gnosticism."*
99. Brakke, *Gnostics*.
100. Brakke, *Gnostics*, 30.
101. Brakke, *Gnostics*, 30.
102. Tugwell, *Apostolic Fathers*, 143. He continues: "Even apart from Gnosticism, we have found in *Hermas* and *Ignatius* signs that there were people exploiting a radical dissociation of flesh and spirit in order to play down the significance of the flesh, with

the use of the word "Gnostic" as a "catch-term" during this early period. He observes that to merit the title literary works "should include the idea that the creation of the material world is the work of a being other than the supreme God and that the world is essentially something alien (and bad) from which one should seek to escape."[103] Second Clement lacks this emphasis. The lack of ethical seriousness addressed in the book "does not clearly point to a Gnostic background: not all Gnostics were necessary libertines, and not all libertines were necessarily Gnostics."[104] What is clear is that the importance of ethical behavior is under threat, but such threats are not necessarily presented by gnostics.

James A. Kelhoffer also has questioned the idea that gnostics are the main "opponents" in 2 Clement. In a more thorough treatment of 2 Clem. 2.1–7, focusing especially on the use of Isa 54 and "another Scripture" (probably Matt 9:13c), Kelhoffer addresses the question of a possible gnostic background in the author's purpose.[105] Kelhoffer cites the recent literature that reexamines how Gnosticism has been handled wrongly by many writers.[106] He then applies those findings to the popular scholarly notions that Gnostics are the opponents addressed in 2 Clement—and he finds those assumptions seriously lacking.[107] To summarize, Kelhoffer stresses the "fuliginous" or obscure nature of the rambling and almost incoherent "expositions" of the texts in chapter 2. He dismisses "as unfounded the attempts to find antignostic polemics in 2Clem 2."[108] Such efforts cloud what the speaker is trying to do with these citations, namely, to engender a response of praying continually (2.1–3) and to remove any brash confidence as "sinners." He declares that "being saved" is a necessity that needs to be realized subsequent to being called. Such ethical results of the soteriological experience address the opponents not as gnostic outsiders but as those within the congregation who are unwilling to recognize that believers have a responsibility to offer "payback" to Christ in the form of repentance and faithfulness. His so-called opponents

---

lamentable consequences both for morality and for honesty in the face of persecution" (143–44).

103. Tuckett, 2 Clement, 50.

104. Tuckett, 2 Clement, 55. Space simply does not permit the inclusion of his other comments on the "Gnostics" issue. See Tuckett, 2 Clement, 47–57.

105. Kelhoffer, "Pigeonholing a Prooftexter?"

106. For example, Williams, Rethinking "Gnosticism"; King, What Is Gnosticism?; Brakke, Gnostics.

107. For example, it has never been convincingly demonstrated that the oft-cited word ἀνάπαυσις (5.5; 6.7) is an expressly gnostic term. See its use by Jesus in Matt 11:29; 12.43/Luke 11:24 and in the Apocalypse (4:8; 14:11).

108. Kelhoffer, "Pigeonholing a Prooftexter?," 294.

are not associated with any doctrinal "heresy" but are the congregants as a whole who need to hear this message.

Who then were the opponents? We simply should not seek to identify them with any philosophical or theological label. That they were persons within the group addressed who were bothering the believers with their teaching is evident. "And if they alone were doing these things (seeking pleasure), it could be endured, but now they continue teaching evil to innocent souls, not realizing that both themselves and their listeners will receive a double punishment" (10.5). They do display some libertine tendencies and ignore any future consequences for their behavior. If we must put a modern label on them, they could be labeled something akin to antinomians.

The Integrity and Structure of 2 Clement

The effort to discern an overall structure to this "discourse" can be a challenge due to its sometimes hectic and scattered character. Before attempting a suggestion, I deem it necessary to address the integrity of the discourse and whether all twenty of its "chapters" should be included in the original address. Pratscher claims, "2Clem 19.1—20.4 does not belong to the original sermon 1.1–18.2, 20.5."[109] Although not mentioned in earlier studies of the book (e.g., Lightfoot), this claim has become almost commonplace among recent scholars.[110] Some impressive evidence can be assembled for this approach to the relationship of the ending (19–20) to the previous chapters (1–18). Verbal differences between the sections include such issues as (1) the address is always "brothers" (ἀδελφοί) in 1–18, while "brothers and sisters" (ἀδελφοί καὶ ἀδελφαί) are addressed in 19.1 and 20.2; (2) the speaker refers to his address as a συμβουλία in 15.1 while in 19.1 it is an ἔντευξις; (3) the major term ἀντιμισθία appears five times in the first section but is absent in the "appendix"; (4) terms mentioned at the end such as εὐσέβεια in 19.1 and εὐσεβής in 20.4 are absent in the earlier part; and (5) words expressing the same idea such as ἐντολή in 3.4; 4.5 are communicated by a different word, like πρόσταγμα in 19.3. It must be acknowledged, however, that some of the differences above (such as number 5) can be explained simply as an author's variation in his vocabulary, and do not demand that there be a different author.

On the other hand, theological differences have also been discerned between the sections. "The motif of God's prevenient grace (1.8; 15.3–5) is

---

109. Pratscher, *Apostolic Fathers*, 72.

110. See, for example, Lindemann, *Clemensbriefe*, 190–91, 255–56; and Parvis, "2 Clement," 34–35.

absent in the appendix. The preacher's strong awareness of sin (16.2-3, 18.2) is weakened by the discussion of the occasional ignorance of evil (19.2)."[111]

Some authors raise the possibility that the "appendix" beginning with the statement "I am reading to you an appeal" belongs to the beginning as an introduction, suggesting that 19.1—20.4 was originally the opening or overture to 2 Clement.[112] It is also possible that the two chapters were part of a different address and attached to the end of 1-18, with 20.5 forming the conclusion when it was placed beside 1 Clement. Kelhoffer has argued that a philological analysis of the two sections reveals such differences between the two sections that most likely point to a later author of chapters 19 and 20.[113]

These arguments appear to be rather persuasive, but not all have detected such a serious degree of difference between 1-18 and 19-20. "But many scholars accept the unity of the work, among them, recently, Baasland, who sees in these chapters the concluding *peroratio* of the entire discourse."[114] While acknowledging the differences between the sections, Tuckett concludes "that the argument against the literary unity of the present text is not completely watertight."[115] There exist, for example, a number of expressions that unite the ideas between the sections. For example, the "wholehearted repentance" in 8.2 and 19.1; the "Father of Truth" in 3.1 and 20.5; the hearers saving both themselves and the speaker in 15.1 and 19.1; and the metaphor of athletics in 7.1-4 and 20.2. While it is true that the signature word ἀντιμισθία does not appear in 19-20, another morphologically related word reflecting "recompense," μισθός, appears five times in 1-18 (1.5; 3.3; 9.5; 11.5; 15.1) and twice in 19-20 (19.1; 20.4). Finally, the appeal in 19:1 is "to pay attention to what is written." While scripture has been appealed to quite often in chapters 1-18, this different expression is best viewed as describing "what is written" in the present discourse, namely, chapters 1-18.

In light of the above factors, I suggest that the argument that there were originally two separate documents, 1-18 and 19-20, is often

---

111. Pratscher, *Apostolic Fathers*, 72.

112. Lindemann, *Clemensbriefe*, 255-56.

113. Kelhoffer, "How Did Second Clement Originally End?" Kelhoffer also acknowledges many similarities between 2 Clem 19-20 and the earlier section and between both 1 Clement and 2 Clement. Those similarities suggest a compositional strategy underlying 19:1—20:5 that involves the *imitation* of both Clementine writings in order to make the secondary addition appear authentic.

114. Moreschini and Norelli, *Early Christian Greek and Latin Literature*, 133. The referenced work is Baasland, "Der 2. Klemensbrief und frühchristliche Rhetorik," 78-157.

115. Tuckett, *2 Clement*, 27.

overdrawn. The most striking difference is the switch to "brothers and sisters" in 19.1; 20.2. This change, however, could be part of the rhetorical strategy of the speaker in focusing on his application to all of his hearers present. The issue, however, may not be that crucial in the end. Since the document has come down to us as a whole, we should still consider it as a whole discourse. In keeping with the rhetorical conclusion of Baasland mentioned above, the approach in this commentary will be to view 19–20 as a concluding *peroratio*, functioning as a summary appeal on the basis of what has gone before. In the end, however, this commentary will examine the book as a whole, while leaving the issue of the integrity of the original 2 Clement as an open issue.

In considering the structure of the entire discourse, the lack of an overall thematic and logical construction is evident to most readers. One can discern, however, that the decisive past salvific events are strongly emphasized in chapters 1–2. Ethical and hortatory concerns, although not limited to chapters 3–14, are quite prominent there. A move to an eschatological thrust can be discerned in chapters 15–18 with the conclusion comprising chapters 19–20.[116] Pratscher discerns exhortation as the central theme, and 1–3 as the primary christological basis of the exhortation while chapters 4–18 compose the eschatological basis of the exhortation, and 19–20 serve as the concluding exhortation. Tuckett does not appear to offer an outline as such.

Donfried's suggested structure is one simple guide.

I. Theological (1.1—2.7)

II. Ethical (3.1—14.5)

III. Eschatological (15.1—18.2)

IV. Final Appeal (19.1—20.5)[117]

Not all authors distinguish chapters 19–20 as a separate section. "The structure suggests a basic division into three primary sections: the first is theological in tone (1–2), the second focuses on the ethical lifestyle (3–14), and the third centers on the final judgment of God (15–20)."[118] Very few authors attempt a two-tiered overall structure to the book. Jefford's "outline of the materials" in 2 Clement, evidently viewing 19–20 as a summary-conclusion, is the outline that will be followed in this commentary.

---

116. See Donfried, *Setting*, vii–viii.

117. Donfried does not include 19–20 in his initial outline of "The Intention of 2 Clement" (*Setting*, viii).

118. Jefford, *Reading the Apostolic Fathers*, 131.

The Role of Jesus Christ for Salvation 1.1—2.7
The Appropriate Response of Humanity 3.1—14.5
    The need to respond to Christ's sacrifice 3.1—4.5
    A Christian's struggles with the world 5.1—7.6
    Appeal for obedient living 8.1—13.4
    The church as the body of Christ 14.1-5
The Need for Urgency in Response to Christ 15.1—18.2
    Appeal to righteousness and holiness 15.1-5
    General appeals for repentance 16.1—18.2
Summary and Conclusions 19.1—20.5[119]

---

119. Jefford, *Reading the Apostolic Fathers*, 137.

2

The Reception and Use of Sacred Tradition in 2 Clement[1]

SECOND CLEMENT EXHIBITS A rich and varied use of previous writings considered authoritative by the author. The book incorporates more references to other "sources" than any other work among those included in the corpus known as the Apostolic Fathers. Before we consider those references and how the author utilizes them, a review of terminology being utilized is appropriate.

Every treatment of 2 Clement has a section devoted to this subject. Donfried refers to "quotations" in a chapter titled "Quotations from Authoritative Sources."[2] Tuckett, in a chapter titled "Citations," refers to Clement's "extensive use of citations."[3] Neither utilizes the more recent terms, "intertextuality" and "reception," in their thorough discussions. In the appropriate section of his introduction to 2 Clement, Pratscher uses the more recent expression, "Intertextual Relationships." He then surveys Clement's "Quotations from Old Testament Jewish Tradition," "Quotations from the Jesus Tradition," and his "Apocryphal Quotations."[4] My use of the terms "reception" and "reception history" reflects a recent trend in both literary and biblical/patristic studies.[5] What is the difference between "intertextuality" (German:

---

1. Expressions such as "Old Testament," "New Testament," and "Apocryphal Books" are anachronistic during the time of 2 Clement and raise canonical questions that are also out of place at this period. I prefer the expression "sacred tradition" to refer to any previous texts or traditions deemed as authoritative for the author. In this I follow the example of Porter, *Sacred Tradition in the New Testament*.

2. Donfried, *Setting*, 49–97.

3. Tuckett, *2 Clement*, 34–46.

4. Pratscher, *Apostolic Fathers*, 75–77.

5. See, for example, de Vries and Karrer, eds., *Textual History*; and Evans, *Reception History*. Strangely, even though both of these works claim to examine how scripture was received in second-century literature, neither mention 2 Clement, although they refer often to other second-century texts known as the "Apostolic Fathers." This oversight,

Intertexualität) and "reception history" (German: *Wirkungsgeschichte*)? The following definitions reflect the treatments of these terms in the books mentioned in footnote 5 as well as the lucid explanations by Wilhite in the inaugural commentary in the current series.[6] *Intertextuality* is the shaping of a text's meaning by another text. Intertextual figures include allusion, quotation, citation, and translation. The term takes into account questions of textual constitution in reference to individual texts and the ways texts stand in relation to one another to produce meaning. *Intertextuality* had its origins in twentieth-century linguistics, particularly in the work of linguist Ferdinand de Saussure (1857–1913). The term itself can be traced to the Bulgarian-French philosopher and psychoanalyst Julia Kristeva in the 1960s. *Reception history*, at least how it is used here, is the study of how biblical texts have changed over time through transmission, translation, reading, retelling, and reworking. It explores all the different ways that people have received, appropriated, and used biblical texts throughout history. The agenda of biblical reception attempts to chart the series of complex interpretive "events" generated by the journey of the biblical texts down through the centuries.[7] In literary studies, reception theory originated from the work of Hans Georg Gadamer in the 1960s and is reflected in his volume translated as *Truth and Method*.[8] This succinct survey also sets the agenda for the rest of this chapter, which will proceed in two stages. First, the tracing of the reception history of the many "citations and allusions" in 2 Clement will address the questions of the sources and how the texts are quoted or cited by Clement. This information is what is meant by the book's "intertextuality," namely, the form of the older text or saying and the how it is quoted in Clement. Second, the explanation of how it was received and utilized by Clement will follow, attempting to be guided by the most recent ideas about the ways that the "receiving" author (Clement) utilizes these sacred traditions to accomplish his goals and purposes. What does Clement do with these texts in general? In chapters 2–17 there are twenty-five citations or clear allusions to previous texts, around one for every four verses, most of which are recognizable as to

---

which is often suffered by 2 Clement, does not reflect these authors' quite thorough description of reception history, nor does it reflect 2 Clement's thorough reception of sacred tradition.

6. Wilhite, *Didache*, 30–59.

7. Evans, *Reception History*, 3

8. A related discipline, *reception theory*, is a version of reader-response literary theory that emphasizes a reader's reception or interpretation in making meaning from a literary text. It emphasizes the history of the meanings that have been imputed to texts and traces the different ways interpreters make sense of texts to make them meaningful for the time in which they lived.

their source but a few that are uncertain as to their origin. The terms "Old Testament" and "New Testament" as well as "Apocrypha" and "canon" are used in this discussion, even though Clement himself would not recognize their exact meanings during his time.

Reception History of "Jewish" Traditional Books

Readers can recognize around fourteen quotations and allusions to OT books. Quotations are obvious citations of a text and are often accompanied, at least in Clement, by a formula such as the name of the author or "the scripture said." Allusions are quotations of a text that involve a greater measure of freedom but maintain enough of the language for most readers to identify the source. These can be summarized as follows: 2.1 (Isa 54:1), clearly a quotation; 3.5 (Isa 29:13); 6.8 (Ezek 14:14–20), clearly an allusion; 7.6 and 17.5 (Isa 66:24); 13.2 (Isa 52:5); 14.1a (Ps 71:5, 17 LXX); 14.1b (Jer 7:11); 14.2 (Gen 1:27); 15.3 (Isa 58:9); 16.3 (Mal 3:19; Isa 34.4); 17.4–5 (Isa 66:18). Two citations are drawn from what probably is an unknown Jewish source: (1) 11.2–4, which is cited as "scripture" (ἡ γραφὴ αὕτη) in 1 Clem. 23.3. Lightfoot suggested that it is from the lost book *Eldad and Modat* that is mentioned in Herm. *Vis.* 2.3.4; and (2) 11.7 (also similar to 1 Clem. 34.8). These citations are usually preceded by a formula including the verb λέγειν, except in 2.1 and 17.5. The speakers of the cited text are identified as God (15.3), the Lord (13.2; 17.4–5), and the scripture (the singular γραφή, 14.1–2).

While more detailed aspects are explained in the commentary, a few general reflections are as follows. Six of the OT quotations are from Isaiah, frequently close to the LXX text, which probably assumes that the author had access to a manuscript of that book. Other quotations are quite close to the LXX, but some vary slightly. The purpose of citing these texts is almost always hortatory, with 2.1 (no citation formula) and 14.1–2 ("scripture") utilized to make a specific theological point.[9]

Reception History of Jesus *Logia*

Seven quotations have close parallels to the sayings of Jesus in the canonical Gospels. These are: 2.4 (Matt 9:13; Mark 2:17; Luke 5:32); 3.2 (Matt 10:32; Luke 12:8); 4.2 (Matt 7:21; Luke 6:46); 6.1 (Matt 6:24; Luke 16:13);

---

9. The treatment of "Intertextual Relationships" by Wilhelm Pratscher was helpful in formulating some of the above ideas. Pratscher, *Apostolic Fathers*, 75–77.

6.2 (Matt 16:26; Mark 8:36); 9.11 (Matt 12:50; Mark 8:35; Luke 8:21); and 13.4 (Matt 5:44; Luke 6:27–28). Each of these is introduced by some sort of citation formula (except 6.2). As in the OT citations, the verb used is the present tense of λέγειν (except 9.11, εἶπεν). As the speaker in these formulas, Jesus is referred to as Christ (3.2); Lord (6.1); and God (13.4). An interesting feature is how the quotation in 2.4 is traced to "another scripture" (ἑτέρα δὲ γραφή). This usage raises the possibility of at least one written Gospel that was utilized. Apart from 2.4, it is difficult to be dogmatic about the specific sources of these quotations, whether written or oral. While the Matthean tradition seems fairly visible, sometimes the quotation is closer to Luke (for example, 3.2 and 4.2). The specifics of this important issue will be addressed in more detail in the commentary.

As was the case with the OT quotations, the purpose of citing these sayings is almost always hortatory; that is, they serve the author's purpose to exhort hearers about ethical behavior. The exception is 2.4, where a clearly soteriological application is made, namely, salvation from the hearers' heathen background (see 1.8). In keeping with the speaker's stress on a "payback" owed to God and Christ, hearers are to learn from Jesus to confess with their deeds, not just with their mouths (3.2; 4.2). A follower of Jesus does the will of the Father (9.11). To be inconsistent in one's words and deeds is to blaspheme the name of Christ (13.4). Consistent with the hortatory thrust of the entire discourse and with the quotations from the OT, these citations of Jesus *logia* have as their purpose the promoting of obedient behavior in a disciple of Jesus. This behavior is essential for entering into the life that is now and is to come.

Are there any other quotations from the NT apart from the Jesus tradition? Words in 11.7 are cited as scripture by Paul in 1 Cor 2:9 ("ear has not heard nor eye seen nor the heart of man imagined"), but the statement is very similar to Isa 64:4 and does not prove dependence on Paul. A general response among scholars to the question of Pauline citations in has been a rather firm no. On the other hand, some possible allusions to NT texts appear in a few places, such as the athletic analogies in chapter 7 (see 1 Cor 9:24–47).[10] Dissenting from the majority view that Clement offers no Pauline citations, Donfried offers a very thorough discussion of the sources (Jewish and Christian) for Clement's extensive citations.[11] His general conclusion is worth consideration as to Clement's general naming of his authoritative sources. "Given the whole of 2 Clement, we note three sources of authority:

---

10. After a thorough review of possible Pauline allusions in 2 Clement, Foster agrees with earlier conclusions that Pauline references are simply absent. Foster, "Absence of Paul in 2 Clement."

11. Donfried, *Setting*, 49–97.

τὰ βιβλία (the Jewish Scriptures), ὁ κύριος (especially with reference to the Jesus *logia*), and οἱ ἀπόστολοι (including Paul)."[12]

Second Clement's possible use of NT texts has been addressed by two major works on the subject. In 1905 the Committee of the Oxford Society of Historical Theology sought to handle the entire issue of the use of the NT in the Apostolic Fathers.[13] The general conclusion about 2 Clement is that in regard to possible Gospel texts, "our homilist quotes throughout from a single Evangelic source, if we were at liberty to imagine it a sort of combined recension of two or more of our Synoptists . . . an earlier local type of harmony than Tatian's *Diatessaron*." "As regards the NT Epistles, the phrase 'The Books and the Apostles' prepares us to find pretty free use of them, even though they are not formally quoted."[14] A century later, another major project addressed the important issue again, though more in-depth. Gregory and Tuckett concluded as follows about 2 Clement's use of the NT.

> 2 Clement . . . clearly uses material that has been shaped by Matthew and Luke, although not necessarily directly, but it also contains Jesus tradition that may originate elsewhere. Parallels with material elsewhere in the New Testament locate it firmly in the same general milieu, but none demands a literary relationship with any of those texts. The strongest evidence for such dependence is found with respect to Ephesians and Hebrews, but these parallels, though tantalizing, are insufficient to raise dependence to the level of probability, rather than mere possibility. Thus we have found firmer evidence for the use of Matthew and Luke than was claimed in 1905, but less secure evidence for Hebrews.[15]

In the later commentary on specific texts, there will be opportunity to interact further with these two important works.

Reception History of "Apocryphal" Texts

At least four quotations in 2 Clement are taken from noncanonical sources (4.5; 5.2-4; 8.5; 12.2-6). The speaker in the citation is sometimes the "Lord," but in 5.4 it is Jesus, and in 12.6 no personal subject is expressed. In contrast to the prominent use of the present tense of λέγειν in the "Jesus" sources,

---

12. Donfried, *Setting*, 95.
13. Bartlet et al., *New Testament in the Apostolic Fathers*.
14. Bartlet et al., eds., *New Testament in the Apostolic Fathers*, 125.
15. Gregory and Tuckett, "2 Clement and the Writings," 292.

the use of εἶπεν is prominent in 4.5; 5.4; and 12.2. While the oral nature of the sayings is stressed, in 8.5 a written source is mentioned, where the speaker utilized what has been called an "apocryphal gospel." The question of specific sources of these sayings is one of the most interesting issues in the study of 2 Clement. Each of these will be discussed in turn at its appropriate location. While three of these have similar ideas in some gospel texts (for example, 8.5 in Luke 16:10-12), the quotation in 12.2-6 has no NT parallels. It may be from the nonsurviving Gospel of the Egyptians but has some interesting echoes also in the Gospel of Thomas 22.

In a volume titled *Intertextuality in the Second Century*, Christopher Tuckett reviews the possible use of the NT by 2 Clement. After analyzing both the methods of the citations and the citations themselves, Tuckett concludes that "it is thus hard to establish with any certainty any clear evidence that Clement knew and used specific Pauline texts."[16] Therefore, he concludes that the reference to "the apostles" (14.2) refers to what Justin Martyr later called "the memoirs of the apostles," that is, the canonical Gospels. Regarding the "canonicity" of these sources, Tuckett's conclusion is as follows.

> The evidence of 2 Clement reinforces the general picture of what many have painted of the situation in the first half of the second century C.E., with quite a lot of fluidity and freedom in relation to the issue of Scripture and canonicity. 2 Clement certainly seems to know texts that later would become a firm part of the Christian NT, that is, the Gospels of Matthew and Luke; but it knows other traditions too and is not in the slightest way embarrassed to use them alongside what would become later the 'canonical' texts.[17]

Having examined the textual way Clement cites sacred tradition, I must inquire about the specific ways Clement "receives" these sacred traditions. The ways he uses these authoritative texts indicates he recognizes that his "argument" is based on an authoritative tradition. His summary statement in 2 Clem. 14.2 indicates such a dependence on authority: "Also, the scrolls and the apostles (τὰ βιβλία καὶ οἱ ἀπόστολοι) say that the church does not belong to the present, but has existed from the beginning." It is widely recognized that this is a general reference to the Jewish Scriptures and to the writings of the apostles, recognizing that the terms "Old Testament" and "New Testament" would be anachronistic at this point, and that many of those NT books were not yet recognized as "canonical."[18] More

---

16. Tuckett, "2 Clement and the New Testament," 34.

17. Tuckett, "2 Clement and the New Testament," 36.

18. Lightfoot, trans., *Apostolic Fathers*, I.2, 245; Donfried, *Setting*, 93-95 (noting the similar phraseology in 1 Clem 42 and 43); and Tuckett, *2 Clement*, 253-54.

attention will be given to the meaning of this expression in the commentary. As has been his custom, the speaker does not delve into the theological implications found in these unnamed texts, but his intent is again hortatory. He utilizes these texts or sayings to stress the importance of reciprocating to God what we owe him because of his great salvation extended to us. "The use of that many quotations in 2Clement 2–17 shows how important it was to Clement to demonstrate that other authoritative traditions supported his exhortations and argumentation."[19]

In expounding on how *Wirkungsgeschichte* (reception history) takes place in Christian writers in the second century, Evans explains that "in the patristic period, reception of the subjection paraenesis is indeed in doctrinal and practical commentaries, homilies, apologias, letters and similar writings. Reception of these texts outside of these parameters has not survived, and is not easily conceived."[20] Although Evans does not mention 2 Clement specifically, our document fits his description well, whether or not it is an example of a true homily.

In addressing the reception of these sacred traditions by 2 Clement, an important question concerns how these texts function in the speaker's purpose. In other words, what does he desire them to do? Donfried has discerned a common pattern.[21] The citations are often inserted after a theme is introduced. Often a "paraenetic theme" is followed by a "paraenetic allusion." "In chapter 3, verse 1 contains the theme in the form of a theological summary of chapter 1. Verse 2 contains a quotation from the gospel tradition which both illustrates and supports the points previously made. The paraenesis proper is found in verses 3–4, and this is followed by a quotation from Isaiah, which again illustrates and supports what precedes."[22] This pattern is followed in chapters 4, 6, 7, 8, 9, 11, and 13. At two points a quotation is taken up and an "exegesis" of that quote is attempted (chapters 2 and 12). At no point, however, do the citations play a role in an extended argument as one can find in the NT (for example, Rom 4; Gal 3; or Rom 9–11). The texts are cited in either an illustrative or supportive function, most often in a context of paraenesis. As the above quotation from Kelhoffer also affirms, Clement's appeal is to the authority of the Jewish and Christian traditions, not only to illustrate but also to provide authoritative support for what is being communicated.

---

19. Kelhoffer, "Pigeonholing a Prooftexter?," 267.

20. Evans, *Reception History*, 144. The word "subjection" refers to submission to an authority.

21. Donfried, *Setting*, 96–97.

22. Donfried, *Setting*, 96.

3

The Theology of Second Clement

MOST COMMENTARIES AND GENERAL treatments of the book have a section titled something akin to "The Theology of Second Clement."[1] At the same time, commentators recognize the difficulties that accompany a theological analysis of what is a very practical document. "The preacher is no theologian, as his efforts in chapters 9 and 14 make clear."[2] "While there is some theological reflection, especially about the nature of Christ and the church, it is ethically right behavior rather than closely nuanced theology that concerns the author, and, presumably, his congregation (or at least its leaders)."[3] Others have recognized the difficulty with analyzing the book's "theology as such" and have preferred to understand the "message" of the book within an overall theological framework.[4] The latter will be the approach of this section on the book's message. The concern will be to understand how the author's beliefs about God, Christ, the Spirit, salvation, the church, and last things impact and help to shape his main message—that is, that believers must render a "payback" to God for his great salvation (1.3, 5; 9.7; 15.2). We will attempt to discern what that "payback" consists of and why hearers and readers of the book must do that. In considering the theology of 2 Clement, the message must be viewed as always oriented toward an overarching hortatory purpose. Clement is not interested in delivering a theological lecture. As will become evident, what was later called *orthodoxy* is important to him, but it is *orthopraxy* that is his main concern.

---

1. Tuckett, *2 Clement*, 65–82; Pratscher, *Apostolic Fathers*, 77–81; Lightfoot, trans., *Apostolic Fathers*, I.1, 396–400.

2. Grant and Graham, *First and Second Clement*, 109.

3. Ehrman, ed., *Apostolic Fathers*, I, 161.

4. See also Donfried, "Theology of Second Clement." Donfried, however, does not deal with traditional theological loci, but with how the original setting of 2 Clement impacts its overall message. Parvis also addresses the overall "message" of the book ("2 Clement," 37–41).

Theology Proper

The God of 2 Clement is one who has acted in the past, who is active in the present, and who will act decisively in the future ("Eschatology"). He is the Creator (15.2) and is the author of a new creation as well. The church was created before the sun and moon (14.1). God sent his son on his mission of salvation (1.4–8; 20.5). God is described not in abstract terms, but as the one who saves (9.7), who cares for his people (2.3), who is benevolent (15.5), and who is willing to give (15.3–5). Note that these attributes are not presented abstractly but are mentioned in connection with his relationship to others. Some expressions, however, convey a few of the traditional theological attributes. For example, God is all-knowing (9.9) and is the only God (20.5), who is invisible to the created eyes (20.5). He is the Father and the God of Truth (3.1; 19.1). A number of these themes are brought out in the heavily "theological" benediction (20.5).

Christology

No one would criticize this work as being in any way heretical or non-orthodox in regard to the person of Jesus. The preexistence of the Son is evident (14.1–2), but this is expressed in his relationship to the also spiritually preexistent church. Pratscher uses the term *syzygy* to express that relationship.[5] Jesus is the one sent to save "us," and that mission is expressed by God sending the light and his mercy by Jesus's suffering for us (1.4–8). While the Father sent the Son, Christ stands beside God and should be viewed as divine (1.1). The verbs for "calling" (1.8; 2.4; 10.1; 16.1) and "saving" (1.4–7; 10.1) and "teaching" (4.5; 8.4; 17.3) are all used of both God and Christ with no distinction. In the initial passage so often noted (1.1), Christ is thought of as God and exercises the eschatological function of judge. The familiar Jesus *logion* of loving one's enemies is introduced as something that "God says" (λέγει ὁ θεός).

The exact relationship between Father and Son is not expressed as one would expect in later Nicene theology. Platonic concepts of substance and/or idealism are not his concern, but rather functional definitions of Jesus's person and role. The writer of 2 Clement assumes that God and Christ, if they are not identical, are inseparable. Thus he follows the example of other early Christians, who, as one writer has expressed it, affirmed that Jesus simply shares in the divine identity.[6] In his final benediction (20.5) the author

---

5. Pratscher, *Apostolic Fathers*, 78.
6. Bauckham, *God Crucified*, vii. See also Hurtado, *Lord Jesus Christ*, 487–518. The

further calls Jesus the "Savior" (σωτήρ) and then couples with it the title "Pioneer/Founder" (ἀρχηγός). This title echoes the preaching of Peter (Acts 3:15) and the author of Hebrews (12:2).

Pneumatology

The teaching of 2 Clement about the Spirit is one of the most controversial aspects of the book.[7] The word πνεῦμα is virtually confined to chapter 14, where it appears five times. The reference in 9.5 is disputed, and the occurrence in 20.5 references the human spirit. The rarity of the word in light of its abundant use in the NT and in the second-century Fathers is striking.[8] As his other doctrines are related directly to his ethical concerns, the references to the Spirit are all found in a christological context. Jesus was "spirit" before he "became flesh" (9.5), and currently Jesus in heaven is again equated with "spirit" (14.4). Absent is any clear reference to the presence of the spirit of Jesus among believers. While we might be tempted to make certain gnostic conclusions, perhaps we should not read too much into this relative paucity of references. Tuckett warns against a polemical conclusion in this regard. Perhaps it is simply that Clement is not writing like Paul or Luke! "It simply seems to be part and parcel of his theological vocabulary and language which appears here in an unreflective way."[9] We should remember that the Letter of James also did not refer to the Spirit by name.

After describing what we can conclude about theology proper, Christology, and pneumatology in the book, at this point it is appropriate to mention the relevance of 2 Clement to later Trinitarian discussions. Clement's description of the Godhead still operates within the ancient Jewish concept of monotheism. Recent Jewish scholars, however, have argued

---

implications of this approach for later Trinitarian discussion follow under Pneumatology.

7. Thiselton addresses the broader issue of the role of the πνεῦμα in the rest of the Apostolic Fathers. See Thiselton, *Holy Spirit in Biblical Teaching*, 163–72. He traces the use of πνεῦμα in Didache, Ignatius, Barnabas, and Hermas, He focuses on the role of the πνεῦμα in the inspiration of the Old and New Testaments in the past (164–65) and the role of the πνεῦμα as inspirer of prophets in the present (165–67). Not surprisingly, Thiselton does not mention the few references to the πνεῦμα in 2 Clement.

8. The noun πνεῦμα as referring to the divine spirit appears over 100 times in the LXX and approximately 380 times as the divine spirit in the Greek NT (*NIDNTTE*, 3, 807). The noun πνεῦμα appears in a heavenly association (rather than the human spirit) approximately 177 times in the corpus of writings known as the "Apostolic Fathers," many of these (84) in the Shepherd of Hermas (Goodspeed, *Index Patristicus*). The total number in the AFs is approximate because of a few references in which the human πνεῦμα may be referenced.

9. Tuckett, *2 Clement*, 73.

that ancient Judaism was more "binitarian" than many have thought.[10] At the same time, it would be anachronistic and would violate Clement's language to expect that he should use the terminology of Nicaea and finely distinguish between the "persons" of Father, Son, and Holy Spirit. Clearly, however, Clement associates the Son with the Father's divine identity. The few and at times unclear references to the "spirit" make any claims to offer an incipient Trinitarianism as unwise at best.

An incipient modalism may be tempting since Clement speaks about the preincarnate Jesus also as a preincarnate spirit (see above). Yet the same chapter also seems to distinguish the two, so we should not insist on Jesus being described in two modes by the language of chapter 14. While some divine characteristics may be discerned in his few references to the "spirit," it is best to view Clement's Godhead without any clear inclusion of a divine person called the Holy Spirit. Hurtado describes the theology of the New Testament as having a "triadic shape."[11] Building on that approach, I recommend that the best we can say is that Clement's theology reflects a "dyadic shape."[12]

Ecclesiology

What 2 Clement says about the church is also connected to Christ and the spirit. The preexistent and spiritual church was united with Christ (14.1) and came to earth as the "flesh of Christ" (14.3). In the present time the spirit is again united with him in heaven, thus completing three periods of the spirit's "theological history." Apart from its appearance in chapter 14, the only reference to "church" is in 2.1. The barren woman in the Isaiah citation is equated with the church who also was barren before she produced offspring. In a rather muddled explanation, at least to modern readers, he further asserts that the "flesh" is the antitype (τὸ ἀντίτυπον) of the genuine reality (τὸ αὐθεντικόν), which again is the Spirit (14.3). One is left with the impression that the purpose of all this discussion is not to formulate a developed ecclesiology but again to emphasize the importance of ethical behavior. Tuckett concludes, "Ideas about the church arise probably from

---

10. Drawing on the ancient Jewish concept of "two powers in heaven," Boyarin, *Jewish Gospels*, argues that Jesus as a divine messianic figure was an expression of widely held opinions among ancient Jews about the Messiah and his identity.

11. Hurtado, *God in New Testament Theology*, 99–105. See also Hurtado, *Lord Jesus Christ*.

12. For a positive approach to what could be called the "proto-orthodoxy" of Clement and other writings from this period, see Kruger, *Christianity at the Crossroads*.

the context in which the author is writing and living; they are not necessarily part and parcel of his key ideas."[13]

Eschatology

In regard to "last things" the author could wear the modern theological label of a "futurist." He has a surprisingly modern, although brief, discussion of the "two ages" (6.3; 19.3–4). In connection with the future day of God's appearing (12.1; 19.3–4) he references the future "kingdom of God" (also 12.1). While the author makes no reference to the prominent NT term παρουσία, God's future judgment is vividly described (16.3; 17.6), with Jesus as judge (1.1). Entering God's future kingdom (5.5; 6.9; 9.6; 11.7; 12.1) will be in connection with the resurrection (9.1; 19.3) and the passing of the heavens and earth (16.3).

The scattered references and lack of one overarching passage that covers this eschatological drama is indicative of the hortatory appeals that appear at so many intervals in the discourse. His work again is NOT a textbook of systematic theology; it is a fervent appeal for proper behavior. The speaker deals with the problem of the delay in the second coming by reference to what is an apocryphal text (11.1–5). With the aid of another apocryphal text (12.1–6) he declares that the timing of that coming will be when the outward and inward as well as the male and female differences are removed and an original unity restored. Unlike the NT writers, he expresses no expectation about the nearness of the parousia, but he does counsel an expectation of it. Finally, as one would expect, he counsels an ethical behavior that is consistent with the future expectation. As long as we are in this world (8.1–2), we have an opportunity for salvation (9.7), because God is kind (16.1). Repentance is a necessary response that is always counseled (8.1–2; 13.1; 17.1).

Soteriology

In regard to the doctrines associated with salvation, the opening chapter is foundational. Christ has brought about salvation by the giving of "light," by his recognition of recipients as "sons," and by "saving" the lost. Second Clement also includes the importance of Christ's "passion" (he suffered) in terms of what would later be called "atonement." In 3.1 this saving action was based on his "mercy." Christ's "saving" is not only mentioned in the early

---

13. Tuckett, *2 Clement*, 73.

foundational chapter (1.4, 7), but also in 2.7; 3.3; and 9.5. Second Clement 2 also conveys a "then–now" theme, echoing a pattern of the "before and after" aspects of salvation. NT passages such as Rom 6:17–22; Gal 4:8–10; Eph 2:11–22; and Col 1:21–23 also convey this eschatological schema. In addition to these "past" references to salvation, there exist many other texts that clearly imply that this salvation depends on a proper behavioral response in the present, thus focusing this aspect of salvation in the future (8.2; 13.1; 14.1; 15.1; 17.2; and 19.3).[14] Therefore, the very current "praxis" of soteriology cannot be separated from its "completed" nature, although it is related very much to that past event. The references to keeping the seal of baptism "pure" (6.9; 7.6) and to "redemptive almsgiving" that is as good as repentance must also be viewed in this light.[15]

Another related soteriological doctrine is the importance of "repentance." The verb μετανοέω (8.1–13; 9.8) and the noun μετάνοια (8.2; 16.4) describe the expected continual actions of the saved. However, unlike Herm. Vis. 2.2.5 (6.5), no "only one time" possibility of repentance is mentioned. "That penance is required of the baptized assumes its repeatability—otherwise anyone who sins again must be excluded from the possibility of repentance."[16] The speaker sees himself as a sinner who is also in need of this repentance (8.2–3; 18.2). All of this extensive praxis, however, is "the appropriate response to grace which has already been given to the hearers in the salvation achieved through Christ."[17]

Theological Praxis

The above reflections, especially on soteriology, anticipate what I consider to be the main "theological message" that the original hearers should receive, namely, what I call the "theological praxis" of 2 Clement. Modern systematic theologians would probably group the following discussion under the rubric of "sanctification." Not all writers on 2 Clement have discerned the importance of this theme in the book. That central "message," related closely to the previous topic of soteriology, is that believers have an ongoing obligation to render "payback" or "repayment" to Christ or God (2 Clem. 1.3, 5; 9.7; 15.2). This "repayment" should be rendered in the form of "works,"

---

14. Donfried especially develops this pattern (*Setting*, 108–9).

15. Lampe, *Seal of the Spirit*, 100–104; and Downs, "Redemptive Almsgiving and Economic Stratification." More attention will be paid to both Lampe's volume and Downs's article in the commentary on chapters 6, 7 and 14.

16. Pratscher, *Apostolic Fathers*, 84.

17. Tuckett, *2 Clement*, 70.

as the proper response to God's gracious initiative. Failure by ungrateful believers to repay Christ would put them at risk of their supposed salvation and liable to eternal punishment (17.5–7). Being "saved" is both the result of God's gracious initiative (1.4; cf. 1.7; 2.7; 3.3; 9.2, 5) and something that needs to be realized through reciprocity (8.2; 14.1; cf. 4.1–2; 13.1; 14.2; 15.1). In other words, he saved us that we may also be saved!

To recognize the significance of this divine–human salvific relationship as a payback for grace granted, we must first recognize that such language has led some authors to describe 2 Clement as an example of "moralism" at best, if not an outright denial of salvific grace. Bultmann concluded that the Christianity of 2 Clement was "a peculiar kind of Christian legalism" influenced by "certain Hellenistic tendencies of asceticism and flight from the world."[18] Another critical assessment was made by Thomas F. Torrance, an author whose influence, especially in evangelical circles, colored an approach to the book for decades. Torrance summarizes his critical assessment of the "doctrine of grace" in 2 Clement by a reference to God as the subject of the verb ἐχαρίσατο in 1.4.

> Here there is a conception of Christianity as a religion in which God puts us in His debt, rather than one in which we put God into our debt by our righteous works demanding His recognition (therefore, χάρις). This is a genuine Christian thought, but it is not maintained throughout the epistle which we must leave with the judgment that it is the least evangelic of all the writings of the so-called Apostolic Fathers.[19]

In recent years, James A. Kelhoffer has contributed a number of articles exploring some important features of 2 Clement. His seminal article, "Reciprocity as Salvation: Christ as Salvation Patron and the Corresponding 'Payback' Expected of Christ's Earthly Clients according to the Second Epistle of Clement" has informed the concluding observations about the applied theology of the book.[20]

> The article analyzes the widely misunderstood concept of 'payback' or 'repayment' (αντιμισθία) that . . . believers owe to Christ. Much of the secondary literature is laden with

---

18. Bultmann, *Theology of the New Testament*, I, 169, 171.

19. Torrance, *Doctrine of Grace in the Apostolic Fathers*, 132. An additional judgment by Torrance about the book was that its theology "does not leave any room for a doctrine of grace" (131). Tuckett's observation is telling: "It is clear in Torrance's work that the standard of comparison is the Pauline doctrine of justification by faith alone, as interpreted by the Reformers" (79n27).

20. Kelhoffer, "Reciprocity as Salvation."

theological polemics (e.g., the author perverts Paul's gospel of grace, rather than an attempt to understand this concept relative to social relationships in antiquity). I argue that *Second Clement* presents Christ as salvific benefactor and patron. Christ offers salvation to those who accept the terms of his patronage, terms that include the obligation to render 'payback'—for example, in the form of praise, witness, loyalty, and almsgiving. A failure to accept these terms would jeopardize the relationship between Christ and his earthly clients and thus call their salvation into question. As a corollary, I propose that a likely purpose for *Second Clement* was to convince a Christian audience that the benefits of salvation come with recurring obligations to Christ, their salvific patron.[21]

Kelhoffer's insights point the way ahead for understanding the relationship between correct behavior and soteriology in this writing and thus its ultimate message. A summary of these thoughts follows, supplemented by my own comments. As a background to his argument, Kelhoffer explores the sociology of the patron–client relationship in Roman society.[22] This feature of the ancient world has also drawn the attention of other authors.[23] For many, the consistency with the NT teaching about salvation by grace is a major concern (see the comments above by Bultmann). Years ago, however, J. B. Lightfoot called attention to the parallel idea expressed by the author of Ps 116:12–14: "What will I return to the Lord for all his goodness to me? I will lift up the cup of salvation and call on the name of the Lord. I will fulfill my vows to the Lord in the presence of all his people." The LXX in 115:3a employs a verb (ἀνταποδίδωμι), which conveys the same sentiment of the psalmist's desire to pay back the Lord for his gracious blessings.[24] Danker defines this verb as "to practice reciprocity with respect to an obligation, repay, pay back, require."[25] While this verb does not appear in 2 Clement, a similar noun, ἀντιμισθία, conveys the crux of the author's message. This noun appears in 1.3, 5; 9.7; 11.6, and 15.2. The word is without a prehistory to the NT but appears there in 2 Cor 6:13 in a positive sense and in Rom 1:27 in a negative sense.

---

21. Kelhoffer, "Reciprocity as Salvation," 433.

22. Kelhoffer, "Reciprocity as Salvation," 434–38.

23. New Testament scholars have contributed significantly to this discussion. See deSilva, "Patronage and Reciprocity." DeSilva argues that "when the magnitude of God's grace is considered, gratitude and its fruits must fill our speech and actions." See also Barclay, *Paul and the Gift*, 24–50. Barclay applies these ideas of reciprocity to the Pauline theology of the gift and finds consistency with the doctrine of grace in the NT.

24. Lightfoot, trans., *Apostolic Fathers*, I.2, 212, on 2 Clem. 1.3.

25. BDAG, s.v. ἀνταποδίδωμι, 87.

This noun has been found thus far only in Christian writers and "expresses the reciprocal (ἀντί) nature of a transaction as **requital based upon what one deserves,** *recompense, exchange,* either in the positive sense of *reward* or the negative sense *penalty,* depending on the context."[26]

This word occurs at the very beginning of 2 Clement in connection with his vivid description of God's grace in salvation (1.6–8). The noun describes a "reciprocal exchange of goods and services: in return for the gift of salvation (1.4) believers are to offer, for example, 'fruit' and 'holy acts' (καρπόν ... ὅσια, 1.3), 'praise' (αἶνον, 1.5), and a change in perspective (or repentance: μετανοήσωμεν, 8.1–2; 13.1; 16.1–17.1)."[27]

Kelhoffer then describes no less than twenty-four ways in 2 Clement in which believers are to reciprocate that "Divine Beneficence."[28] Consistent with this approach to reciprocity, the gift of salvation requires the preservation of the patronage relationship between Christ (or God) and his earthly clients. "Salvation entails not simply the receipt of a gift but also requires reciprocity from those who would receive that gift."[29] He suggests that possible precedents in the NT for this approach to balancing grace with orthopraxy, are in such passages as Matt 6:14–15; 22:11–14; Rom 15:27; and 1 John 3:16.[30] He concludes that a likely purpose or occasion for this writing is "to convince a Christian audience that the benefits of salvation come with recurring obligations to Christ, their salvific patron."[31]

As mentioned previously, Clement may not evidence any actual citations from James and Paul. The idea of payback for grace, however, is consistent with the relationship between "faith" and "works" in James, as well as with the teaching of that champion of "justification by faith," the apostle Paul. He also taught about a "faith working through love" (Gal 5:6), wrote often about the necessity of "good works" (Eph 2:10; Titus 3:8), taught that believers should prove themselves worthy of Christ (1 Thess 2:12; Col 1:10), expected fruitful deeds in believers' lives (Phil 1:11), and emphasized that the final judgment of believers would be according to their works (Rom 2:6–10). "It would be unfair to set 2 *Clement's* emphasis on *antimisthia* ('recompense, exchange'—2 Clem. 1.3, 5; 9.7; 11.6; 15.2) in contrast to Paul's teaching ... since Paul was also concerned that his converts produce 'good works' (2 Cor 9:8; Col 1:10) and prove themselves worthy of their Lord (Col

---

26. BDAG, s.v. ἀντιμισθία, 91 (italics, boldface, and boldface italics added).
27. Kelhoffer, "Reciprocity as Salvation," 437.
28. Kelhoffer, "Reciprocity as Salvation," 448–54.
29. Kelhoffer, "Reciprocity as Salvation," 455.
30. Kelhoffer, "Reciprocity as Salvation," 456n84.
31. Kelhoffer, "Reciprocity as Salvation," 456.

1:10; 1 Thess 2:12), and he looked for 'the harvest or fruit of righteousness' in their lives (2 Cor 9:9–10; Phil 1:11)."[32] A message about salvific grace abounds in chapter 1. Anything that he then says about "payback" must be understood in light of this opening chapter.[33]

The nature of the Christian life as marked by obedience is the dominant theme in 2 Clement, as every reader of the book can discern. What motivated the author's strong emphasis on obedience and proper behavior? "There are not many early Christian texts with such a distinct orientation on ethos as Second Clement. The author is deeply concerned about the correct way of life."[34] While discerning no formal system in Clement's view of the Christian life, Pratscher does point out a variety of divine motivations for this evident ethos. God's salutary action plays an important role, namely, in creation, devotion, and granting a time limit to turn back. The salutary action of Jesus Christ is stressed similarly, namely, in vocation, salvation, liberation from darkness, and granting a status of being God's sons as consequences of Christ's suffering.[35]

Something, however, is missing. "One point is especially noticeable: the motivation of ethos by the presence of the Spirit, which was typical for the early Christians (e.g., Gal 5:25), is completely lacking."[36] If a Corinthian context is valid for 2 Clement, the church must have shed much of the pneumatological fervor that was so evident in 1 Corinthians.

Group Identity

For Clement, ethics and theology were not two separate theological subjects for abstract reflection. How the truths of this new faith impacted individual as well as group identity animated both this author and his fellow writers during this period. When forming a group identity, people often define themselves by how they differ from other groups.[37] While Clem-

32. Dunn, *Neither Jew nor Greek*, 696–97.

33. Most authors, in my opinion, have not seriously interacted with the reciprocity ideas found in 2 Clement. While defending the book against the attacks of Torrance and Bultmann, the normally thorough commentary by Tuckett does not actually engage the meaning of ἀντιμισθία in light of patron/client reciprocity (Tuckett, *2 Clement*, 79). There are a few exceptions to this neglect. See, for example, Moreschini and Norelli, *Early Christian Greek and Latin Literature*, 1:134.

34. Pratscher, "Motivations of Ethos in 2 Clement."

35. Pratscher, "Motivations of Ethos in 2 Clement," 608.

36. Pratscher, "Motivations of Ethos in 2 Clement," 609.

37. An adequate assessment of social, cultural, and theological issues facing the original hearers and readers of 2 Clement is outside the parameters of this commentary.

ent does not spend much time describing the people who were outside, he accomplishes this forming of a self-conscious identity by exhorting his hearers to be different from their unbelieving neighbors. Consider 13.4: "For when they hear from us that God says: 'It is no credit to you if you love those who love you, but it is a credit to you if you love your enemies and those who hate you,' when they hear these things, they are amazed at such extraordinary goodness." Furthermore, the abundant use of sacred tradition in Clement also is evidence that rather than identity being found in a group like a church, it is these scriptures that offer the strongest influence in shaping the Christian identity of his hearers.[38]

For a current treatment of these issues, see Paget and Lieu, eds., *Christianity in the Second Century*, part 4: "Modelling Identities" (233–308), whose chapters address ethnicity by Gruen (235–49) and Skarsaune (250–64). Lieu describes the various "models" that have been proposed for studying the second century and describes the period as the "age of the laboratory" (294–308). This metaphor was "the setting where a number of similar materials were mixed together by very different individuals with very different outcomes" (298). This model "has undoubtedly helped expose some of the weaknesses of conventional accounts of the second century and has suggested alternative ways of addressing the elusive dynamics of diversity and continuity" (308).

38. For discussions of how a specific *Christian* social identity was formed during this early period, see the following. Holmberg, ed., *Exploring Early Christian Identity*; Zetterholm and Byrskog, eds., *Making of Christianity*; Lieu, *Christian Identity in the Jewish and Graeco-Roman World*; Lieu, *Neither Jew nor Greek?*.

Part 2

Commentary

Theological Section

The Role of Jesus Christ for Salvation (1.1—2.7)

Chapter 1

1. Brothers, we must think of Jesus Christ as of God, as of "the Judge of the living and the dead." And we ought not to undervalue our salvation,

2. for when we undervalue him, we also hope to receive little. And those who listen as if it is a little matter are sinning, and we also are sinning if we do not recognize from where and by whom and to what place we were called, and what great suffering Jesus Christ endured for our sake.

3. What repayment, then, should we give to him, or what fruit should we offer that is worthy of what he has given us? And what holy deeds do we owe him?

4. For he gave us the light, as a Father he called us "sons," he saved us when we were perishing.

5. What praise, then, will we give him, or what repayment for what we received?

6. We were maimed in our understanding, worshiping stones and wooden objects and gold and silver and copper, the products of men, and our whole life was nothing else than death. We were thus covered with darkness, and our sight was filled with mist, but we have received our sight, and by his will we have cast off the cloud that covered us.

7. For he had pity on us and saved us by his mercy, even though he had seen in us great error and destruction, when we had no hope of salvation except what comes from him.

8. For he called us when we did not exist, and out of nothing he willed us into existence.

Literary Structure

The first chapter develops in three movements. The first section (1–2) is an exhortation to think about Christ as God and the resulting importance of thinking correctly about him. The second section (3–5) communicates by two questions the repayment that believers are to render to Christ because of being called his sons, even though "we" (first person plural) were perishing. The third section (6–8) graphically describes the dismal and lost condition of "our" idolatrous past from which we are saved. We did not exist, but he willed us into existence.

Comments

The familial address to the hearers as "brothers" (ἀδελφοί) is repeated an additional fourteen times in the discourse (in 12.5 it is singular and not used as a form of address). The noun later appears combined with "and sisters" (καὶ ἀδελφαί) in 19.1 and 20.2. Holmes translates the word in 1.1 as "brothers and sisters."[1] While this translation does reflect the generic nature of addressing the congregation in this way, the rendering blurs the conscious difference in addressing these hearers by the two nouns in 19.1 and 20.2. Familial language such as this is also employed in direct address in other writings from the period (see, for example, 1 Clem. 1.1; 4.7; 13.1; 14.1; Ign. *Eph.* 16.1; Ign. *Rom.* 6.2; Ign. *Phild.* 3.3; Barn. 2.10; 3.6; 4.14; 5.5), and often by James and Paul in the NT (for example, Jas 1:2; Rom 12:1). Clement makes no claim to authority here nor anywhere else but appeals to the salvific experience of his congregation, including himself, and will later base that experience on scriptural texts as the basis for his appeal (2.1–7). He rarely uses a first person verb (15.1), and he utilizes the first person plural in his appeals beginning with 1.5. No apostolic appeal to authority, which often appears in NT epistles, is evident here. "This is an intra-community discourse, not a polemical attack on those regarded as 'outsiders.'"[2]

While commentators often observe that 2 Clement clearly affirms the deity of Jesus,[3] even this bold opening sentence is expressed by the language

---

1. Holmes, ed., *Apostolic Fathers*, 139. See also 5.1; 7.1; 10.1; 13.1; 14.1; 16.1.
2. Tuckett, *2 Clement*, 128.
3. Tuckett refers to the "apparently very high Christological claim" (Tuckett, 2

of exhortation, not instruction: "we must think of Jesus Christ as of God" (οὕτως δεῖ ἡμᾶς φρονεῖν). The use of the impersonal verb δεῖ, while not abundant, appears elsewhere also in hortatory contexts (2.5; 4.4; 6.6; 7.4; 9.3; 17.1). This reference is the only time the exhortation is to "think" (φρονεῖν) about something. The reason for this language is that 2 Clement, from the very beginning, is concerned about making a behavior-related statement, namely, that if we "undervalue" Christ, we will undervalue our salvation and thus lessen the importance of our "repayment" to him through correct behavior, a theme that he will take up as early as 1.3. Translators have basically rendered the expression μικρὰ φρονεῖν in 1.2–3 two different ways, namely, "think little"[4] or "belittle."[5] Rothschild has argued that such translations reflect outdated language and should be revised in light of the arguments of James Kelhoffer about 2 Clement indicating ancient patronage.

> Rather than warning believers against "thinking little of" or "belittling" Jesus and salvation, 1a exhorts addressees to estimate, reckon, or value Jesus as God and judge and, not to "underestimate," "undervalue," or "devalue" salvation. Low value assessments of Jesus or salvation—estimating, for example, that salvation costs Jesus little or affords believers insignificant rescue or reward—are based on wrong information about items affecting value and misrepresent a believer's assets and liabilities. By undervaluing assets (e.g., σωτηρία), believers underestimate corresponding liabilities (e.g., ἀντιμισθία).[6]

A careful review of the subsequent verses about how much Jesus endured for our sake (1.2) shows that every believer's debt is significant (1.5), and it is this repayment that cannot be undervalued in response. Through Rothschild's suggested translation "the first two verses effectively set the stage for the upcoming tractate."[7]

While this "thinking" about Christ as "God" appears as a rather bold theological declaration, the additional statement places it in a functional context. Clement does not describe Jesus as the second person in the Godhead (an incipient binitarianism) but invokes Jesus as God in his role "as judge of the living and the dead." This title for Jesus can be traced to Acts

---

Clement, 128).

4. Lake, *Apostolic Fathers*, I, 129; Ehrman, ed., *Apostolic Fathers*, I, 165; Brannan, *Apostolic Fathers*, 56.

5. Holmes, ed., *Apostolic Fathers*, 139.

6. Rothschild, "'Belittling' or 'Undervaluing' in 2 Clem. 1:1–2?," 121. The arguments of Kelhoffer about patronage have been explained in the Introduction.

7. Rothschild, "'Belittling' or 'Undervaluing' in 2 Clem. 1:1–2?," 123.

10:42, although it is difficult to assume that it is a direct allusion to that text (see also 1 Pet 4:5 and 2 Tim 4:1). Other texts, such as Barn. 7.2 and Pol. *Phil.* 1.3—2.2; 8.1-2; 10.1-3, may support the idea that this is a Petrine allusion or simply part of early Christian phraseology. This eschatological reference appears later as a motive for present behavior. This first of his four references to "salvation" (σωτηρίας ἡμῶν; see also 1.7; 17.5; 19.1), stresses its future nature, which leads at least one commentator to discern a "now" and "not yet" in our author's soteriological thinking.[8]

This future orientation is continued in 1.2 as Clement refers to "what we hope to receive." A future perspective will impact the present behavior of believers. To undervalue these things (or "think little about them") is not simply a poor choice, but those who do so are "sinning" (ἁμαρτάνουσιν). He then makes the point more personal by switching to the first person: "and we also are sinning" (καὶ ἡμεῖς ἁμαρτάνομεν) when we do this. He follows this with a temporal, or possibly causal, participle: "because we do not recognize" (οὐκ εἰδότες) three important soteriological realities. These realities are (1) from where we were called, (2) by whom we were called, and (3) to what place we were called. He thus combines the past, present, and future blessings enjoyed by believers and then adds an insight into the relevance of the salvation experience by supporting behavior that he will advise throughout the discourse.

Finally, he closes this concise introductory appeal (1.1-2) with a reference to the salvific work of Jesus, again in a hortatory context. Those who sin because they undervalue their salvation also do not recognize "what great suffering Jesus Christ endured for our sake." While some might desire that the speaker says more about the atoning death of Jesus, he is content with this plain statement about Jesus's substitutionary suffering. No further reference is made in the discourse to Jesus's death, because this forceful passage lays the groundwork for his main message, namely, the responsibility to repay the Lord for this costly salvation through ethical behavior. While some authors see a polemic against gnostic ideas here,[9] nothing in this language evokes Gnosticism as a target for these statements. The language is again not polemical but focuses rather on a soteriological basis for the life of obedience, which Clement will expound throughout the subsequent discourse.

In the second section in chapter 1 (1.3-5). Clement rhetorically asks a single question: (how can we repay the Lord for all these blessings?) through two similar questions. The questions are "what repayment *will* we return to

---

8. Lindemann, *Clemensbriefe*, 200. Such a suggestion may too quickly import a modern soteriological schema into our author's theology.

9. See, for example, the comments in Donfried, *Setting*, 101-2. See also the Introduction to this commentary on "opponents" for further discussion of this issue.

him in the form of 'fruit' or 'holy acts'" (1.3), and "what praise *should* we give as a repayment for what we have received?" (1.5).¹⁰ The important noun ἀντιμισθία is mentioned at this point, both in 1.3 and 1.5. The comments by Danker on this noun are as follows: "so far found only in Christian writers . . . expresses the reciprocal (ἀντί) nature of a transaction as **requital based upon what one deserves**, *recompense, exchange,* either in the positive sense of *reward* or the negative sense *penalty,* depending on the context."¹¹ Its "negative" sense (as reflected in Rom 1:27) does not occur in 2 Clement in its five occurrences, here in 1.3, 5 and also in 9.7; 11.6; and 15.2.

The importance of this concept cannot be overestimated. The Introduction of this commentary explained this word as embodying the central message of 2 Clement, namely that believers are expected to render a "payback" or "repayment" in the form of "works," as the proper response to God's gracious act of salvation. The fact that believers cannot *fully* repay such an act of grace is conveyed by it being expressed by two questions at this point. Later references (9.7; 11.6; 19.1) convey the idea by an assumed affirmation. This positive response to these questions on the part of the believer will comprise the main message of the following chapters.¹² Before he declares the divine mercies in 1.6-8, the speaker in 1.4 mentions three salvific deeds as the basis for our responsibility to offer "repayment." (1) God gave us light in our darkness; (2) he called us his children; and (3) he saved us while we were perishing. This is a clear expression of "salvation by grace." The verb ἐχαρίσατο and the verb ἔσωσεν in the first and third statements reflect word groups with abundant NT examples (see the summary expression in Eph 2:8-9). The idea of "saving" (the verb σώζω) appears throughout the book in both past and future manifestations (1.7; 2.5, 7; 3.3; 8.2; 9.2, 5; 13.1; 14.1; 17.2; 19.3). We "have been saved" in the past (as here) "that we may be saved" in the future (14.1). The second description of believers as "sons of God" reflects the teaching of a number of NT texts, from Jesus (Matt 5:45) to Paul (Rom 8:14) and John (John 12:36; 1 John 3:1). The third section of the chapter (1.6-8) is a rhetorically powerful description of the state we were

---

10. The italicized words *will* and *should* reflect a variant reading. The Constantinople text (H) has the future indicative δώσομεν in both verses, while the earlier Alexandrian text (A) has the subjunctive δώσωμεν in 1.5. While Ehrman (*Apostolic Fathers*, I, 164) adopts the indicative δώσομεν, Holmes (*Apostolic Fathers*, 138) favors the subjunctive δώσωμεν since it is earlier and the Syriac version favors it also. Tuckett (*2 Clement*, 84) adopts δώσομεν but does not comment on the relevance of the Syriac version. Lightfoot adopted the subjunctive δώσωμεν (*Apostolic Fathers*, 2:43).

11. BDAG, s.v. ἀντιμισθία, 90 (italics, boldface, and boldface italics are original to BDAG).

12. Strangely, Donfried has no discussion of ἀντιμισθία at the location, where it would be expected (*Setting*, 102-5), and only prints the word in a quotation on page 38.

in and from which we were "saved." Donfried argues that in this passage, including 1.4, we have a sort of "hymnic confession," and he lays out the poetic structure and some of what he thinks are unique grammatical examples. On the basis of this structure he concludes that the "hymn" expresses ideas foreign to the author/speaker, reflected in the congregation he is addressing.[13] While this is a creative analysis, Donfried's description, in this writer's opinion, is greatly overdrawn. Donfried has not succeeded in demonstrating how these ideas are foreign to the rest of the discourse.[14]

This passage is filled with an abundance of metaphors and verbal images that describe the serious nature of our "lostness" prior to being saved. The characteristics pile upon each other through circumstantial participles that describe us as "maimed" in our understanding and "worshiping" dead objects while our life was nothing but "death." The rare adjective translated "maimed," πηροί, is absent from both the LXX and the NT. Furthermore, the word appears only here in the corpus of the Apostolic Fathers. It is further defined as *"crippled, mutilated, ineffective, mad, foolish"* and derives its specific meaning from the context.[15] Thus here it is *"blind in mind"* due to the following τῇ διανοίᾳ.[16] Other participles describe our presalvation state as "wrapped" in darkness and "filled" by a thick mist, but we recovered our sight when we put away that cloud in which we were wrapped.

The graphic language exceeds even the desperate state of the unsaved described in the NT in such passages as Rom 1:18–32 and Eph 4:18–19. The diatribe against idolatry rivals some of the OT prophetic denunciations of this practice by the "Gentiles" (Isa 44:9–20; see also Dan 5:4–23). Our author in this entire passage (1.6–8) strongly suggests that at least the original hearers of this diatribe were from Gentile backgrounds. The language, it must be admitted, is not only strong but strange.[17] The end of 1.6, however, turns to the positive condition of our receiving sight by putting away the cloud of darkness upon conversion. The grace involved in this conversion is conveyed by the expression that all of these conditions were removed "by his will" (τῇ

---

13. Donfried, *Setting*, 103–7.

14. He elaborates in an earlier article in an even more detailed way how the rest of the message interprets and seeks to correct this hymnic confession (Donfried, "Theology of 2 Clement").

15. GE, s.v. πηρός, 1661.

16. BDAG, s.v. πηρός, 812. Codex H (also called Codex C) has πονηροί probably because of the rarity of the adj. πηρός.

17. Tuckett observes that "ἀμαύρωσις ('dimness of sight') and ἀχλύς ('mistiness') occur only here in early Christian literature" (*2 Clement*, 136n34). He overlooks, however, the use of ἀχλύς to describe the literal condition that fell upon the sorcerer Elymas in Acts 13:11 (ἀχλὺς καὶ σκότος).

αὐτοῦ θελήσει). This is the only appearance of this noun in the Apostolic Fathers, and it only occurs once in the NT (Heb 2:4). This emphasis on the "will" of Christ/God again stresses his sovereign salvific act of deliverance. Benecke argued that some key words in 2 Clem. 1.6 indicate that the writer was "influenced" by the language of Hebrews.[18] I would add that the use of the rare word θελήσει in Heb 2:4 strengthens his assertion.

Further examples of these vivid word images occur in 1.7 in a description of the salvific events that delivered us from the vivid images of destruction and calamity. The condition from which we were delivered was marked by "much deception" (πολλὴν πλάνην) and "destruction" (ἀπώλειαν) and absolutely "no hope of salvation" (μηδεμίαν ἐλπίδα ἔχοντας σωτηρίας). One translation renders this last expression as having "not an ounce of hope."[19] Three familiar NT words express how God showed us "mercy" (ἠλέησεν); and "compassion" (σπλαγχνισθείς); and "saved" us (ἔσωσεν). The emphasis in this passage is not on eschatological salvation, but on the present experience of being saved.[20]

This section closes in 1.8 with a positive statement about the cause of deliverance from "our" pitiful state just described in 1.6–7. God called (ἐκάλεσεν) us out of nonexistence to a new existence. This verb has already been used to describe conversion (1.2: ἐκλήθημεν). Its use here functions to prepare the hearer/reader for the "scripture" quotation in 2.4: "I came not to call (καλέσαι) righteous ones but sinners." It will often be used later to describe that experience (2.7; 5.1; 9.4, 5; 10.1; 16.1). The metaphor of our nonexistence leading to existence also prepares the way for the metaphor in 2.1–3 of the church as "barren" in the past but now becoming "fruitful." While not all see a clear reference to Paul at this point, it is possible that "God's (Christ's) calling the nonexistent is based on Romans 4:17."[21]

---

18. Benecke, "II Clement," 125–26. More recently, others argue that the differences in application make this unlikely (Gregory and Tuckett, "2 Clement and the Writings," 290–91). These authors do not mention the use of θελήσει, which, in my opinion, strengthens the Hebrews connection.

19. Brannan, *Apostolic Fathers*, 57.

20. Tuckett remarks that it is noteworthy that "the descriptions of the 'lost' state of human beings do not include any reference to 'sin' or sinfulness" (Tuckett, *2 Clement*, 136n360). This appears a bit harsh, given the metaphorical language that obviously describes the effect of sin. It also overlooks the fact that in just a few verses (2.4), a "scripture" is cited that says "I came not to call righteous ones but *sinners*."

21. Grant and Graham, *First and Second Clement*, 113. The expression "things that were not" (τὰ μὴ ὄντα) in Romans 4:17 bears a striking resemblance to the ἐκ μὴ ὄντος in this verse.

Chapter 2

1. "Rejoice, O barren woman, who bears no children. Break forth and cry, you who have no labor pains, because the deserted woman has more children than the one who has a husband." In saying, "Rejoice, O barren woman, who bears no children," he spoke about us, for our church was barren before children were given to her.

2. And when he said, "cry, you who have no labor pains," he means this: that we should offer our prayers sincerely to God, and not grow weary like women who are giving birth.

3. And when he said, "the deserted woman has more children than the one who has a husband," he meant that our people seemed to be deserted by God, but now we who have believed have become more than those who seem to have God.

4. And another scripture also says, "I came not to call righteous ones, but sinners."

5. He means that those who are perishing must be saved,

6. for that is a great and marvelous thing, namely, to support not those things that are standing but those that are falling.

7. So Christ also desired to save the perishing, and he saved many by coming and calling us who were already perishing.

Literary Structure

Chapter 2 is clearly divided into two sections, each anchored by a scripture quotation.

Second Clement 2.1–3 consists of a quotation from an unannounced source, Isa 54:1 (2.1a), immediately followed by a brief exposition in (2.1b–3) of that text. Verses 4–6 consist of a quotation from what the speaker calls "another scripture" (2.4) followed by a brief exposition of that saying (2.5–7).

Comments

The chapter opens with a straightforward quotation of Isa 54:1 from the LXX. The citation has no accompanying citation formula such as "it says" or "the Lord said" (the verb λέγει or εἶπεν). See 3.5; 6.8; 7.6; 13.2; 14.1; 15.3;

17.4 for this language. The reason for this absence is difficult to discern, although the 17.5 citation from Isa 66:18 also lacks any citation formula. If one takes 2 Clement to be a sermon, then one might surmise that Isa 54:1 is the sermon text and so does not need to be referenced by location in the OT. This explanation faces the fact that the text is not at the beginning, and, apart from its immediate exposition in 2.2–3, the rest of the discourse is not really based on the sentiments expressed in Isa 54:1. There exists also the problem discussed in the Introduction that this book does not really display the features of a scriptural homily. Before moving on to the interpretation of Isa 54:1 in 2.1b–2.3, it would be good to see how other Christian texts interpret this verse. The context of Isa 54:1 indicates no evidence that it applies to any individual apart from desolate Israel in general. It could also refer to the city of Jerusalem as a metaphor for the people since architectural metaphors occur later, in Isa 54:11–12. In Gal 4:27 Paul quotes the context of the Sarah-Hagar "allegory" that he is applying to the controversy of Jews and Gentiles, which forms the background of that letter. He interprets the "barren woman" in Isa 54 as symbolizing the new group of believers (Sarah) contrasted with nonbelieving Jews (Hagar). "So brothers, we are not children of the slave (Hagar) but of the free woman (Sarah)" (Gal 4:31).Justin Martyr utilizes the text in both his *First Apology* and in his *Dialogue with Trypho* (*Dial.* 13.8). His usage is similar to Paul's, but he applies the text not as an allegory but rather as an explanation for why Gentile believers were more numerous than Jewish believers. "And the prophecy in which it was predicted that there should be more believers from the Gentiles than from the Jews and Samaritans we will produce." He then cites Gal 4 and adds: "For all the Gentiles were 'desolate' of the true God, . . . but the Jews and Samaritans . . . did not recognize Him when He came" (*1 Apol.* 53.5).

How then does Clement handle Isa 54:1? His focus is not on any numerical superiority of Gentiles in the relationship between Jews and Gentiles. The "barren woman" he calls "our church," but he does not clearly define the "woman who has a husband." No attack on nonbelieving Jews is offered here, or at least it is not clearly stated as such. He proceeds logically in three steps, namely, 2.1b, 2.2, and 2.3. Clement quotes the first part of the Isaiah text in 2.1b when the "barren woman" is addressed and then gives the interpretation: "he spoke about us, for our church was barren before children were given to her." Does this language imply that "our church" had some preexistence before having any human members? A similar idea is expressed in 14.1 where he will say that the church existed before the sun and the moon. But how is it described as being at one time "barren"? Lindemann suggests that there may have been a period of "stagnation" (*Stagnation*) for the church before the present children.[22] This, however, implies a period when there were no children and creates a problem while trying to solve another. Tuckett provides a way through this conundrum. "Perhaps the language and imagery should not be pressed too far and the verbal imagery should not be taken over-literally."[23] The message is that the church benefits from God's amazing grace in providing her with spiritual children, which should cause her to "rejoice." Clement proceeds in 2.2 to explain the next clause in Isa 54:1: "shout, you who have no labor pains." The expression "this says" (τοῦτο λέγει) conveys the idea of "this means that." But then the interpretation offered seems rather foreign to that of the previous clause. It becomes a command for believers to pray and not be weary in doing so! "We should offer our prayers sincerely to God, and not grow weary like women who are giving birth." The imperative βόησον is taken as commanding believers to "cry" out in prayer. This does echo Luke 18:7, where the elect are described as crying out to God day and night (τῶν ἐκλεκτῶν αὐτοῦ τῶν βοώντων αὐτῷ ἡμέρας καὶ νυκτός). Another verbal link with the Luke passage is found in the words προσευχάς and ἐγκακῶμεν as they appear in Luke 18:1 as "men ought always to pray (προσεύχεσθαι) and not to faint (ἐγκακεῖν)." Tuckett thinks an intended allusion is doubtful, but the similarities may be more than accidental. In an insightful article, Kelhoffer points out the main similarities in the two passages, and that the parable of the widow between 12:1 and 7 does not mention her praying.

> These similarities make all the more startling the contrast between the function of Luke's widow, who is unmistakably a positive example, and Clement's laboring mothers, who become *negative* examples of what Clement *does not* want his community to do . . . These two 'prayer' interpretations of materials that are not about prayer illustrate how such a general exhortation could be brought to bear on diverse texts and traditions.[24]

The third part of the interpretation of Isa 54:1 returns to the subject of the first clause above, the church. The deserted woman having more children than the married one means: "our people seemed to be deserted by God, but now we who have believed have become more than those who seemed to have God." The last expression ("those who seem to have God") is usually explained as describing nonbelieving Jews. Clement anticipates Justin Martyr's interpretation of the numerical contrast between Gentile and Jewish believers in his day. The present number of "our people" appears to be describing a time

22. Lindemann, *Clemensbriefe*, 204.
23. Tuckett, *2 Clement*, 142.
24. Kelhoffer, "Pigeonholing a Prooftexter?," 278. "Except for the quotidian insight that Christians should unreservedly cry out to God in prayer and not 'lose heart,' we have not gleaned anything substantial about Clement's theology" (281–82).

after the break between "church and synagogue" has taken place, and "seems to link Christians, as a 'people' (λαός), with the ancient Israelites but not with non-Christ-believing Jews of Clement's day."[25]

The second section of this chapter (2.4-7), follows the pattern of the first section (2.1-3) and cites a scriptural text. This one, however, is from the NT, and as before Clement proceeds to offer an explanation and application of it. The two texts are not unrelated, at least to Clement's thinking, but this one further illustrates his main point in 2.1-3. The quotation, "I have not come to call righteous ones, but sinners," is prefaced by the expression, "and another scripture (καὶ ἑτέρα δὲ γραφή) says . . ." The use of the word γραφή suggests a written source, especially since the word is applied to OT scriptures in 6.8 (Ezek 14) and 14.1-2 (Jer 7:11 and Gen 1:27). While the text has great similarities to Matt 9:13 and Mark 2:17, the former is probably the source. At least for the Matthew/Mark citation these texts were beginning to acquire a status of equal authority with OT books.[26] It should be noted that Barn. 5.9 also cites this text but puts the verb in the third person: οὐκ ἦλθεν καλέσαι δικαίους ἀλλὰ ἁμαρτωλούς. First Timothy 1:15 also has similar language while naming the one who came into the world to save sinners as "Christ Jesus."

The initial interpretation (τοῦτο λέγει) of the Jesus *logion* in 2.5—"that it is necessary to save those who are perishing"—is not a sudden shift so that the hearers become the ones who are to "save the perishing." This is not a move to express the necessity of evangelism on the part of the hearers. Lindemann suggests that a mission to outsiders plays no role in the exhortations, but that this is a call to convert others *inside* the community.[27] This again seems forced in light of the lack of evidence for such opponents, and also is foreign to the immediate context (for example, 2.7). Attention to similar language in 15.1 and 17.1 (dragging people from idols) influences the statement in 2.5 as a general one directed toward unbelievers.[28] The use of the first person plurals "we" and "us" and "our" in the context (vss 1, 2, 3, 6) indicates that Clement and his hearers were once those in need of saving. Here and elsewhere in the book "he saved us" (ἔσωσεν, see 1.4 and 2.7) balances the hopeful "that we may be

---

25. Kelhoffer, "Pigeonholing a Prooftexter?," 282. Both Tuckett (*2 Clement*, 143-44) and Kelhoffer ("Pigeonholing a Prooftexter?," 280-81) resist efforts to identify an antignostic polemic in this verse. See Lindemann (*Clemensbriefe*, 205) and Pratscher's identification (*Apostolic Fathers*, 79) of "Valentinian opponents" who had been larger than Clement's group.

26. See Tuckett (*2 Clement*, 144-45) for an affirmation of this approach to Matthew as written "scripture" as well as Donfried (*Setting*, 57-60), who prefers the "words of Jesus transmitted orally."

27. Lindemann, *Clemensbriefe*, 205.

28. Kelhoffer, on the other hand, does see Clement as issuing "an invitation to mission" ("Pigeonholing a Prooftexter?," 289), although he admits that it is not a developed theme in 2 Clement.

saved" (σωθῶμεν in 8.2; 13.1; 14.1; 17.2; 19.3: "in the end"). Clement attempts to keep both ideas in creative tension, perhaps not always successfully. That tension is between the "now" and the "not yet" in their salvation.

The demonstrative pronoun ἐκεῖνο fronts the sentence in 2.6 to bring to greater prominence an effusive expression that the author uses to describe the wonderful character of this salvation. "That is great and marvelous thing (μέγα καὶ θαυμαστόν), namely, to support not those things that are standing but those that are falling." A similar expression, μεγάλη καὶ θαυμαστή, describes the promise of Christ in 5.5. The exact expression in 2.6 also describes the resurrection earlier in 1 Clem. 26.1 as well as love in 1 Clem. 50.1.[29] While some may not conclude too much from this common usage between the books, this is another often overlooked verbal connection between the two works. The reason for hesitance is that the language may simply reflect early Christian expressions.

"The things that are standing" and "those that are falling" are neuter participles. The expressions thus may not be describing people but may be borrowed from construction and reconstruction. The analogy, however, is not lost. For people to be perishing is to be as things that fall. To be saved is to "support" (στηρίζειν) those falling things. To do that is to do something "great and marvelous." Clement closes this chapter and this early section in 2.7 with a summary statement, utilizing a number of words he previously employed: "save" (twice) and "perishing" and "called." What is new is the statement that Christ was deliberate and willed (ἠθέλησεν) to save the many who were perishing. This is the third time that the author has used the participle ἀπολλυμένους ("perishing") to describe the condition of those who need to be rescued. It is the object of the verb σῴζω ("save") in 1.4 and again in 2.5. Here it is the object of the verb καλέω ("call"). This word appears to be his summary term for the state of those whose lost condition was so graphically described in 1.6–8. This theological section (1.1—2.7) thus ends with a summary description of the work of Jesus Christ, whom we must think of as "God" and as the judge of the living and dead (1.2). While he *will* judge those who perish, he also rescues "many" (2.7) by his "great and marvelous" salvation (2.6). Tuckett's conclusion to this chapter is appropriate because of the way it looks both backward and forward. "This opening section . . . has made clear the wonderful nature of what Christ has already achieved for the Christian hearers. What this implies for the present life of the Christian will now be developed much more strongly in what follows."[30]

---

29. It is used in 1 Clem. 53.3 to describe a reconstituted nation of Israel in a quotation from Deut 9:13–14. The rich expression was also employed in Rev 15:1 to describe a sign in heaven and in Barn. 6.4 to describe a "day that the Lord made."

30. Tuckett, 2 *Clement*, 147.

Ethical Section

The Appropriate Response
of Humanity 3.1—14.5

The Need to Respond to Christ's Sacrifice 3.1—4.5

Chapter 3

1. Seeing, then, because he has shown mercy towards us—first that we who are living do not sacrifice to the dead gods and do not worship them, but through him we have come to know the Father of Truth—what is the true knowledge about him if it is not refusing to deny him through whom we have come to know him?

2. And he himself also says, "Whoever acknowledges me before men, I will acknowledge him before my father."

3. This, therefore, is our reward, if we acknowledge him through whom we were saved.

4. But how do we acknowledge him? By doing what he says, and not disobeying his commandments, and honoring him not only with our lips, but "from all our heart and all our mind."

5. And he also says in Isaiah, "This people honors me with their lips, but their heart is far away from me."

Literary Structure

This brief chapter revolves around two questions. 1. What is knowledge about him if it is not refusing to deny him? (3.1); and 2. How do we acknowledge him? (3.4). The answer to each question is conveyed by quotations from sacred tradition. The first question is answered by a Jesus *logion* (3.2) and the second is answered by an allusion to the Shema in Deuteronomy (6:4) and to a passage from Isaiah (3:5), both of which are also cited by Jesus.

Comments

Chapter 3 commences with a summary of the salvific confession in chapter 1. This summary serves as a transition from the theological section (1–2) to the ethical section (3–14). The message of this chapter is that because of Jesus' mercy he has brought us to know the Father. This knowledge consists in not denying the one through whom we were saved. If we now confess him, he will also confess us before his Father, and we should confess him not by our lips only but also by our lives.

The reference to "mercy" (ἔλεος) in 3.1 recalls the verb "showed mercy" (ἠλέησεν) in 1.7. From this point the author begins to press forward the behavioral implications of that mercy which "we" received. The four first person verbs (θύομεν, προσκυνοῦμεν, ἔγνωμεν [2]) and the two first person pronouns (ἡμᾶς and ἡμεῖς) portray a hortatory practice that will prevail throughout the work.[1] The speaker identifies with his hearers and exhorts them by including himself.

The theme of the hearers'/readers' former worship of "dead gods" formed part of the Didachist's warning as well (Did. 6.3). The language also reflects the anti-idolatry passages in Wisdom of Solomon 15, although it would be difficult to be dogmatic about the conscious use of those two texts by Clement. This condemnation of idolatry again recalls the pagan practices that he describes in the colorful language of 1.4–8, but no indication appears of a concern for a possible reversion to those practices. The depths from which they came serve to point out not only the great divine mercy but also the measure of "payback" which is expected in return—a major purpose of the message to which he has referred (1.3, 5), and which will soon concern him even more (9.7; 15.2).

The reference to knowing the Father of Truth has led some commentators to posit a negative reference to gnostic language and practice (see the discussion of "opponents" in the Introduction). Most acknowledge, however, that the speaker "while taking over certain 'gnosticizing' phraseology, is at the same time reinterpreting it."[2] Kelhoffer has criticized the idea that

---

1. In a work of only 128 verses, there are around 70 first person plural hortatory subjunctives, at least 20 of which are in chapters 16–20.

2. Donfried, *Setting*, 112. The texts usually cited that use the expression "Father of Truth" are *Gospel of Truth* 16:31–33 and *Treatise of Seth* 53.3–4.

2 Clement consciously takes up an "antignostic" argument. He reasons that "the writing's copious warnings and direct criticisms bespeak an author who would have possessed the boldness to criticize directly any gnostic false teachers had he wished to do so. Therefore, it is unfounded to infer that the author only indirectly, or implicitly, criticizes non-distinctively gnostic aspects of his supposedly gnostic opponents' theology."[3]

What then does the language of 3.1 reflect? A very clear biblical tradition about "knowing God" is evident. In addition to examples in the OT (Hos 6:6: "the knowledge of God"), similar sayings attributed to Jesus appear in John 14:7; 16:3; and 17:3; the Pauline examples of knowing God or Christ (Rom 1:21; 2 Cor 5:16; Gal 4:9); and those in the Johannine Epistles (1 John 2:3, 13; 3:1, 6; and 5:20). The verse itself defines and also refines this "knowing" in a very practical way. It simply means not to deny him (3.1c). While we should not conclude that "confessional orthodoxy" is unimportant to Clement, here and elsewhere it is a "confessional orthopraxy" that is his chief concern. When this refusal to deny the Lord is expounded further in the following verse, the language of behavior is what dominates.

The corresponding contrast with "not denying" the Lord in 3.1 is to confess or acknowledge him (3.2). This contrast is expressed by another Jesus *logion*, most likely taken from Matt 10:32, with some similarities also with Luke 12:8.[4] One may forget that an author also could simply be quoting such a saying from memory, adapting it for the purpose of the speech or writing at hand! The statement, both in its original Jesus-setting and in its usage here, is future oriented ("I will acknowledge before my Father"). The past salvific action governs current actions and will also require a future approbation—or condemnation. "The future salvation carried out by Jesus Christ is expressed in his function as an advocate in court. Jesus will avow himself to those who have avowed themselves to him in their lives."[5]

Continuing the focus on the future, 3.3 states that "this" is our "reward" (μισθός). This is the second appearance of this noun, the first (1.5) referring to our "repayment in return" (μισθὸν ἀντιμισθίας) to God. The other usages of the word refer to the "reward" of the righteous (9.5; 11.5;

---

3. Kelhoffer, "*Second Clement* and Gnosticism," 124.

4. Lightfoot notes the omission of "before men" (ἐνώπιον τῶν ἀνθρώπων) in the Syriac version. "The omission in S is probably correct, the words having been inserted by scribes from a well-known evangelical passage, Luke xii. 9. For a similar instance, where S preserves the true reading, see Clem. Rom. 46. Our preacher is in the habit of dropping out words in his quotations, and presenting them in skeleton" (Lightfoot, trans., *Apostolic Fathers*, I.2, 216). Both Holmes (*Apostolic Fathers*, 140) and Ehrman (*Apostolic Fathers*, I, 168) retain the expression on the strength of the two Greek witnesses.

5. Pratscher, "Motivations of Ethos in 2 Clement," 604.

15.1; 20.4) and a "reward" to the speaker (19.1) by their obedience. The language of reciprocity, which we have already noted and will see again, permeates the author's thinking.

We return to that demonstrative pronoun "this" at the beginning of the verse. As part of the fronted apodosis of a conditional sentence, it points to the following protasis: "if we acknowledge him through whom we were saved." While it is possible that the confession actually is the reward,[6] "the reward is thus probably the divine reward we will receive, not the response we are expected to make."[7] This is consistent with the broader context. There will from now on be an increasing emphasis on the promises of that reward based on present obedience, and on the threats to that reward based on present disobedience. The past salvation that is based on the work of Christ ("through whom we were saved"), so stressed in the first two chapters, now begins to emerge as a future reward dependent on "our" payback to Christ.

In 3.4 Clement asks another question (see 3.1) to clarify further the meaning of the act of "confessing Christ before others." How do we confess Christ—only with our mouths? Clement offers three responses to this question: (1) We confess Christ by doing what he says; (2) we confess Christ by obeying his commandments; and (3) we confess Christ by honoring him with our lives, not just our lips. This recalls the LXX version of the Shema (Deut 6:5) in Mark 12:30 (cf. Matt. 22:37; Luke 10:27). Compare Deut 4:29: "You will seek there the Lord your God and you will find Him when you seek Him with your heart (ἐξ ὅλης τῆς καρδίας σου)." Lightfoot comments: "as both words διανοίας and καρδίας do not seem to occur in that passage [Deut 6:5] in any one text of the LXX, we must suppose that the writer had in his mind the saying rather as it is quoted in the Gospels, esp. Mark xii. 30 ἐξ ὅλης τῆς καρδίας σου καὶ ἐξ ὅλης τῆς ψυχῆς σου καὶ ἐξ ὅλης τῆς διανοίας σου καὶ ἐξ ὅλης τῆς ἰσχύος σου (compare Matt xxii. 37; Luke x. 27)."[8] The words "from all our heart" appear again in how we are to "serve God" in 17.7 and also in how we are to "repent" in 8.2; 13.1; 17.1; and 19.1.

Even as scripture was previously employed to back up the answer to the proposed question (3.1–2), so another scripture is now quoted in 3.5. "This people honors me with their lips, but their heart is far away from me." Surprisingly the source of the quotation is mentioned as "in Isaiah" (ἐν τῷ Ἡσαΐᾳ). The fact that Clement mentions the identity of the scriptural author makes it clear that it is the Isaiah text he is citing and not its use by Jesus in Matt 15:8–9. It certainly also is possible that he consciously knows that

---

6. Lindemann, *Clemensbriefe*, 207.
7. Tuckett, *2 Clement*, 154–55.
8. Lightfoot, trans., *Apostolic Fathers*, I.2, 217.

Jesus also is citing Isaiah. That helps to clarify the subject of the verb λέγει, namely, "it says"—the scripture is speaking. The message is clear, no matter the specific identity of the speaker. Obedience to God is not manifested by what one professes or declares. It is "shown" by what one does in ethical actions. "The author is well acquainted with Jesus' summary of the Law. Deeds are contrasted with words not only here but also in 4.1–2; 9.10; and 13.3"[9] This strong message not only echoes the influence of Jesus' words, but it is also reflected in such NT authors as James (for example, 2:14–26).

Clement's use of this Isaiah reference raises an interesting hermeneutical issue with paraenetic and homiletical implications. Tuckett comments that "this verse from Isaiah is applied directly to a Christian audience. No evidence exists of an awareness of the context in the synoptic gospels, where the verse is applied to the opponents of Jesus . . . As with all the scriptural citations in 2 Clement, the words of scripture are presumed to address Christian readers directly."[10] This practice of Clement is a general trait seen in a number of patristic authors, and some would say also in NT authors as well. While this is not the place to settle this hermeneutical issue or even to evaluate it, it is the first of many other intertextual characteristics that we will encounter as we wrestle with Clement's hermeneutical method.

From the first three chapters, the tone and thrust of the remaining chapters of the discourse have now been announced. What is required both for now and for the future is a proper "payback" for the amazing salvation shown to people who were previously "maimed" and "perishing." This proper response consists of not only obeying the commands of scripture, but in performing that obedience from one's entire heart and mind, thus manifesting itself in a devoted life.

Chapter 4

1. Let us, therefore, not just call him "Lord," for this will not save us.

2. For he says, "Not everyone who says to me, 'Lord, Lord,' will be saved, but only the one who does righteousness."

3. So then, brothers, let us acknowledge him in our deeds by loving one another, by not committing adultery nor slandering one another nor being jealous, but by being self-controlled, compassionate, and good. And we ought to sympathize with one another, and not love money. By these actions we should acknowledge him and not by their opposites.

---

9. Grant and Graham, *First and Second Clement*, 114.
10. Tuckett, *2 Clement*, 156.

4. And we must not fear men but rather God.

5. Because of this, you who do these things, the Lord said, "If you have gathered with me in my breast but do not obey my commandments, I will throw you out, and I will say to you: 'Depart from me; I do not know where you are from, you who commit iniquity.'"

Literary Structure

The structure of this chapter centers on three exhortations (3.1, 3, 4). The readers are exhorted in 3.1 not merely to call Jesus Christ Lord; in 3.3 to confess or acknowledge him in their actions; and in 3.4 not to fear men but God. The first and third exhortations are then supported by a citation of a saying by the Lord (3.2, 5) while the second is elaborated by a series of virtues that are to be practiced (3.3).[11]

Comments

Donfried sums up the content of this chapter with the expression, "acknowledgment by action."[12] A summary of this "action" then follows. Although our salvation is evidenced by calling Jesus our Lord, we should also acknowledge his Lordship by our deeds, specifically by our love and purity and sincerity. We should only fear God, and not be afraid of other people. Jesus himself has warned us that although we are his followers, he will accept us only if we obey his commands.

The divine title "Lord" (κύριος) appears for the first time. The warning about its inadequate use thus anticipates the quotation in the next verse. The title will appear a total of twenty times in 2 Clement, most of the examples referring clearly to Jesus (for example, 5.2; 6.1; 8.5), but occasionally as a reference to the OT *Yahweh* (13.2; 17.4). Here "Lord" clearly refers to Jesus, as the following quotation makes clear.

This chapter explains further what the author intended by "confessing" or "acknowledging" Jesus in chapter 3. The verb changes to "call" (καλῶμεν,

---

11. The chapter divisions did not exist in the original document or in the manuscripts in which our text survives. The divisions are artificial and derive from Bryennios's publication following his discovery of Codex H (also called Codex C) in the 1870s. Lightfoot's original text and translation contained the chapter divisions but no verse numbers. The 1891 edition of *Apostolic Fathers*, edited with J. R. Harmer, also did not contain verse numbers, which were added in subsequent editions, beginning with the first Loeb edition edited by Lake (*Apostolic Fathers*, 1:1912).

12. Donfried, *Setting*, 114.

the subjunctive of καλέω). This word describes the salvation experience in 1.2 and 8, appears to be synonymous with σῴζω in the book, and will continue to be a favorite word of the author (for example, 5.1; 9.4–5; 10.1; 16.1). In 4.1 we encounter the negative side of calling Jesus Lord, that is, what it does not mean. Simply addressing Jesus by that title "will not save us." The future tense of this verb (σώσει) is significant because up to this point it has appeared in 2.7 and 3.3 in the past tense (aorist) as something that has taken place. From this point onward, it becomes clear that a past experience cannot be counted on because a future salvation is for those who respond by paying back the Lord for what he has done for them.

The support for this idea is a quotation from the "Lord" himself in 4.2, that is, "he says." Clement includes the future passive of σῴζω (σωθήσεται) in the quoted saying, replacing the "will enter into the kingdom of heaven" (εἰσελεύσεται εἰς τὴν βασιλείαν τῶν οὐρανῶν) of Matt 7:21 with "will be saved." This does not imply that he is not utilizing Matthew.[13] It does indicate that he is adapting the Matthean saying and simply inserting his own synonymous expression to fit his overall purpose in stressing future salvation.[14] Justin Martyr will later quote the exact words of Matthew (1 Apol. 1.16). He does not condemn the use of "Lord" but the act of saying the "right" religious words without the appropriate accompanying behavior. Holmes translates the final adversative clause that describes the demanded behavior as "the one who does what is right."[15] Ehrman renders ὁ ποιῶν τὴν δικαιοσύνην as "the one who practices righteousness."[16] At this point Clement prefers this phrase to the Matthean "the will of my Father," but without doing violence to the original Jesus *logion*. He rather expresses it in a different way. Clement also aligns himself with a more "synoptic" use of this word as an action rather than the more Pauline abstract idea of "righteousness." He will use the plural of δικαιοσύνη in 6.9 to convey "acts of righteousness,"[17] which is consistent with the meaning of the word as "justice and mercy" conveyed in Matt 6:1.[18]

What those "acts of righteousness" look like appears in 4.3. In one of the longer verses in the book, broken up into two or three sentences in the translations, Clement portrays the "righteous deeds" consistent with the confession

13. Donfried, *Setting*, 114.

14. Lightfoot (*Apostolic Fathers*, I.2, 217) and Tuckett (*2 Clement*, 158, 162) affirm the source as Matthean, as does Lindemann (*Clemensbriefe*, 209), although cautiously.

15. Holmes, ed., *Apostolic Fathers*, 143.

16. Ehrman, ed., *Apostolic Fathers*, I, 171. See Brannan, *Apostolic Fathers*, 58.

17. Ehrman, ed., *Apostolic Fathers*, I, 175. Holmes renders the plural as "righteous deeds" (*Apostolic Fathers*, 147); Brannan as "righteous works" (*Apostolic Fathers*, 60).

18. BDAG, s.v. δικαιοσύνη, 248, 3b.

of Christ in both negative and positive ways. Addressing the hearers the second time as ἀδελφοί (1:1), he conveys first by four infinitive clauses the "righteous deeds" that are the evidence of our true "confession" of the Lord,

1. by loving one another
2. by not committing adultery
3. by not slandering each other
4. by not being jealous.

In an adversative contrast (ἀλλ᾽), conveyed by another infinitive complement (εἶναι . . . ὀφείλομεν), he then states that "we ought"

1. to be self-controlled
2. to be compassionate
3. to be good
4. to have sympathy for one another, and
5. not to be "lovers of money" or "avaricious."[19]

The verse closes with an effective explanation: "By these actions let us acknowledge (hortatory subjunctive ὁμολογῶμεν) him, and not by their opposite."

Clement's use of the verb ἀγαπάω (in the infinitive clause ἐν τῷ ἀγαπᾶν) to head the list may be instructive. Tuckett takes effective notice of this.

> The general exhortation to love is in some way similar to Paul in making 'love' the overriding ethical category (cf. 1 Cor 13; Gal 5:14; also 1 Clem. 49). Here, love is explicitly related to relationships within the community ('one another'). The concern for good internal relations within the community is underlined here by the threefold reference to 'one another' (loving one another, not slandering one another, sympathizing with one another).[20]

One need not posit a direct Pauline influence at this point to recognize that this role of love as the governing virtue is consistent with the ethical admonitions throughout the NT Gospels and Epistles (Matt 7:12; 22:40; John 13:34; Jas 2:8; 1 Pet 4:8; and the above Pauline references). The danger is always near of "mirror hermeneutics" in assuming that the original hearers were guilty of transgressing these admonitions. These exhortations, however, would be appropriate for any congregation. A good assumption, however, is

---

19. Holmes, ed., *Apostolic Fathers*, 143.
20. Tuckett, *2 Clement*, 163.

that any problems that might be addressed at this point are problems "primarily related to relationships within the community."²¹

The list of adjectives conveying desirable virtues is headed by ἐγκρατής, followed by ἐλεήμων and ἀγαθός. That this virtue is very important for our author is evident from the fact that he uses its noun form ἐγκράτεια as a one-word summary of his message thus far in 15.1: "Now I think that I have not given unimportant advice about self-control (περὶ ἐγκρατείας)." As the first in its own sublist of triads, practicing "self-control" corresponds to the first behavior in the vice triad (following the counsel to "love")—that is, "not committing adultery" (μὴ μοιχᾶσθαι). Whether or not the words are intended to be parallel, that the word group ἐγκρατής/ἐγκράτεια refers to self-control in sexual matters is most probable. The adjective appears only once in the NT (Titus 1:8) as a character trait of an ἐπίσκοπος, while the noun occurs in two NT virtue lists (Gal 5:23; 2 Pet 1:6 [2x]) and once as a "sermon theme" (Acts 24:25). Its scarcity in the NT stands in contrast to its prominent use as an ethical trait in Socrates, the Stoics, Plutarch and Philo.²² Other Apostolic Fathers also use it (1 Clem. 30.3; 35.2; 38.2; 62.2; 64.1; Hermas, *Vis.* 2.9; 3.8; *Mand.* 1, 6, 8; *Sim.* 51. 9.15).

Readers should resist any temptation to view the author of 2 Clement as an Encratite. As mentioned in the Introduction, Harris thought that these words indicated that Julius Cassianus the Encratite was the author of 2 Clement.²³ However, 1 Clement used the same noun four times (35.2; 38.2; 62.2; 64.1), but no claim is heard that he was encratitic. The virtue of "self-control" is commended so widely in secular and Christian literature that the use of the word does not indicate a commitment to any extreme asceticism.²⁴ It is not necessary to conclude that the counsel about self-control in sexual matters implies that the author either practiced or encouraged abstention from sexual activity.

The admonition to be concerned for one another, literally to "have mutual sympathy for each other" (συμπάσχειν ἀλλήλοις), points out the concern that marked early Christian communities, especially as they faced the majority culture around them. This "group identity" was forged through these commands and evidently became evident to others around them. The exhortation against "loving of money" (μὴ φιλαργυρεῖν) need not be addressing a specific issue in the community. This counsel was part

21. Tuckett, *2 Clement*, 163.

22. See Donfried, *Setting*, 116; Tuckett, *2 Clement*, 165-66; BDAG, 274, for both the noun and adjective. See also the excursus in Lindemann, *Clemensbriefe*, 244-45.

23. Harris, "Authorship of the So-Called Second Epistle of Clement."

24. See discussion about this issue in Donfried, *Setting*, 16, 77, 116; and Tuckett, *2 Clement*, 165-66.

of the general paraenesis appearing throughout early Christian communities (1 Tim 6:10; 2 Tim 3:2; Did. 3.5), employing admonitions that took their cues from their founder, Jesus (see Luke 16:14).

The admonition in 3.4 not to fear men but to fear God could be an allusion to a Jesus *logion* found in Matt 10:28. This prepares the way for a fuller treatment of this antithesis of fear in the "citation" recorded in 5.2–4. It is difficult to see its connection to the final "citation" in the following verse. The counsel is probably intended to end the virtue list in 4.3.

The genitive absolute participle clause that begins 4.5 (ταῦτα ὑμῶν πρασσόντων) combined with the causal "because of this" (διὰ τοῦτο) marks a sort of conclusion to this chapter.

As citations give support to the previous admonitions, so this quotation functions here. The exact causal connection of the preceding with the quotation, as well as the source of the quote, perplexes one seeking to analyze it!

The author was familiar with a source that has no real parallel in any Gospel, but perhaps was known to others apart from Clement. See the section "The Intertextuality of Second Clement" in the Introduction for a survey of this and other quotations from sources that have not come down to us. We simply cannot know the source for the unique language like "being gathered with me in my breast." Tuckett mentions a similar marginal gloss to Matt 7:5 found in MS 1424 which is said to be from "the Jewish Gospel," which could be the Gospel of the Nazarenes, and which also has not survived.[25] Lightfoot's suggestion, while not providing anything like a final solution, is at least worth considering:

> Not found in the canonical Gospels, and perhaps taken from the *Gospel of the Egyptians*, . . . The image and expressions are derived from Is. 40:11 τῷ βραχίονι αὐτοῦ συνάξει ἄρνας καὶ ἐν τῷ κόλπῳ αὐτοῦ βαστάσαι. The latter clause, though absent in BSA [i.e., standard LXX texts], is found in several MSS, in other Greek Versions, and in the original; and must be supposed to have been known to the writer of the Gospel in question. For the expression συνάγειν ἐν κόλπῳ, 'to gather in the lap,' see LXX Prov. xxx. 4 (xxiv. 27). The image is carried out in the language of the next chapter, ἔσεσθε ὡς ἀρνία κ.τ.λ.[26]

The final words of the citation ("Depart from me; I do not know where you are from") echo the words of Jesus in the judgment of the sheep and goats (Matt 25:41 combined with a judgment statement in Matt 7:23). The purpose of the citation, however, is evident and proclaims an idea alluded to in 1:1 that

---

25. Tuckett, *2 Clement*, 161.
26. Lightfoot, trans., *Apostolic Fathers*, I.2, 218.

ETHICAL SECTION 71

will be expounded at length in subsequent chapters. That point is that failure to display these expected ethical virtues will result in being rejected by the "Lord" (Jesus) who is the judge of the living and the dead.

A Christian's Struggles with the World 5.1—7.6

Chapter 5

1. For which reason, brothers, let us turn away from our temporary sojourn in this world, and do the will of him who called us, and let us not fear to depart from this world.
2. For the Lord says, "You will be like lambs among wolves."
3. But Peter answered and said to him, "What if the wolves tear apart the lambs?"
4. Jesus said to Peter, "Let the lambs have no fear of the wolves after their death, and have no fear of those who kill you, and can do nothing more to you, but fear him who after your death has power to cast body and soul into the flames of hell."
5. And be assured, brothers, that our temporary stay in this world of the flesh is a little thing and lasts a short time, but the promise of Christ is great and wonderful, and brings us rest in the coming kingdom and eternal life.
6. What then will we do to secure these things except to live a holy and righteous life, and to regard these worldly things as not our own, and not desire them?
7. For when we desire to acquire these things, we fall away from the right way.

Literary Structure

This chapter is marked by three references to the "world": "this world" in 5.1 and 5, and "these worldly things" in 5.6. The first reference is part of an opening exhortation to leave behind this world (5.1). Then follows the reason why we should do this, namely, an extended saying of the Lord (5.2-4). Then follows an affirmation about our stay in "this world" (5.5), followed by a question about "the things of this world" (5.6). The chapter concludes with a warning against desiring "these things." The six appearances of demonstrative pronouns (5.1[2]; 5.5[2]; 5.6; 5.7) serve to focus attention on "this" world and "this" flesh in contrast to the promise of the coming kingdom.

Comments

This chapter is both a summary of and a fitting conclusion to the admonitions of chapters 3 and 4. The exhortation that we turn away from this temporary location and not to fear departing from this world should not be viewed as an exhortation to become martyrs. This verse clearly introduces the contrast between the current and the coming worlds for the believer. The combination of a unique adverbial marker translated as "for which reason" and the familial address as "brothers" lends a sense of urgency to the exhortation.²⁷ The two worlds comprise two ways of life; one is temporary (5.1) and the other is eternal (5.5). The encouragement not to "fear" the departure leads to describing this relocation as something "great and wonderful" that results in an eschatological "rest" (5.5). Before describing the nature of that "promise" (5.5), it is necessary to examine in greater detail the reason given for turning from this world (5.1) in the citation conveyed in 5.2–4. This "quotation" is described as a saying of the Lord (5.2), which is followed by Peter's response (5.3), which is then followed by another saying of Jesus (5.4). This passage contains two sayings of Jesus connected by a saying of Peter. While the passage has affinities to Matt 10:16 and Luke 10:3 in its beginning and Matt 10:28 and Luke 12:4–5 in its ending, the question by Peter and Jesus' initial response have no parallels at all in the canonical Gospels. A good place to begin is with Lightfoot. "This is a close parallel to Luke x. 3 ἀποστέλλω ὑμᾶς ὡς ἄρνας ἐν μέσῳ λύκων (comp. Matt x. 6). As however Peter is not mentioned in the context, and as the continuation of the quotation is not found in the canonical Gospels, the whole passage was probably taken from some apocryphal source, perhaps the Gospel of the Egyptians."²⁸ This suggestion, however, is not more than an educated guess, and has not found many advocates since Lightfoot. The issue is complicated by an added response by Jesus about "not fearing" those who would kill you (5.4), which does appear in some other patristic sources (see Hermas, *Mand.* 12.6.3). This raises the possibility that these sayings circulated independently, but

---

27. The adverb ὅθεν is "a marker of the basis for an action or procedure, *for which reason*" (BDAG, 693–94). This is the first and only occurrence of this word in Clement, although it is often used by Ignatius. It is used in this sense in Matt 14:7; Acts 26:19; Heb 2:17; 3:1; 7:25; 8:3; 9:18; 11:19.

28. Lightfoot, trans. *Apostolic Fathers*, II, 218–19.

Clement attributes the entire unit to "the Lord" and gives no indication that he patched together independent traditions. Therefore, most authors have concluded that the sayings, although possibly independent, survived in some sort of composite form.[29] The alternative is the suggestion that the author is citing from an apocryphal gospel that is now lost.[30]

The discovery of papyri from the Egyptian sands postdates authors like Lightfoot, and the delay in publishing them makes another suggestion possible. Lührmann and Parsons's publication of P.Oxy. 4009 suggests that the fragment of an exchange between Peter and Jesus is from the Gospel of Peter, since the saying about not fearing death overlaps our "citation" in 2 Clem. 5.3–4.[31] Examination of the sayings in both 2 Clement and the Gospel of Peter, however, indicates that they are not as close to a Jesus saying as the authors wish, given that the authors of 2 Clement and the Gospel of Peter themselves make assumptions about what parts of the "saying" are missing. It remains an interesting suggestion, but the fragmentary nature of the papyrus text makes certainty impossible. One further observation remains on the features of the text. The comments by Peter preserved in 5.3 seem very typical of those in other apocryphal gospels, which also tend to expand the language of the canonical texts. This also points to the whole story as being from a written noncanonical source—one that is probably closer to Luke's account than to Matthew's.[32]

The best solution, therefore, given our knowledge of these texts, is that this conversation between Jesus and Peter derives from a noncanonical gospel source that has not survived. This tradition also probably developed after the Synoptic Gospels of Matthew and Luke were finished, perhaps even surviving in some sort of harmony, long before Tatian would write his *Diatessaron*. In the context of the exhortation in 5.1, the saying functions in an eschatological manner. Because we should not be afraid to depart for that future world (5.1), we should not be afraid of dying by being killed by people who have no control over our afterlife (5.4). The statement in 2 Clem. 5.1 (bidding hearers not to be afraid to depart from the world) best supports that 2 Clem. 5.4 (the exchange between Jesus and Peter) may well be an exhortation to martyrdom, although the context of

29. See Donfried, *Setting*, 68–71; and Tuckett, *2 Clement*, 169.
30. Lightfoot, trans., *Apostolic Fathers*, I.2, 219; Lindemann, *Clemensbriefe*, 213.
31. Lührmann and Parsons, "4009, Gospel of Peter?"
32. Justin Martyr (*1 Apol.* 19.7) has occasionally been pointed out as preserving a form of this conversation (Donfried, *Setting*, 68–70). Examination of Justin's text, however, shows that he only mentions the references to "fearing" and "not fearing." He mentions nothing about the initial conversation between Peter and Jesus. Clement and Justin are not appealing to the same text.

what the original hearers were facing does not seem to include persecution. It serves as paraenesis for all who face death no matter the means. The appeal to the hearers' shared knowledge is "be assured" or "you know" (γινώσκετε), and the word "brothers" adds familial urgency to this appeal to their knowledge. Clement reiterates the point he has made in 5.1 about the temporary nature of our current lives. This life is a "little thing" and it endures for a "little time" because the "promise" of Christ (Matt 25:46) will bring us "rest" as part of our "eternal life" (5.5). The word for "temporary stay" (ἐπιδημία) is a synonym for the "sojourn" (παροικία), used in verse 1. The adjective "little thing" (μικρά), possibly echoing its use in 1.2–3, although paired with the temporal adjective "short time" (ὀλιγοχρόνιος), may imply "small in importance" rather than duration. The contrast is with the elegant repetition of a "great and wonderful" (μεγάλη καὶ θαυμαστή) promise, also an echo of an earlier expression (2.6).[33]

The eschatological "rest" in 5.5 again raises the possibility of gnostic echoes. We have previously argued against this being an antignostic polemic. See the "Opponents" in the Introduction. Its use in previous Jewish biblical contexts (Josh 21:44; Matt 11:29; Rev 4:11) argues for a more Jewish or at least Hellenistic Jewish association. The Christian use of another synonymous term for "rest" (κατάπαυσις) in Heb 3:11, 18; 4:1, 3, 5 should not be disallowed by the slight difference in spelling. Both terms here and in Hebrews refer to an eschatological rest, typified by the physical rest in Joshua. Whatever be those details, no pressing need emerges for seeing gnostic associations in the use of this word here in 2 Clement.

The writer reverts to posing a rhetorical question in 5.6, echoing his questions in chapter 1 about what we can give in return or payback for this great grace (1.3, 5). The answer here, as it was there, is obvious. We can attain to these promises by the same answer given in 5.1, namely, by obeying the will of the one who called us. Here in 5.5 he describes the same response, leading a holy and righteous life and not desiring "these worldly things." As mentioned before, the demonstrative pronoun points out what is to be avoided, as in 5.1, 5 (see "Literary Structure," above). While the things to be avoided are not mentioned, the reader should recall the "adultery, or speaking evil of one another, or cherishing envy" so recently condemned in 4.3. The chapter concludes with a temporal infinitive clause: "when we desire to acquire (ἐν γὰρ τῷ ἐπιθυμεῖν ἡμᾶς) these things, we fall away from the right path." The last word, δικαίας, is a genitive of

---

33. Tuckett mentions that the coupling of "small" and "short in time" may be a hendiadys, both words together referring to the same shortness of length (Tuckett, 2 Clement, 176).

description, namely, "the right path"[34] and is preferred to "the path of righteousness."[35] This is the first and only use of this verb for "fall away" (ἀποπίπτω) in 2 Clement and elsewhere in the Apostolic Fathers. A possible semantic connection, however, exists with the strong warning in Heb 6:6 where the verb for "fall away" (παραπίπτω) is only slightly different in spelling. This is the first of many strong warnings against failing to obey and to pay back Christ for what he has done. In the following chapter Clement will describe this danger of falling away as failing to "keep the baptismal seal as pure and undefiled" (6.9).

The reference to the "right way" as contrasted with the wrong way also points out a very Jewish and Jewish Christian paraenetic device. Two choices or ways are open to people, something developed largely in the Wisdom tradition of Prov 1–9, namely, the Way of Wisdom and the Way of Folly. Jesus also taught about the two ways, one to death and one to life (Matt 7:13–14). The Jewish Two Ways tradition is exemplified also in the Letter of James, the Lord's brother, as the way of wisdom from above contrasted with the way of wisdom from below (Jas 3:13–18). Too often 2 Clement is viewed as arising from a very Hellenized context. One does not need to argue that the author or his congregants were Jewish Christians to ignore that these were wild Gentile branches grafted onto a very Jewish tree (Rom 11:17–19). It has become obvious thus far that these people were rooted in some very Jewish literature. The Jewish Two Ways theme will be developed throughout the rest of this document, and this theme cautions against the tendency to Hellenize the document too strongly. This language is not so otherworldly that it should become construed as docetic or encratitic or ascetic. Donfried at times tilts too much in this direction by characterizing the language as gnostic and "anti-worldly."[36] Clement is not promoting a negative orientation toward physical things. "These things" that are so roundly condemned in this chapter are attitudes and behaviors, not the physical flesh or things as objects. The warning is against sinful human attitudes that manifest themselves in sinful actions.

Chapter 6

1. Now the Lord says: "No servant can serve two masters." If we desire to serve both God and Mammon, it is harmful to us.

---

34. Ehrman, ed., *Apostolic Fathers*, I, 173.

35. Holmes, ed., *Apostolic Fathers*, 145; or "way of the righteous" (Brannan, *Apostolic Fathers*, 59).

36. See, for example, Donfried, *Setting*, 121–24.

2. "For what is the advantage if someone gains the whole world but loses his soul?"
3. Now this age and the coming one are two enemies.
4. This age speaks of adultery and corruption and love of money and deceit, but that age renounces these things.
5. Therefore, we cannot be the friends of both, but we must renounce this age in order to make the most of that one.
6. We think that it is better to hate the things that are here, because they are insignificant and short-lived and corruptible, but to love those things that are good and incorruptible.
7. For if we do the will of Christ, we will find rest; on the other hand, nothing will rescue us from eternal punishment if we disobey his commandments.
8. And the scripture also says in Ezekiel, "Even if Noah and Job and Daniel arise, they will not rescue their children in the captivity."
9. Now if even such righteous men as these are not able to save their children by their own righteous deeds, with what confidence will we enter the kingdom of God, if we do not keep our baptism pure and undefiled? Or who will be our advocate if we are not found to have holy and righteous deeds?

Literary Features

The citation of two authoritative texts provides the literary backbone of this chapter. The first quotation is what "the Lord says" (5.1, followed by another Jesus *logion* in 5.2). The second quotation is what "the Scripture says" (5.8), the Jewish Scriptures (that is, the "Old Testament"). Each citation is then followed by a brief explanation and exhortation (5.3–7 and 5.9). Conditional clauses (5.7 and 5.9) and hortatory questions (5.9) heighten the paraenetic issues related to each text.

Commentary

The dualism in the previous chapter: this world/the coming kingdom (5.1, 5), is developed in greater detail in this chapter. Here appear "two masters" (6.1) and "two ages" (6.3). One cannot serve both masters or be friends of both ages. We can only serve one master (6.1), and we must also renounce one of these ages (6.5). The rejection of the practices of this age must be expressed by nothing less than hatred of them (6.6). The reward of obedience in this matter is the "rest" mentioned in the previous chapter. The consequence of disobedience is eternal punishment (6.7). The chapter concludes with a lesson from the examples of OT worthies who could not even rescue their own children from captivity by their godly example (6.8). This negative lesson is applied by an appeal to maintaining our baptism commitments, because if we fail in this regard, no one, not even Jesus (implied), can stand up for us.

Unlike the uncertain source of the quotation in 5.2–4, the sources of the Jesus *logia* in 6.1–2 are easy to identify. The first is a rather explicit citation of either Matt 6:24 or Luke 16:13. This reflects a greater agreement with Luke because of the presence of "household servant" (οἰκέτης) in Luke, which is absent in Matthew. The second "saying" in 6.1, referring to serving God and Mammon, is more a paraphrase of the synoptic sayings. While there are similarities with the same saying in the Gospel of Thomas, uncertainty about the dating of Thomas's composition counsels that Clement is probably citing Luke.[37] Whatever their sources, the purpose in citing these sayings is clear. That purpose marks a clear separation between "these things" and "the things to come" (as in chapter 5). The former represents the wrong master (that is, "Mammon"), and the latter represents the right master, (that is, "God"). The two "ages" are set apart as "enemies" (6.3). Donfried calls this portrayal a "radical cosmological and ethical dualism."[38] While one is tempted by such a portrayal to discern gnostic expressions, Clement is more likely borrowing and adapting language from the NT. See, for example, 2 Cor 4:4; Gal 1:4; Col 1:4; Jas 4:4; and 1 John 2:15–17. His purpose is not cosmological but ethical, and this is expressed in the intervening comment of 6.2 about gaining the world but losing one's "life" (ψυχήν). Nothing is said about gaining some form of new "knowledge," but rather about gaining salvation. The worldly/behavioral things that are to be rejected are the actions mentioned in 6.4 as "these things": "adultery, and corruption, and love of money, and deceit." This list of vices characterizes the "age," and they are to be "renounced" (6.4–5). In a similar passage in chapter 4, there was also a vice list and a virtue list (4.3), but no list of virtues

---

37. For the text of the Gospel of Thomas and the secondary literature as well as a judicious handling of the issues surrounding the work, see Gathercole, *Gospel of Thomas*. This commentator agrees with Perrin's argument that the finished form of *Thomas* must be after Tatian because it utilizes Jesus *logia* that resemble the way these are rendered in that author's *Diatessaron*. See Perrin, *Thomas, the Other Gospel*. If Perrin is correct, then it is unlikely, if not impossible, that 2 Clement made use of *Thomas*.

38. Donfried, *Setting*, 124.

appears here. The renouncing of friendship with this age recalls Jas 4:4: "You adulterous people, do you not know that friendship with the world means enmity against God? Therefore, anyone who chooses to be a friend of the world becomes an enemy of God." This passage displays the ethical dualism witnessed to in 2 Clement.

The verb "renounce" in 2 Clem. 6.4–5 does introduce an idea not clearly expressed in the NT. Whereas the NT is satisfied with the command "not to love" these things (1 John 2:15–17), Clement goes even further than the corresponding language of James with this verb, which in the NT is not quite as strong as it is in this context.[39] The closest parallel to what is being portrayed here appears in Luke 14:33: "In the same way, those of you who do not give up (ἀποτάσσεται) everything you have cannot be my disciples." The reference again to what is "insignificant" (2 Clem. 6.6) reflects not so much smallness or insignificance in length, like the following word ("short-lived"), but rather that which is small or insignificant in relative importance; the word was also used in 5.5. With Holmes, I prefer the rendering "insignificant."

The final contrast in this dualism of 6.1–5 lies in the contrast between hating what is "perishable" (φθαρτά) *here* and loving what is "imperishable" (ἄφθαρτα) *there*. While rejecting any gnostic dualism in favor of ethical dualism, Tuckett still concludes that "the language is perilously close to a position where there seems to be a radical denial and rejection of everything to do with the present world order."[40] While recognizing this "position" as possible, I suggest an approach that recognizes an "exaggeration for effect." This language reflects more the passion of the speaker and his recognition of the danger of "these things" rather than a philosophical view that approaches asceticism.

Our speaker now returns in 6.6 to his familiar method of exhorting his hearers to obey the ethical demands of Christ, who is now mentioned by name for the fifth time (see also 1.1, 2; 2.7; 5.5). "If we obey the will of Christ" (the first person plural including the speaker), we will find that reward already mentioned, namely, the eschatological "rest" (see 5.5). The expression to "find" rest follows the language of Jesus in Matt 11:29.[41] This is also a reminder that the approximately twenty-five citations of authoritative writings do not include allusions to the same and possibly other scriptures. This rest is again an eschatological rest, because the consequence of

---

39. The verb appears more often in the active voice as meaning "say farewell" (Luke 9:61; Acts 18:18, 21). In the middle it expresses more strongly the idea of "renounce, give up" as in Luke 14:33 (BDAG, s.v. ἀποτάσσομαι, 123).

40. Tuckett, *2 Clement*, 183.

41. Lindemann, *Clemensbriefe*, 216.

disobedience is an eschatological judgment described as "eternal punishment." This expression (αἰωνίου κολάσεως) is identical with Matt 25:46 (κόλασιν αἰώνιον), but again may be one of those unconscious allusions to a Jesus *logion* that fills the mind and mouth of the speaker.

The last section of this chapter (6.8–10) focuses on the quotation and adaptation of a passage in Ezek 14:14, which is abridged for its use here. It is one of the very few times that Clement names his scriptural author (Ezekiel). He previously named Isaiah as his source in 3.5. The reference to Noah, Job, and Daniel not rescuing their children during the captivity is not stated in the canonical books of Genesis, Job, and Daniel. It is a summary of Ezek 14:14 as well as 14:20, perhaps even recalled from memory. The point taken is that these paragons of virtue could not rescue their own children (6.8). The children themselves had to decide whether to obey God, and the hearers of 2 Clement too must decide to obey God or not. While no mention is made of Ezekiel's children in the biblical text, problems with Noah's and Job's children are mentioned (Gen 9; Job 1). The reference to "captivity" is interesting since only Ezekiel was involved in a literal captivity. Rather than some oblique gnostic allusion, this references a metaphorical captivity or bondage like the language used with cognate verbs in Rom 7:23 and 2 Tim 3:6 or even Luke 4:18. The analogy between the children of these righteous heroes and Clement's hearers may not be clear to all. Perhaps the analogy is intended to convey that the hearers must consider their own choices to obey rather than depend on the speaker's or the elders' righteousness.

A rhetorical question intended to focus again on the tenuous character of the future state of the hearers concludes 6.9, and the chapter ends on another somber note. If "we" are not marked by "righteous deeds," how can we hope to enter the "kingdom of God"?[42] But the danger of not entering that eschatological reward comes if we "do not keep our baptism pure and undefiled." In 7.6 the same verb (τηρέω) refers to those who have not "kept the seal," and in 8.6 we are exhorted to "keep the seal spotless." The similarity of language in all three passages points to the interpretation that this reference in 6.9 refers to behavior associated with baptism. There is no need to adopt a sacramental meaning of breaking a spiritual seal associated with the ordinance. The context is behavior, and if people do not keep their behavior pleasing to Christ, then they will betray the obligations that they undertook when making their baptismal vows. As a result, the words for "baptism" and "seal" are synonymous in Clement. Pauline parallels are in 2 Cor 1:22; Eph

42. The noun βασίλειον is not "kingdom," which is βασιλεία, but "palace" or "royal residence," as in Luke 7:25. However, Danker, on the basis of its other NT use in 1 Pet 2:9, states that here in 2 Clement its meaning is the same as βασιλεία, namely "kingdom" (BDAG, s.v. βασίλειον, 169).

1:13 and 4:30, references to the Holy Spirit's seal. Paul associates the gift of the Spirit with baptism in 1 Cor 12:13.

Perhaps the felt need of this exhortation was that some people among Clement's hearers were viewing baptism as the culmination of their salvation, and "they may have stressed the 'already' and neglected the 'not-yet' character of the Christian life."[43]—hence the eschatological context of the urgency in Clement's strong exhortations. Perhaps they simply needed to be reminded of the full implications of their baptism and the accompanying vows. A final rhetorical question in 6.9 introduces a new semantic term to the discussion. If we do not keep our baptism seal pure, then "who will be our *advocate* if we are not found to have holy and righteous deeds?" While an allusion to 1 John 2:1 may be easy to make, this raises other problems. The statement in the Johannine text expresses just the opposite, namely, if someone sins, we *do* have such an advocate, who is Jesus Christ the righteous one! While it is possible that Clement is attempting to correct John, it is more probable that he had no knowledge of this text. Pauline references to a future judgment of believers by Jesus when he finds "wood, hay and stubble" may also be in view (1 Cor 3:12–15), or Clement simply may not have been familiar with these texts.[44] Thus he is making conclusions based on the parts of "scripture" with which he was familiar (for example, Matt 25:41: "Depart from me into everlasting fire") that advocate a judgment by works."[45] How is the use of "advocate," the only occurrence of παράκλητος in the book, associated with the necessity of holy and righteous deeds? Jesus will not be our advocate then if we are not marked by that behavior now. "In other words, the heavenly Jesus Christ appears as our advocate, but only if solid evidence is available. And this evidence has to be brought forward by the defendant."[46]

Chapter 7

1. So then, my brothers, let us compete, knowing that the competition is at hand, and that many are arriving by boat for corruptible prizes, but

---

43. Donfried, *Setting*, 126–27.

44. Lindemann, *Clemensbriefe*, 217; Tuckett, *2 Clement*, 186.

45. "The last sentence of this verse reproduces the thought of 2 *Esdras* 7.102–106 and may be taken as an echo thereof if that book is thought to be in reference in chapter 17" (Grant and Graham, *First and Second Clement*, 117). Clement's possible use of this pseudepigraphal book at this point is interesting to consider, but we will follow Graham's suggestion and wait until more consideration can be given to it at that point in the commentary.

46. Pratscher, "Motivations of Ethos in 2 Clement," 604.

not all are crowned, except those who have trained hard and competed well.

2. Let us therefore compete that we may all be crowned.
3. Let us run the straight course, the incorruptible competition, and let many of us sail to it and compete, that we may also be crowned. And if we all cannot receive the crown, let us at least come close to it.
4. We must remember that if someone taking part in the contest for a corruptible prize is found cheating, he is flogged, disqualified, and thrown out of the stadium.
5. What do you think? What will he suffer who cheats in the contest for what is incorruptible?
6. Concerning those who have not kept the seal he says: "Their worm will not die, and their fire will not be quenched, and they will be a spectacle for all flesh."

Literary Structure

Chapter 7 follows the now familiar pattern of (1) issuing an exhortation in 7.1–5, and (2) citing a "text" to support the exhortation in 7.6. The exhortation is to compete in the games (7.1), but it is soon clear that an analogy is being drawn from the athletic competitions to which participants travel (7.2). The exhortation is then reissued as a command concerning the heavenly race (7.3). The analogy continues with statements about the participants obeying the rules if they are to win (7.4). Two rhetorical questions follow about cheating in the heavenly competition (7.5). The chapter then concludes with a scriptural citation conveying a strong warning about the seriousness of cheating (not keeping the "seal") in the Christian race (7.6).

Commentary

This chapter uses an analogy from athletic competitions to convey that believers who compete well and according to the rules will receive a reward, namely a "crown." The cognate verb (στεφανόω) and noun (στέφανος) occur a total of five times in 7.1–3. Readers familiar with the NT readily recognize that this metaphor was also utilized by Paul (1 Cor 9:24–27; Phil 3:12–14). Clement's use of it, however, differs in that (1) he mentions sailing as well as running, and (2) he describes a severe punishment for those who cheat in the games.

NT authors utilize the metaphor of running in the race (1 Cor 9:24–27; Gal 2:2; 5:7; Phil 2:16; 3:12–14; Heb 12:1). The famous Isthmian Games occurred near Corinth, and it is possible that this fact contributed to the original setting of the references in 1 Corinthians and also may have implications for the original setting of 1 Clement. (See "Authorship and Provenance" in the Introduction). Paul refers to "running" and "boxing" and mentions the reward for winners as "imperishable" and as a "crown." He also used a Greek word related to running in a prayer for the speedy progress of the word (2 Thess 3:1). Clement refers to running as well (7.3), although not with the normally expected Greek verb.[47] He refers to no other specific sport, since the reference to "sailing" refers to the contestants traveling to the games. The writer of Heb 12:1, like Paul, also uses the verb τρέχω for "run."

Other ancient writers employed the metaphor of the athletic contest to describe the struggles and challenges of life. "Latching on in part to the widespread disillusionment with the games, many philosophers and other teachers use the image of the athletic contest to talk about the struggle in the moral life which was demanded of the true sage. So too the language and imagery was taken up in Hellenistic Judaism especially in the writings of Philo (*Spec.* 2.910; *Leg.* 3.72; *Agr.* 119–21)."[48] Furthermore, 1 Clem. 2.4; 5.5; and 35.4 allude to the running imagery.

What is unique in 2 Clement 7 are the two references to "sailing" (7.1, 3) to the games. The verb does not mean simply "sail" but refers to the goal of the voyage, namely, "sailing to" a destination.[49] This specific use of the verb should point us to an actual event that then serves as a metaphor for entering the contests of the Christian life. As important as these

---

47. Both Holmes (*Apostolic Fathers*, 146) and Ehrman (*Apostolic Fathers*, I, 174), following Lightfoot (*Apostolic Fathers*, II, 225), adopt the reading θέωμεν, the aorist subjunctive of θέω meaning "run" (BDAG, s.v. θέω, 454). This choice is against both A and H, which have θωμεν, aorist of τίθημι, meaning "put, place" (BDAG, s.v. τίθημι, 1003). This choice is based on the reading of S where the Syriac verb means "run." The difficulty of understanding the meaning if the verb τίθημι is followed by "the way" (τὴν ὁδὸν) is the motivation for following the Syriac manuscript.

48. Tuckett, *2 Clement*, 188.

49. The verb καταπλέω, which appears only here in the Apostolic Fathers, means "to put in" not "to depart from" ("sail down" BDAG, s.v. καταπλέω, "sail down," 524). In this sense it appears in its only reference in the NT ("sail down to the country of the Gerasenes," Luke 8:26). Two other verbs function for the meaning "sail away" (BDAG, s.v. ἀποπλέω, 119; see Acts 20:15) and "sail past" (BDAG, s.v. παραπλέω, 770; see Acts 20:16).

major events were, Clement agrees with Paul that they are "perishable" and that we should faithfully run the imperishable race. Not all authors, however, think that the verb should bear the weight of this specialized meaning.[50] The objection that "sailing" was not one of the contests disappears if the verb means transport to the games. The ancient evidence for such a sport in the games is rather thin. Clare Rothschild has argued that the alternating of sailing and running in this passage recalls the voyage of Aeneas recorded in the fifth chapter of the *Aeneid*.[51] She relates how Virgil describes funeral games that Aeneas staged on Sicily in honor of the anniversary of his father's death. The entire episode is modeled on Homer's *Iliad* 23. Both sources deploy the convention of funeral games. The *Aeneid* substitutes a ship race for Homer's chariot contest. "As such, this chapter of Virgil contains several important parallels with 2 Clement 7."[52] Her chart sets out the parallels.[53] Her conclusion is, "In 2 Clement 7, the Aeneid is not recast, just summoned to mind. The parallels are vague at best."[54] They help to make sense of some conundrums in 2 Clem. 7, namely the mixed metaphor of sailing and running and why all the competitors receive a reward. In this regard she recalls 2 Clem. 7.3b: "And if we all cannot receive the crown, let us at least come close to it." Aeneas's act of prayer for his father is also the literary example of the believer's "payback" in 2 Clement. Here Rothschild draws on the contribution of Kelhoffer's reciprocity theme that has been mentioned in an earlier chapter as well as in the comments on 2 Clem. 1.[55] "Although Clement asks his audience to part with their money, chapter 20 specifies the importance of the intention behind such acts of charity. One ought to be upright for the sake of piety, not profit (2 Clem. 20.4). Aeneas exemplifies his ideal."[56] The parallels that Rothschild draws between these two literary works are fascinating. One struggles, however, to recognize that Clement had Aeneas in mind as he wrote and delivered his address. The value of Rothschild's study may lie in its attempt to understand better the ancient attitude toward sailing, competing, and finishing well.

---

50. See Tuckett, *2 Clement*, 145; and Stanton, "2 Clement VII and the Origin of the Document."
51. Rothschild, "Sailing Past the Competition."
52. Rothschild, "Sailing Past the Competition," 149.
53. Rothschild, "Sailing Past the Competition," 151.
54. Rothschild, "Sailing Past the Competition," 150.
55. See, for example, Kelhoffer, "Reciprocity as Salvation."
56. Rothschild, "Sailing Past the Competition," 156.

Another literary parallel may help to shed light on the statement in 7.4: "And if we all cannot receive the crown, let us at least come close to it." Those who do not receive a crown for finishing in first place will still get recognition for striving. Philo expresses it like this: "Nor let those be downcast who have been held worthy of the second or third prize. For these, like the first, are prizes offered as a reward for the acquisition of virtue, and those who cannot reach the topmost virtues are gainers by the acquisition of the less lofty ones, and theirs is actually, as is often said, a more secure gain since it escapes the envy which ever attaches itself to preeminence."[57] Clement's (and Philo's) more compassionate approach to those who lack the ability to win a crown is contrasted with Clement's strong condemnation of those who cheat in the races. For Clement, cheaters convey the metaphor of those who stumble badly in the heavenly competition. They are "flogged, disqualified, and thrown out of the stadium" (7.4). This comment then prompts Clement to deliver one of his strongest condemnations, toward those who do not live up to the high ethical behavior that marks the necessary "payback" expected of believers. Clement conveys this judgment through two rhetorical questions. "What do you think? What will he suffer who cheats in the contest for what is incorruptible?" (7.5). Following the analogy of being flogged and kicked out of the stadium, their future is a fiery judgment (7.6).

The disobedience of these who start the race but are eliminated is described with the figure of "not keeping the seal." In Greco-Roman religion, a seal could be a physical object that was a visual guarantee of either protection or ownership.[58] In Jewish tradition, the same word (σφραγίς) could refer to the physical sign of circumcision (Rom 4:11; see also Barn. 9.6). While uses of this word to refer to the Spirit occur in Christian Scriptures (2 Cor 1:22; Eph 1:13; 4:30), Paul also calls the believing community the "seal" of his ministry (1 Cor 9:2). The association of the word with baptism in 6.9 and its use for baptism in other Fathers (Hermas, *Sim.* 8.2.2–4; 9.16.3–7) indicates that the seal here refers to baptism.[59] Lampe has traced the word in its various expressions throughout the NT and the early Fathers as uniformly referring to baptism.[60] No "sacramental" associations are attached to the sealing at this point, although later texts seem to express the coming of the Spirit in that way. Its association with baptism is always in the context of a behavioral praxis, the expected accompanying ethical behaviors probably

57. Philo, *Agr.* 120–21.
58. See Tuckett, *2 Clement*, 191, citing Knopf, *Zwei Clemensbriefe*, 162.
59. Lightfoot, trans., *Apostolic Fathers*, I.2, 226; Donfried, *Setting*, 125; Tuckett, *2 Clement*, 192. For lack of dogmatism on the matter, see Lindemann, *Clemensbriefe*, 221.
60. Lampe, *Seal of the Spirit*. For specific references to 2 Clement, see Lampe, *Seal of the Spirit*, 100–103.

associated with baptismal vows. The language of "keeping the seal" does not imply permanence. In other words, it is a seal that would be "broken" by the wrong behavior that is condemned in the analogy and now comes under such strong language in the concluding verse of this chapter. To describe the severe judgment for not keeping the seal, Clement cites verbatim from the LXX of Isa 66:24: "Their worm will not die, and their fire will not be quenched, and they will be a spectacle for all flesh." Mark 9:48 quotes part of the Isaianic text with only slight modifications. The citation is introduced by the general "he says."[61] Isaiah denounces "the men who have transgressed," and the context there does not contain any reference to a broken seal. The rather lurid language of the text paints the fate of those experiencing the severity of eternal punishment, and is the spiritual parallel to the physical experience of the cheating athlete flogged and thrown out of the stadium in 7.5. If some readers seem stung by this strong language applied to believers who have been baptized, they should know that equally strong NT language describes those who have received the truth but have "gone on sinning." They face a "fearful expectation of judgment, and a fury of fire that will consume the adversaries" (Heb 10:26–27, ESV).

Appeal for obedient living 8.1—13.4

Chapter 8

1. Therefore, while we are still on earth, let us repent.
2. For we are clay in the hand of the craftsman. For in the same way as the potter, if he makes a vessel, and it becomes misshapen or breaks while it is in his hand, he reshapes it; but if he has put it into the kiln, he no longer is able to mend it. So also, as long as we are in this world, let us repent from all our heart from the wicked things we have done in the flesh, so that we may be saved by the Lord while we still have time to repent.
3. For after we have departed the world, we are no longer able there to confess or to repent anymore.
4. So, brothers, if we have done the will of the Father and have kept the flesh pure and have obeyed the commandments of the Lord, we will receive eternal life.

---

61. There does not appear to be any significance to the use of φησίν here (also in 12.6 of a Jesus *logion*), rather than the more common λέγει, which is used over two dozen times.

5. For the Lord says in the Gospel, "If you have not observed what is small, who will give you what is great? For I tell you that whoever is faithful in what is little is faithful also in what is much."

6. He means this then: keep the flesh pure and the seal unstained so that we may receive life.

Literary Structure

This chapter, as do so many previous ones, opens with a consequential conjunction (οὖν) and a hortatory subjunctive (4.1; 5.1; 7.1; see also 10.1; 11.1; 12.1; 13.1; 16.1; 17.1; 18.1). Then follows a causal conjunction (γάρ) that introduces a statement about clay in a potter's hands (8.2). The analogy is applied again to the urgent need to repent in order to be saved (8.3), which is further described as keeping the flesh pure and thus receiving eternal life (8.4). This entire exhortation is again affirmed by a citation from an authoritative source, this time "the Gospel" (8.5) followed by its explanation (8.6).

Commentary

The verb and noun for "repent" dominate 8.1–3 as well as appearing prominently in 9.8; 13.1; 15.1; 16.1, 4; 17.1; and 19.1. The message in this chapter is that repentance, further clarified as keeping the flesh pure, is demanded if we are to receive eternal life. Definitions of "repentance" sometimes are dominated by expressions of inner regret or sorrow over sin.[62] A NT text like 2 Cor 7:10 may lend support to such an approach: "For godly grief produces a repentance that leads to salvation without regret, whereas worldly grief produces death" (ESV). Clement's exhortation to "repent from all our heart" (8.2) also may underscore the idea of an accompanying inner sense of remorse. The noun also can bear a literal sense of "a change of mind."[63] The word group conveys a change of mind that leads to a change of behavior if it is to be a genuine repentance. The constant appeal for ethical behavior is what dominates Clement's exhortation to repent. Repentance, without denying some sort of grief arising from the heart, stresses more a change in actions on the part of the hearers. It is a change from moral laxity to ethical behavior that is stressed in the context of all these exhortations. Both inward and outward change is reflected in the statement that we must

---

62. BDAG, s.v. μετανοέω, 640: "feel remorse, repent, be converted."
63. BDAG, s.v. μετάνοια, 640.

"repent with all our heart from the wicked things we have done in the flesh" (8.2), and we must "keep the flesh pure" (8.4). As always, it is ethical praxis that concerns Clement. This does not mean that the audience has changed and he is now addressing nonbelievers who must initially repent. This is not a repentance for initial conversion, as is described in such NT texts as Mark 1:15 and Acts 2:38. These people in 1 Clem. 8 are those who have experienced to some degree the salvific elements described so vividly in 1.4–8. They have been baptized but have failed to "keep their flesh pure and the seal [of baptism] unstained" (8.6). Clement also addresses his hearers in this context as "brothers" (8.4), believers who have failed to behave in a morally upright manner. They now must repent, that is, change that behavior. The focus here is not on a backward-looking sorrow but on a forward-looking change of direction that will be witnessed in their deeds. Rather than label the problem of these hearers as Gnosticism, it is better to call these people libertines, who are lax in their morality and perhaps even defending their moral laxity. I suggest that they may have seen baptism as the *end* instead of the *beginning* that it should have been.

Hermas would also have much to say about repentance, but there is no indication here about a limited number of such acts of repentance as in Hermas. The language of repentance coupled with keeping the seal also appears there. "Sir, now explain to me about those who have returned their sticks, that is, what kind of person each of them is, and where they live, in order that when those who have believed and have received the seal and have broken it and have not kept it sound hear this, they may recognize what they are doing, and repent and thereby receive a seal from you, and glorify the Lord because he has had mercy on them and sent you to renew their spirits."[64] Donfried also calls attention to the similarity of this concern in 2 Clement to the exhortation in Rev 2:5: "Remember therefore from where you have fallen; repent, and do the works you did at first. If not, I will come to you and remove your lampstand from its place, unless you repent" (ESV).[65] The initial exhortation to repent leads to the clause, "while we are on earth" (8.1). This is the idea that is repeated in the following passage. It shows up in the analogy of the potter and the clay "while it is in his hand" (8.2a). In the next exhortation it appears by "as long as we are in this world" (8.2b). These expressions stress the fact that the hearers need to repent now while they have an opportunity to do so, because "after we have departed the world, we are no longer able there to confess or to repent any more" (8.3). The figure of the potter and his clay could be derived from Jer 18:4–6, but Clement

---

64. Hermas, *Sim.* 8, 6, 3 (quoted in Holmes, ed., *Apostolic Fathers*, 609).
65. Donfried, *Setting*, 132.

adds the important point that serves his purpose here, namely, that once the vessel is in the kiln it can no longer be reshaped. We are to reshape our lives now, because after death there will be no second chance to do so. "The idea that no further repentance is possible in the other world seems to be based on the parable of Dives and Lazarus (Luke 16:19–31), especially its ending."[66] Since the message is a commonplace in Jewish and Christian teaching, a definite reference is probably not needed here.

In his final exhortation based on this idea, the author addresses his hearers again as "brothers" and tells them that "eternal life" is dependent on their doing three things: (1) doing the Father's will, (2) keeping the flesh pure, and (3) obeying the Lord's commands (8.4). This is a summary of his message of orthopraxy and will be developed in a number of ways in the chapters ahead. He used the verb "keep" (τηρέω) earlier when he stressed the importance of keeping our baptism "pure" (6.9) and of keeping pure the "seal" (7.6). Here he employs the same verb to discuss keeping the flesh "pure" (8.4) and then again keeping the "seal" unstained (8.6). He will finally use this verb to exhort how we should "keep" or "guard" the flesh of Christ, of which we are spiritual partakers (14.3). Such references to flesh and purity could be viewed as a particular reference to sexual activity, perhaps even implying asceticism. The accompanying language, however, points more toward this being a general command to obey the ethical demands expressed as the "Lord's commandments" (8.4). No denial of all sexual activity (such as celibacy or abstention within marriage) is implied, particularly in light of the command against adultery in 4.3.[67]

The promise accompanying this obedience is that "we will receive eternal life" (8.4). While the verb "receive" (λαμβάνω) can be pressed to convey that "eternal life" is something we "receive" and not earn, we should be careful about reading back into the discussion certain "Reformation" issues.[68] This is language that conveys that those who have truly experienced salvation by grace (1.4–9) will display that "salvation" by their behavior. Teachings in James (2:14–26) as well as in Paul (Rom 2:6–10; Gal 5:6), although using different language for their purposes, similarly convey what Clement is demanding.

The reference to observing the Lord's "commandments" raises the question of what commandments? Are these the Mosaic commands or those of Jesus or the apostles? Clement does not answer that question here. John

---

66. Grant and Graham, *First and Second Clement*, 119.

67. See the discussion in Lindemann, *Clemensbriefe*, 222–23; as well as in Tuckett, *2 Clement*, 199.

68. Lindemann, *Clemensbriefe*, 223.

speaks with a bit more precision when he focuses on the commandments to love others (1 John 2:3-6). "One can surmise from 2 Clem. 4.3 that the writer has something similar in mind, but it is not stated with the same degree of precision as in 1 John."[69] The language of 2 Clem. 4.3 makes clear that Clement would agree with Jesus' summary of all those commandments in Matt 22:37-40, namely, to love the Lord with all the heart and the neighbor as one's self. For more specificity, 4.3 is clear: "not committing adultery nor slandering one another nor being jealous, but by being self-controlled, compassionate, and good." Clement again supports his exhortation in 8.1-4 with a quotation in 8.5 of what "the Lord says in the Gospel." While Clement utilizes a number of what could be called *logia* of Jesus (see the discussion in the Introduction about "The Reception and Use of Sacred Tradition in 2 Clement"), this is the only one that is actually described as "in the Gospel." This "citation" reflects the use of a written text or of written texts, such as in Did. 8.2; 11.3; 15.3-4. The first part of the quotation (8.5a) has no clear parallel example in any of the canonical Gospels. The second half of the quotation (8.5b), expressing that "whoever is faithful in what is little is faithful also in what is much," looks much like Luke 16:10. The first part ("If you have not observed what is small, who will give you what is great?") echoes a nearby verse in Luke (16:12). The "small" Clement interprets as this life; the "great" is eternal life. The interpretive challenge is discerning how this entire citation supports the exhortation in 8.1-4. I suggest that Clement may be utilizing a rabbinic hermeneutical method of finding a common word in two texts and thus making an interpretive connection.[70] That common word is his use of "keep" (τηρήσαντες) in 8.4 and the verb's use in the quotation, "if you have not kept (ἐτηρήσατε) what is small . . ." Whatever modern interpreters think of Clement's hermeneutics, the point is that whoever "keeps" or observes the Father's will (by "keeping" the flesh "pure"), even if it is a small command, will receive a great reward. An explicit interpretation of the saying appears in 8.6. "Life" will be received by those who "keep the flesh pure and the seal unstained."[71] As in 7.6, the seal here refers to baptism, and both Lake and

---

69. Donfried, *Setting*, 133.

70. The practice was called *gezera shevah*, one of the seven hermeneutical "rules" attributed to Hillel (Babylonian Talmud, *Pesahim*, 70b). For a brief explanation, see Longenecker, *Biblical Exegesis in the Apostolic Period*, 20.

71. Holmes (*Apostolic Fathers*, 148) follows Lightfoot's (*Apostolic Fathers*, II, 228) preference for the Syriac single word "life" (ζωήν) rather than the fuller expression "eternal life" (αἰώνιον ζωήν), which reading is found in both A and H. At this point, Ehrman (*Apostolic Fathers*, I, 176) has made the better textual choice of αἰώνιον ζωήν. While it is possible that the Syriac may preserve the original, the documentary evidence of the only two surviving Greek witnesses, one being much earlier, should not be lightly rejected. In this reading the article would be an anaphoric reference back to the fuller

Ehrman translate the single word "seal" (σφραγῖδα) as "seal of baptism."⁷²
While that may be a correct interpretation, one's translational philosophy
may prefer the "formal equivalence" rendering as simply "seal" and leave the
"functional equivalence" rendering for the commentary.⁷³

Chapter 9

1. And let none of you say that this flesh is not judged nor rises again.
2. Understand this. In what condition were you saved? In what condition did you receive your sight, if not while you were in this flesh?
3. We must therefore guard the flesh as a temple of God.
4. For just as you were called in the flesh, you will also come in the flesh.
5. If Christ the Lord who saved us, although he was originally spirit, became flesh and called us, so we will also receive our reward in this flesh.
6. Therefore, let us love one another, so that we all may come into the kingdom of God.
7. While we have time to be healed, let us give ourselves to God, who heals us, making a payback to him.
8. What sort? Repentance from a sincere heart.
9. For he is the one who knows all things beforehand and knows what is in our heart.
10. Therefore, let us then give him eternal praise, not only from the mouth, but also from the heart, so that he may receive us as sons.
11. For the Lord also said: "My brothers are these who do the will of my Father."

Literary Structure

The chapter begins with a command, expressed not with a hortatory subjunctive, but with the singular indefinite pronoun and imperative (9.1). This is followed by a direct command followed by two direct questions

---

expression in 8.4 ("that eternal life").

72. Lake, *Apostolic Fathers*, I, 140; Ehrman, ed., *Apostolic Fathers*, I, 176.

73. See Tuckett, *2 Clement*, 192, on 7.6, where he refers to this fuller translation as "an interpretive gloss."

(9.2). The exhortation that follows embodies a hortatory subjunctive (9.3) with reasons supporting the command (9.4–5). A renewed hortatory subjunctive then conveys a new command (9.6) with an additional exhortation (9.7). Another rhetorical question is answered by an incomplete sentence (9.8). A reason for the answer is based on a divine attribute (9.9). The chapter closes with a final exhortation (9.10) supported by an appeal to a Jesus *logion* (9.11).

Commentary

The "flesh" (σάρξ) is the dominant theme of this chapter, with the noun appearing seven times in 9.1–5. This is not a new theme, however, but is an elaboration of the command to keep the flesh pure in the immediately preceding verse (8.6). Tuckett refers to the chapter opening as "a small excursus . . . on the importance of the flesh, especially in relation to the resurrection."[74] The form of the imperative in 9.1, "let none of you say . . ." implies that this is not a general exhortation but one based on familiarity with a specific problem among the hearers. In other words, someone was actually saying that the flesh would not rise and be judged. While a number of authors have described those concerned as "gnostics," prudence may caution that this has been overstressed.[75] Kelhoffer, supported by Tuckett, has convincingly argued that it is unfounded to conclude with any certainty that the author of 2 Clement criticizes any distinctive aspects of gnostic beliefs.[76] It is not necessary to detect a gnostic opponent in this chapter, because Hellenistic Greek philosophy in general was widespread enough to be the culprit being addressed. In a dated but still valuable work, Oscar Cullmann provides a concise summary of the influence on the original Corinthian hearers of this warning.

> Indeed for the Greeks who believed in the immortality of the soul it may have been harder to accept the Christian preaching of the resurrection than it was for others. About the year 150 Justin (in his *Dialogue*, 80) writes of people, "who say that there is no resurrection from the dead, but that immediately at death their souls would ascend to heaven."[77]

---

74. Tuckett, *2 Clement*, 202.
75. See "The Opponents in 2 Clement" in the Introduction.
76. Kelhoffer, "*Second Clement* and Gnosticism."
77. Cullmann, *Immortality of the Soul or Resurrection of the Dead?*, 59.

Donfried has offered many supporting quotations from a number of patristic sources in support of this quotation.[78] The mockery of the Pauline preaching of the resurrection by those Greeks on the Areopagus is a graphic example of how "foolish" such a belief was held to be by Greeks trained in Platonic thought (Acts 17:32). The situation in Corinth went beyond the general Greek distaste for a resurrection of the flesh. These specific opponents were probably from the believing community and thus were exercising influence on the hearers from within, not simply from the outside. Paul had to deal with two specific individuals, Hymenaeus and Philetus, who were saying that the resurrection was already a thing of the past (2 Tim 2:18). Perhaps they were stressing the realized resurrection, even appealing to such Pauline teachings of a past spiritual resurrection as Eph 2:6 and Col 2:12. Because of this, Paul countered by stating in Rom 6:5: "For if we have been united in a death like his, we will be united with him in a resurrection like his." It would be too much to conclude that our author was drawing on Pauline teaching about bodily resurrection in 1 Cor 15, but the passage would have served his purpose well.

At the point of similarity between Clement's and Paul's concerns, a significant difference also emerges. While Paul affirms that there will be a resurrection of the body, it was still a different body both for Jesus and for the future resurrection—that is, the resurrection body will be a glorified body (1 Cor 15:50–53). Clement mentions nothing about a changed body, only that it will be a body of flesh. "For 2 Clement man will be raised in the same flesh . . . and he will receive his rewards in the same flesh."[79] Clement ignores the Pauline teaching of a "same but different" body in favor of a pragmatic argument that the future body of the believer is identical "flesh" with the one in present life. To Clement the dangerous denial ("one who says," 9.1) is that the present flesh in this body will have a place in the future body of the resurrection. Even destroyed by death, there will be a full involvement of this "flesh" in that next body. It is vital to recognize again the practical, ethical, and praxis-related purpose of Clement. This is not a doctrinal discussion divorced from the purpose of his overall message. It is imperative that since we will be resurrected in flesh, we must now keep the flesh pure and spotless (9.3, echoing 8.6). The Savior became flesh, but the reason for this statement is not theological: it is to make the point that he did this in "the flesh," supporting the argument that our deeds must be done in a flesh that is kept pure. While not operating from a heavy doctrinal orientation, Clement still offers one of his few attempts at approaching a confessional

---

78. Donfried, *Setting*, 134–42.
79. Donfried, *Setting*, 145.

formula by affirming the salvific act of the incarnate Christ. "If Christ the Lord who saved us, although he was originally spirit, became flesh and so called us, so we will also receive our reward in this flesh" (9.5).[80] Both this statement and one earlier in 9.2 appeal to their salvation as something in the past. The clear reference to the preexistence of Christ should be noted as well. This is also the first reference to his existence as "spirit" (πνεῦμα), but it is a theme Clement will take up again in 14.3–5 in much greater detail. But even this christological affirmation is not issued for its own sake but is concluded by a reference to the reward for actual behavior: "so we will also receive our reward in this flesh." This brief but weighty digression is followed by a paraenetic appeal to "love one another, so that we all may come into the kingdom of God" (9.6). The consequences of Clement's argument about the "flesh" for praxis and ethical behavior he expresses in 9.6–7. We should love one another so that all of us can come to the kingdom of God. Our author has mentioned before this concern for mutual love (4.3). A medical metaphor follows that has not before been employed, namely, that we should give ourselves to God so we can be healed. Healing as a metaphor for salvation employs imagery found in both testaments (Jer 3:22; Jas 5:16).

Clement takes up again one of his most important themes, namely, our responsibility of "giving payback to [God]" (9.7c). The noun translated "payback" (ἀντιμισθία) occurs first as part of the opening thematic statement in 1.3 and 5 and will appear again at 11.6 and 15.2. Kelhoffer's contention, as presented in the "Theological Praxis of 2 Clement" section in the Introduction, is that "Second Clement presents Christ as salvific benefactor and patron. Christ offers salvation to those who accept the terms of his patronage, terms that include the obligation to render 'payback' in the form of praise, witness, loyalty, and almsgiving."[81] This payback is gratitude for how much he suffered for us (1.2). The context in this case makes clear what constitutes the believer's "payback," namely, "repentance from a sincere heart" (9.8). This change in one's lifestyle should not be only an outward act, but should

---

80. The εἰ Χριστός reading survives in none of the three codices—A, H, or S—which have the preposition εἰς. Because it is difficult to make any sense out of this construction, Lightfoot (*Apostolic Fathers*, II, 230) proposed that the reading should be εἰ, which has been followed by Lake (*Apostolic Fathers*, I, 142) and Holmes (*Apostolic Fathers*, 148). Ehrman offers a creative conjecture that the εἰς was confused for the conditional particle plus an uncial iota and sigma standing for Jesus (ΕΙΙΣ). His suggestion, first proposed by Lightfoot (*Apostolic Fathers*, II, 230), is that the text initially read εἰ Ἰησοῦς Χριστός, the reading he has adopted in his text (Ehrman, ed., *Apostolic Fathers*, I, 178). His suggestion also helps to smooth out the following words in the sentence by making it no longer a conditional sentence. The conjectural reading is well-argued, but one wishes that at least one of the surviving texts supported it.

81. Kelhoffer, "Reciprocity as Salvation," 433.

stem from within, as Clement describes in 3.4 with an allusion to the Shema (Deut 6:5) and its use by Jesus (Matt 22:37 and parallels). This change in lifestyle is not another example of Clement's legalistic moralism but is the proper response to the salvation mentioned in 9.2 and to the grace through which "he saved us" as described in Clem. 1.2–8. An additional component of that payback is giving God "eternal praise," not only from the mouth but from the heart (9.10).[82] This stress on the role of the heart in this payback has just been strengthened by the affirmation that God "knows all things beforehand and knows what is in our heart" (9.9).[83] The result of this return to Christ for what he has done is that he will "receive us as sons" (9.10). While the earlier reference to being called "sons" in 1.4 appears to be a present reality, this later statement focuses on sonship as an eschatological adoption. Perhaps Clement saw no contradiction in both being true, just as we were saved in the past and will be saved in the future. Paul also expounded this eschatological sonship (Rom 8:19). The saying of Jesus in response to his being sought by his "brothers" (and family) in Mark 3:35 receives a new setting when quoted as a saying of the Lord in 9.10: "My brothers are these who do the will of my Father." Upon first examination, one might wonder how this text (the only one cited in this chapter) could form any solid basis for the previous exhortation. Tuckett offers a simple answer when he suggests that the quotation "neatly sums up the twin themes of the writer: salvation (or divine sonship) is promised as a gift from God, but only to those who behave in an ethically responsible and upright way ('those who do the will of my Father')."[84] I only wish that this was as clear to this commentator as it is to Tuckett! It was said earlier that chapter 9 appears to follow closely the argument in chapter 8; no transitional conjunctions appear in chapter 9 until the very end: δῶμεν οὖν αὐτῷ αἶνον (9.10a). The two chapters echo each other in delivering the message "to repent" (8.1; 9.8) and "to guard the flesh" (8.6; 9.3). Each also ends with believers being "received" in the future: in 8.6 to "eternal life" and in 9.10 as "sons."

---

82. Codex A has αιωνον while Codicies H and S have αινον. Lightfoot argued for an original conflate reading αἶνον αἰώνιον (Lightfoot, trans., *Apostolic Fathers*, I.2, 231, "doubtless"), and is followed by Holmes, trans. (*Apostolic Fathers*, 148). Ehrman, ed., prefers αἶνον without any indication of the variants (*Apostolic Fathers*, I,178).

83. The agent noun προγνώστης appears only here in the Apostolic Fathers and has left no prehistory in any Greek literature, although the cognate verb occurs often. This noun is utilized by a number of church fathers (Lampe, s.v. προγνώστης, 1142).

84. Tuckett, *2 Clement*, 208.

ETHICAL SECTION

Chapter 10

1. So, my brothers, let us do the will of the Father who called us, that we may live, and let us rather pursue virtue, and let us give up malice as the forerunner of our sins, and let us flee ungodliness so that evil things not overtake us.

2. For if we are eager to do good, peace will pursue us.

3. For this reason it is not possible for a person to find peace when they bring in human fears and prefer the present pleasure to the coming promise.

4. For they do not know what great torment the present pleasure brings, and what delight the coming promise brings.

5. And if they alone were doing these things it could be endured, but now they continue teaching evil to innocent souls, not realizing that both themselves and their hearers will receive a double punishment.

Literary Structure

As a consequence of the exhortation to do the Father's will in 9.10, 10.1 consists of a series of four consequential exhortations (hortatory subjunctives), each accompanied by an intended result of the exhorted action. Three reasons for these exhortations, each introduced by "for," develop further the argument in 10.2–4. A contrary-to-fact conditional clause introduces the final argument in 10.5. No specific citation from any scripture text is made, unless the last clause is a general allusion to a number of NT texts. Donfried calls attention to the rhetorical device of antithesis, which conveys the paraenesis by contrasts in 10.1 where believers are told what to do and what to avoid, and in 10.3 where the "present pleasures" are contrasted with the "future promises."[85]

Commentary

This chapter is different from the preceding ones since it contains no supporting citations, at least none that are accompanied by a citation formula. Furthermore, it is unique in that it is the first time where a clear reference is made to false or "evil" teachers (10.5). The concept of "mirror hermeneutics" conveys that warnings to a congregation imply that the warned-against

85. Donfried, *Setting*, 146–47.

practices are definitely happening among the hearers. Such an assumption, however, is in no way clear and is a principle that simply cannot be applied without some clear contextual evidence to do so.

The opening exhortations again employ antithesis. Doing the will of the Father is further defined as practicing "virtue" while avoiding "malice" and fleeing "ungodliness." "Virtue" (ἀρετή) was a term that had appeared quite often in previous Hellenistic moral treatises. It reflected a wide range of meanings from "eminence" to "glory"; for the Sophists it meant "moral virtue."[86] The term's thirty-two occurrences in the LXX showed its wide semantic range, and in Isaiah it describes a divine attribute (42:8, 12). Philo used ἀρετή extensively in its Greek moral philosophical meaning of "moral virtue."[87] Its rare use in the NT (Phil 4:8 and 2 Pet 1:5; 1 Pet 2:9 and 2 Pet 1:3 describe divine characteristics) as well as in the Apostolic Fathers (only here in 2 Clement and five times in Hermas) probably is a reflection of the following judgment: "At the time of the NT the word ἀρετή had so many meanings that it gave rise to misunderstandings."[88] Hence other words were utilized to carry the weight of Christian moral attributes.

In another possible use of antithesis, Clement sets this concept of "virtue" over against "malice" (κακία). In the larger context "virtue" is a characteristic of the promised future whereas "malice" is a characteristic of the present pleasures. Even though Clement does not continue to use the word in this book, it is clear that the one who pursues virtue will receive life and inherit the future promises (10.4). In the end, ἀρετή cannot be isolated from the larger praxis commended by such passages as 5.6: "to live a holy and righteous life, and to regard these worldly things as not our own, and not desire them."

Clement continues his colorful vocabulary by describing "malice" as the "forerunner" of our sins. This is the only use of this noun (προοδοιπόρος) in the entire surviving Greek corpus, including the rest of the Apostolic Fathers. Its cognate verb appears often as "precede" or "travel first" and is used in a positive sense in 1 Clem. 44.5 for the elders who have gone before.[89] Here in 2 Clement the noun has no such positive connotation. Malice is viewed a "forerunner" in the sense of that which causes or provokes "our sins," much as for Paul money is "a root of all evils" (1 Tim 6:10).

Clement uses another colorful trope in 10.2 when he expresses, in a paraphrase, "if we are eager to do good, peace will pursue us." This is his

---

86. Bauernfeind, *TDNT*, s.v. ἀρετή, 1:457–60.
87. Bauernfeind, *TDNT*, s.v., ἀρετή, 1:459.
88. Bauernfeind, ἀρετή, I, 457.
89. GE, s.v., προοδοιπορέω, 1779; BDAG, s.v., προοδοιπόρος, 873.

first and only use of the word "peace" (εἰρήνη), although it often appears in 1 Clement (twenty times) and the other Apostolic Fathers. It was noted that there are no clear citations in this chapter, but this verse serves to summarize the message of Ps 33:11–14, which also did not escape the notice of a text such as 1 Pet 3:10–12, as well as 1 Clem. 22:1–8.[90] The sense of 2 Clem. 10.3 is fairly evident. A person cannot find peace if they are fearful and prefer the pleasant pleasures over the future promises. But how to get that meaning from the text as it stands is a challenge. The text reads in an overly literal way as "it is not for a man to find" (εὑρεῖν), but no object of the infinitive is expressed. Lightfoot suggested an emendation by adding "peace" as the object (i.e., "to find peace").[91] Others have suggested a similar emendation by adding the pronoun "it" as the object.[92] I do not think either emendation is necessary, since in my opinion the ancient reader would have comprehended the *constructio ad sensum* and provided the required object, namely, the "peace" of the previous sentence. The meaning is plain, namely, that people cannot achieve the peace which they desire if they try to attain it by the wrong efforts described in the rest of the sentence.

The grammar of the rest of the verse is still not without its challenges, since the verb now shifts to the plural, namely, "they bring in . . ." But such a shift from singular to plural is not without precedent, and the meaning remains clear. The plural shift happens probably because in 10.5 Clement will soon take to task the false teachers who are bothering his hearers. Occasionally a commentator discerns persecution as the setting of 10.3–4. In other words, the ones addressed are seeking to avoid persecution by refusing to testify to their faith based on these undue "fears."[93] But the following statement about their preference for "present pleasure" does not seem to fit a situation of persecution and possible martyrdom.[94] Furthermore, the language is simply too general to support this claim. The problem with these people was not just fear but that attitude coupled with a desire for the things that are *now* compared to those things that are *not yet*. In 10.4,

---

90. While Tuckett thinks that their common use may be "simply a coincidence," he admits that Psalm 34 may have been in a collection of proof texts used by both authors (Tuckett, *2 Clement*, 211n10). The possibility cannot be ruled out that this is one of those many indications that the first epistle may have directly influenced the second one.

91. Lightfoot, trans., *Apostolic Fathers*, I.2, 232: εὑρεῖν εἰρήνην.

92. Lindemann, *Clemensbriefe*, 231: αὐτὴν εὑρεῖν.

93. See, for example, Lindemann, *Clemensbriefe*, 231. Tuckett is hesitant about this suggestion (*2 Clement*, 212).

94. There is an alternative reading in both 10.3 and 4 for the noun "enjoyment" (ἀπόλαυσιν), which is supported by A and S. The noun ἀνάπαυσιν ("rest") is found in C, probably influenced by 5.5 and 6.7.

Clement again portrays the antithesis between what awaits the righteous and what awaits those who are too attached to the present "things" against whom he speaks. The contrast is between "torment" for one group and "delight" for the other group. The word for "torment" (βάσανον) describes the eschatological punishment for the wicked. It was used by Jesus in a vivid parable to describe the awful condition of *Dives* (Luke 16:23, 28). In contrast with this negative pole is the antithesis of the future "delight," which is the result of the eschatological promise. This word (τρυφή) can convey a negative sense of "indulgence" or "reveling" (2 Pet 2:13) or the undesirable "splendor" of the rich (Luke 7:25).[95] On the other hand, Jewish Greek literature (for example, Philo, Josephus) as well as other Apostolic Fathers (Hermas, Diognetus) stress its meaning as "joy" or "delight," especially in an eschatological context, as is the case here.[96]

Consistent with the antithesis rhetoric employed throughout this chapter, the very clear point is "the standard apocalyptic motif of the reversal of roles and fortunes in the future eschatological age."[97] Clement makes reference in 10.5 for the first time to people who were actually teaching wrong things to his hearers. His previous concerns certainly reflect wrong attitudes and practices, but here is a clear indication of teachers exerting their baneful influence. The expected word group for "teaching," διδάσκω and its cognates, does not appear in the book. The verb here for "teaching evil" incorporates "evil" (κακοδιδασκαλέω). The probable reason for adding the prefix is because of the "evil" (κακία) that Clement condemned in 10.1. This is the second *hapax legomenon* in this chapter.[98] Any suggestion that the author of 2 Clement may have coined this word for his purpose here must remain a speculation, since we simply do not have access to the vast amount of Greek literature that does not survive. The reader is referred to the section in the Introduction called "The Opponents in Second Clement" for ideas about the identity of these false teachers. Donfried's suggestion should be considered because the gnostic opponents that he suggests are often mentioned by commentators. "This chapter can be best understood as a polemic against a gnosticizing direction toward which 2 Clement's congregation was moving."[99] "Although our author does not exactly specify the nature of this false teaching in chapter 10, he has given clues about it

---

95. BDAG, s.v., τρυφή, 1018, 1, 2.

96. BDAG, s.v., τρυφή, 1018, 3.

97. Tuckett, *2 Clement*, 213.

98. See προοδοιπόρος in 10.1. The cognate noun κακοδιδασκαλία is used in Ign. *Phld.* 2.1, and a similar verb, ἑτεροδιδασκαλέω, is used in 1 Tim 1:3.

99. Donfried, *Setting*, 149.

throughout the discourse. At least one characteristic of this teaching is given in 2 Clem. 10.3: they 'prefer the pleasures of the present to the promises of the future.'"[100] Donfried actually answers his own charge of gnosticizing by calling attention to the real problem being taught, namely that a loose moral lifestyle is permitted in the present that will negatively affect their future. This is not specific Gnostic behavior but is characteristic of a moral libertinism. Loose moral standards were not espoused by these supposed gnostic teachers alone. Perhaps these teachers did not recognize the nature of eschatology as well, especially the "payback" that believers are to render to Christ, which is essential to the enjoyment of that future bliss. Reference has already been made to the seminal criticism by Kelhoffer of this "gnosticizing" view.[101] Perhaps we should be satisfied in defining these teachers by the description of their teaching in the context, namely, malice, ungodliness and a preference for earthly pleasures (10.1–3). If we must find a label for them, let it be the libertines. Clement describes those affected by this teaching as "innocent souls." This at least should remind readers of the Pauline warning against false teachers who creep into houses and capture weak women (2 Tim 3:6). The description of them as "not realizing" or "not knowing" again is not a subtle attack on gnostic assumptions about "knowledge," since it is followed by a severe statement that what they do not realize is the tremendous spiritual danger that faces them. That danger is that both the deceivers and those they deceive "will receive a double punishment." No explanation is given why it is "double," and it may simply be that this refers to the punishment both for these deceivers and for those whom they deceive.

It has been noted previously that no clear citation of sacred texts occurs in this chapter. The attentive reader, however, may discern similar themes in the biblical warnings against false teachers and Clement's teachings here. "Verse 5 seems to echo or be tangential to the idea found in three passages: Matthew 18:6 (causing little ones to sin), Rom 1:32 (doing evil and approving those who do it), and Ezek 3:18 and 33:8 (prophet and sinner both to suffer)."[102] That such teachers and their effect on "innocent souls" were perceived as a serious danger in the second century is witnessed also by a strong warning from a contemporary teacher. "Do not be deceived, my brothers. Those who corrupt households will not inherit the kingdom of God. Therefore if those who do such things physically are put to death, how much more if someone corrupts faith in God by evil teaching, for which Jesus Christ was crucified! Such a person, having corrupted himself, will go

---

100. Donfried, *Setting*, 149.
101. Kelhoffer, "Pigeonholing a Prooftexter?," 282.
102. Grant and Graham, *First and Second Clement*, 121.

to the unquenchable fire, likewise also the one who listens to him."[103] False teaching in this chapter is again related to evil behavior. False theology may lead to this, but it is the false behavior that deeply concerns Clement here and throughout his message.

Chapter 11

1. Let us therefore serve God with a pure heart, and we will be righteous; but if we do not serve him because we do not believe the promise of God, we will be miserable.

2. For the prophetic word also says: "Miserable are the double-minded who doubt in their heart, saying, 'We heard all these things long ago and in the time of our fathers, but waiting day to day, we have seen none of them.'"

3. O foolish ones! Compare yourselves to a tree; consider a vine; first it sheds its leaves, then comes a bud, after these things a sour grape, then the full bunch.

4. So also my people have had turmoils and troubles, but then they will receive the good things."

5. Therefore, my brothers, let us not be double-minded, but let us endure in hope, so that we may also receive the reward.

6. For faithful is the one who promised to pay to each person the reward of his deeds.

7. Therefore if we do what is right before God, we will enter into his kingdom, and we will receive the promises "that ear has not heard, nor eye seen, nor has it entered the human heart."

Literary Structure

As with so many chapters in 2 Clement, chapter 11 begins with the conjunction "therefore" (οὖν), followed by a hortatory subjunctive (11.1), but also ends with the same conjunction and a conditional subjunctive (11.7). This *inclusio* structure surrounds two citations, the first (11.2–4) from an unknown source, and the second (11.6–7) from a pastiche of two possible NT allusions. Between these two appeals to authoritative sources is a

---

103. Ign. *Eph.* 16.1–2. Author's translation.

hortatory subjunctive (11.5) intended to convey the central message of the chapter not to be "double-minded."

Commentary

The opening exhortation is to "serve God," the first time that this verb (δουλεύω) appears independently of being part of a quotation (as in 6.1). The two later usages are also in the expression "serve God" (17.7; 18.1). The exhortation in 17.7 is to "serve God with one's whole heart" while here it is "to serve God with a pure heart." The emphasis on the inner being expressed by the "heart" echoes the Shema (Deut 6) and Jesus' use of it (Matt 22). This inner role of the heart appears also in the book as to "honor God from the heart" (3.4); to offer "praise from the heart" (8.2); and to "repent from the heart" (8.2; 9.8, 10; 17.1; 19.1). This emphasis on inner spirituality as the source of these actions contrasts with criticisms of the excessive "moralism" or even "legalism" that is sometimes leveled at the author.[104]

The future promised result of this service to God is that "we will be righteous" (11.1a), immediately followed by another future antithesis, namely that if we do not serve God, "we will be wretched" (11.1c). This eschatological blessing or judgment is dependent on whether or not we "believe God's promise" (11.1b). These words echo themes in Jas 4:7-10, where readers are exhorted to "purify hearts" and "be miserable," and are addressed as the "double-minded"; all of these expressions appearing also here in 11.1-2.[105]

The reference to being "wretched" prompts the use of a citation from the "prophetic word" in 11.2-4. Nothing like these words exists in the canonical Old or New Testament; neither do they survive in any known apocryphal texts. The citation formula as from "the prophetic word" (ὁ προφητικὸς λόγος) appears only once in the New Testament, namely, in 2 Pet 1:19, where the reference is to the Jewish (OT) Scriptures. Philo uses it to refer to Gen 1:14 (*Plant.* 117) and to Gen 49:22 (*Sobr.* 68). A later reference by Justin Martyr (*Dial.* 56.6) is to Gen 18:10. "In light of its usage elsewhere it is likely that 2 Clement has the Jewish Scriptures in mind when he uses this term."[106]

Where is this "prophetic word" found? Hagner, in his work on the use of scripture in 1 Clement, summarizes one of the most frequently cited answers to that question.

---

104. For example, Bultmann, *Theology,* 1:169.

105. James: ἁγνίσατε καρδίας, δίψυχοι . . . ταλαιπωρήσατε; Clement: καθαρᾷ καρδίᾳ . . . ταλαίπωροι . . . δίψυχοι.

106. Donfried, *Setting,* 52.

Of the various conjectures which have been made concerning these sources, the most convincing is that made by Lightfoot, who suggested that the book *Eldad and Modad* could account for the quotation. Little, in fact, is known of this book, attested in *Hermas, Vis.* II, 3. 4, the Stichometry of Nicephorus (400 στίχοι) and in the Pseudo-Athanasian Synopsis (where it is included among the apocryphal books of the NT), but which has not endured to modern times. The names Eldad and Modad are mentioned in Nu. 11:26–39 where it is said that they, having not gone out to the tent, prophesied in the camp . . . This, in fact, agrees well with the quotation in Clement, and also as found in 2 Cl. 11.2f. This latter passage, as we have seen, agrees with 1 Clement except for some slight changes and the addition of a further sentence . . . This added sentence shows that 2 Clement is not dependent upon 1 Clement for the quotation and that both quotations go back to the same source. The added sentence agrees well with what is known of *Eldad and Modad* from Hermas. Moreover, in 2 Clement the quotation is introduced as ὁ προφητικὸς λόγος, a formula which would particularly suit the prophetic *Eldad and Modad*.[107]

Both the substantive "double-minded" (δίψυχοι) and the cognate verb (διψυχέω) appear in the Shepherd of Hermas in the preceding context (*Vis.* 2, 2, 4 and 7).[108] Not all commentators are convinced about *Eldad and Modad* being the source for this quotation. Tuckett concludes that "this can only remain a conjecture."[109] Martin summarizes the present knowledge about *Eldad and Modad* and mentions that only four Greek words are known from it through the Hermas quotation: "The Lord is near to those in distress." After discussing the Clement citations, he concludes: "These passages are sufficiently obscure that they have been applied also to the *Testament of*

---

107. Hagner, *Use of the Old and New Testaments*, 87. It is unlikely that 2 Clement is drawing from 1 Clement, because of the differences in the citations, and because there is an added sentence in 2 Clement (see Tuckett, *2 Clement*, 217; and Lindemann, *Clemensbriefe*, 233).

108. Lightfoot summarized his suggestion as follows: "I would conjecture that it was *Eldad and Modad*, which was certainly known in the early Roman Church; see Herm. Vis. ii. 3 ἐγγὺς Κύριος τοῖς ἐπιστρεφομένοις, ὡς γέγραπται ἐν τῷ Ἐλδὰδ καὶ Μωδὰδ τοῖς προφητεύσασιν ἐν τῇ ἐρήμῳ τῷ λαῷ, a passage alleged by Hermas for the same purpose as our quotation, to refute one who is skeptical about the approaching afflictions of the last times" (*Apostolic Fathers*, 2:80).

109. Tuckett, *2 Clement*, 216. Note that Lightfoot used that word to describe his own suggestion in the previously footnoted quotation.

Moses and the *Apocryphon of Ezekiel*; hence the most prudent course is to leave these verses anonymous."[110]

The point of the quotation is to address those who doubt the future promise (11.1b, building on "the future promise" of 10.3). They are miserable because they "doubt in their heart" (11.2), an intended contrast with the exhortation to serve with a "pure heart" (11.1). The concept of purifying the heart in Jas 4 is also contrasted with the double-minded in Jas 4:8. While it falls short of a citation, the similarity in concept is striking between 11.2b: "We heard all these things long ago and in the time of our fathers, but waiting day to day, we have seen none of them"; and 2 Pet 3:4: "Where is the promise of his coming? For ever since the fathers fell asleep, all things are continuing as they were from the beginning of creation" (ESV). "At one level, the 'problem' addressed is not dissimilar to that addressed in 2 Peter, and it is striking that the text here displays a number of verbal similarities and agreements with the language of 2 Peter."[111] In this context, the reader should again recall the use of "the prophetic word" also in 2 Pet 1:19. Another possible echo of 2 Pet 2:8 is the phrase "day to day" (ἡμέραν ἐξ ἡμέρας), which appears also in 2 Pet 2:8. Given the hesitance on the part of much of NT scholarship to maintain an early date for 2 Peter, the following statement of Tuckett's is worthy of serious consideration: "It may be then that 2 Clement provides a relatively early witness to the existence, and use, of 2 Peter in early Christianity."[112]

The quotation continues with an invitation to consider the natural processes involved in the growth of a vine (11.3).[113] Clement's hearers are "fools" if they cannot discern the certainty of the stages of its growth from leaves to buds to unripe grapes to the bunch of grapes. The point is that they are foolish if they can discern this steady process in nature and not see God's people steadily and inevitably emerging from turmoil and trouble to the goodness they will receive in the eschaton (11.4). While the sentiments of this verse are not quoted in 1 Clem. 23.4, they were probably part of the original "prophetic word" (from whatever source), because the beginning of 11.5 assumes this with its transitional conjunction "therefore" (ὥστε) and the subsequent application of the quotation to behavior.[114]

---

110. Martin, "Eldad and Modad," 464.

111. Tuckett, *2 Clement*, 221.

112. Tuckett, *2 Clement*, 223.

113. "The words strongly resemble Mark iv. 26 sq (comp. Matt. xxiv. 32 sq, Mark xiii. 28 sq, Luke xxi. 29 sq" (Lightfoot, trans., *Apostolic Fathers*, I.2, 81).

114. Lindemann, *Clemensbriefe*, 84.

The title given to these who will receive good things despite their troubles is "my people." Assuming that this text was considered Jewish scripture, the original referent would have been Old Testament Israel suffering most probably in the wilderness sojourn. The application would be to Christian people during their sojourn in this world, preparing for the future "good things." This is consistent with the earlier application of the Isa 54:1 text to "our people" (2.3), as well as with the NT application of OT texts about the people of Israel to the church (Rom 9:25–26/Hos 2:23; 1 Pet 2:9/Exod 19:6).

Following this fascinating citation and its use of the substantive "double-minded," 11.5 exhorts the "brothers" not to be so, but rather to "endure in hope, so that we may also receive the reward." Here and also in 11.6, Clement displays the other side of the reward/recompense dynamic that should motivate believers to "pay back" the Lord for what he has done for them in their salvation. The use of the nouns "reward" and "payback" recalls the use of these words in 1.5; 3.3; and 9.5 (μισθός) and in 1.3, 5 and 9.7 (ἀντιμισθία) to portray the response that believers should give back to God. The words are used to portray the reward that believers will receive for their faithful endurance in obedience. This repayment will be in accord with each person's "deeds" or "works"—the divine response that again echoes NT promises (Matt 16:27; Rom 2:6).

This promise to reward faithful believers is grounded in the faithfulness of God: "faithful is the one who promised." The expression is remarkably similar to Heb 10:23: "for faithful is the one who promised."[115] This also bears resemblance to 1 Clem. 27.1: "who is faithful in his promises." Because appeals to divine faithfulness are a commonplace in Jewish and Christian Scriptures (see Deut 7:9; 1 Cor 1:9; 10:13), it is difficult to be certain about a deliberate use of Hebrews, especially because no citation formula is employed.[116]

Another possible intertextual connection is in 11.7 when the future reward of the righteous is portrayed as entering the divine kingdom and receiving the promises "that ear has not heard, nor eye seen, nor has it entered the human heart." We have placed these words in quotation marks in the translation because they are a description about the incomprehensibility of the eschatological plan for believers—a description very similar to 1 Cor

---

115. 2 Clem. 11.6: πιστὸς γάρ ἐστιν ὁ ἐπαγγειλάμενος; Heb 10.23: πιστὸς γὰρ ὁ ἐπαγγειλάμενος.

116. Benecke writes that Clement was "unconsciously influenced by Hebrews" (in Bartlet et al., eds., *New Testament in the Apostolic Fathers*, 135). Ehrman (*Apostolic Fathers*, I, 183) and Holmes (*Apostolic Fathers*, 153) cite Heb 10:23 as the source. Tuckett is "doubtful" (*2 Clement*, 225), and that skepticism is shared by Lindemann (*Clemensbriefe*, 234).

2:9. This Pauline affirmation is preceded by "as it is written," although the closest text one can find to Paul's description comes from Isa 64:4. Because of the differences between Isaiah and Paul/Clement, the allusion here must be to 1 Cor 2:9. These words are also cited in 1 Clem. 34.8 where they are described as scripture (λέγει), and they are actually attributed to Jesus in the Gospel of Thomas 17.[117] It is difficult to be dogmatic about the source, and the wise counsel of Tuckett should be considered. "Perhaps the most one can say is that the words of 2 Clement here provide further evidence for the widespread use of the saying in a range of different authors."[118]

The heavy stress on moral rectitude here and in a number of places in our text should be balanced by the fact that our author is as emphatic about the truth that the Lord has "saved us" (1.4–8) as he is about how we will be saved through our fidelity in the eschaton. The balance of the divine and human in this regard had been expressed earlier by Paul: "Therefore, my beloved, . . . work out your own salvation with fear and trembling, for it is God who works in you, both to will and to work for his good pleasure" (Phil 2:12–13, ESV).

Chapter 12

1. Therefore, let us wait hourly for the kingdom of God in love and righteousness, since we do not know the day of God's appearing.
2. For when the Lord himself was asked by someone when his kingdom will come, he said: "When the two will be one, and the outside is like the inside, and the male with the female is neither male nor female."
3. Now "the two are one" when we speak to each other in truth, and there is one soul in two bodies with no hypocrisy.
4. And by "the outside is like the inside" he means this: "the inside" is the soul and "the outside" is the body. Therefore, just as your body is visible, so let your soul be evident by your good deeds.
5. And by "the male with the female is neither male nor female" he means this: that when a brother sees a sister he should not think of her as a female, nor she of him as a male.
6. When you do these things, he says, the kingdom of my Father will come.

---

117. See also Hartog, "1 Corinthians 2:9 in the Apostolic Fathers," 115–18.
118. Tuckett, *2 Clement*, 219.

Literary Structure

The chapter opens with a hortatory subjunctive and a reason for obeying that exhortation (12.1). Then follows a saying attributed to the Lord (12.2), followed by a phrase-by-phrase explanation of the saying (12.3–5). The chapter closes with an affirmation about the future coming of the kingdom (12.6).

Commentary

Clement has said much thus far about the believer's future and how to attain to it. Chapter 10 discoursed about the coming future and its delight (10.3–4). The previous chapter ended with the promise of entering the future kingdom with its rewards for good deeds (11.6–7). Clement and his hearers know very well that this future is still very much in the future! Therefore, what should we do now? The answer in this chapter is that we should learn to wait hourly for it while living obedient lives since we do not know when those future events will come (12.1). While 11.5 exhorted that we should "endure in hope," 12.1 has the first use of the word "wait." "Therefore, let us *wait* hourly for the kingdom of God . . ." The verb for "wait" (ἐκδέχομαι) appears here for the first time and will reappear in the concluding appeal (20.3)—another of the links between the main body of 2 Clement and the concluding two chapters, which are often viewed as not originally part of chapters 1–18.

While definitely short of being a citation, 12.1 echoes ideas found in a number of Jesus *logia* in the Gospels, especially in Mark 13 and Matt 24–25. The noun "appearing" (ἐπιφανεία) occurs a number of times in the Pastoral Epistles, in combination with "God" and "the Lord" (1 Tim 6:14; 2 Tim 1:10; 4:1, 8; and Tit 2:13). It is associated with Jesus' "coming" (παρουσία) in 2 Thess 2:8. Our author's simple but high Christology is evident in that both God and Jesus will have such an "appearing" (cf 17.4). As in 2 Clem. 1.1, this is more of a functional rather than an ontological identity, but it is an identity nonetheless. What is said about God can also be said about Jesus.[119] The statement noting the obvious lack of knowledge about the end-times is a prominent feature in the Gospels, especially in parables (Matt 25:1–13; Mark 13:35–38). In both contexts, the ethical implications are prominent. Therefore, this waiting must be done in "love and righteousness," the first time in the book that these two virtues are linked, although they appear

---

119. For an exploration of this high Christology and how it works in Clement, see Crowe, "Like Father, Like Son."

separately in 4.3 and 9.6 (love) and in 4.2 and 6.9 (righteousness). Tuckett observes that "this emphasis on ethical behavior is what governs the 'exegesis' of the Jesus saying which now follows."[120]

The "Jesus saying" in 12.2, "When the two will be one, and the outside is like the inside, and the male with the female is neither male nor female," has engendered a significant amount of literature, since it appears nowhere in the canonical Gospels.[121] It is sometimes referred to as belonging to the *agrapha*, a term referring to the "unwritten" sayings of Jesus. It is an odd term since the only way we know about these sayings is that they were written, in books like 2 Clement, but not written in the canonical Gospels.[122]

While Clement cites the "Lord" as the source of the saying ("the Lord ... said"; ὁ κύριος ... εἶπεν), he does so in a way unlike the other references to "the Lord said" (4.5; 5.2; 9.11; 17.4). Here what the "Lord said" was in response to a question, "For when the Lord himself was asked by someone when his kingdom will come, he said . . ." His response was, "When the two will be one, and the outside is like the inside, and the male with the female is neither male nor female" (12.2). This statement is then followed by a three-part exposition of each part of the statement in 12.3-5. Our author, however, intends us to think that the quotation does not stop with 12.2. After his exposition, he continues the quotation accompanied by a citation formula using a different verb and tense: "When you do these things, he says (φησίν), the kingdom of my Father will come" (12.6). The words in 12.6 should be taken as part of the quotation.[123]

Clement of Alexandria quotes a similar saying as coming from the Gospel of the Egyptians, a work no longer extant apart from a few quotations preserved by various writers over the next few centuries. The other possible source is also the similar words found in the Gospel of Thomas 22.[124] None of the three quotations is in exact agreement with the others.

120. Tuckett, *2 Clement*, 230.

121. For commentary discussions of this passage, see Lindemann, *Clemensbriefe*, 234-36; Grant and Graham, *First and Second Clement*, 123-24; and Tuckett, *2 Clement*, 226-35. Other treatments of the passage include Donfried, *Setting*, 73-77, 152-54; Gregory and Tuckett, "2 Clement and the Writings"; and Tuckett, "2 Clement and the New Testament," 34. For the most thorough discussion of issues related to the passage, see Baarda, "2 Clement 12."

122. For discussions of issues surrounding the *agrapha*, see Jeremias, *Unknown Sayings of Jesus*; Stroker, *Extracanonical Sayings of Jesus*; and Stroker, "Agrapha."

123. Baarda, "2 Clement 12," 547-49; Donfried, *Setting*, 75; Ehrman, ed., *Apostolic Fathers*, I,185. For the contrary view, see Lightfoot, trans., *Apostolic Fathers*, I.2, 240; Lindemann, *Clemensbriefe*, 237; Holmes, ed., *Apostolic Fathers*, 153.

124. A synopsis of the three quotations in Greek and Coptic, accompanied by English translations, is in Tuckett, *2 Clement*, 226-27.

Because of dating issues and the differences in a number of details between the accounts, it is doubtful that Clement is directly citing either of the other two, but that all three are reflecting a common tradition and do not reflect a direct literary relationship. The version in the Gospel of the Egyptians is more developed, as can be seen in the citation by Clement: "When Salome enquired when she would know the things about which she had asked, the Lord said, 'When you tread on the garment of shame, and when the two become one, and when the male with the female is neither male nor female.'"[125] While the Thomas version is a bit closer to Clement, it adds: "and you fashion eyes in the place of an eye, and a hand in the place of a hand, and a foot in the place of a foot and a likeness in the place of a likeness, then will you enter the kingdom."[126] The best approach is that the three texts represent separately a tradition of a Jesus saying, with Clement conveying the earliest form of the saying.[127]

What is 2 Clement's purpose in using this saying? Clement of Alexandria said that this gospel was used by the gnostic Julius Cassianus to support his Encratite views. The ascetic, possibly even gnostic, orientation of the Gospel of Thomas is well known. Was 2 Clement also espousing similar ascetic views in quoting this saying? The best way to answer that question is by examining the way he interprets the saying. Only two times does Clement offer an exposition of a quoted saying: 2.1–3 (Isa 54:1) and here. In the first example, he offers a positive argument. Here it is also a positive explanation, but he actually is providing a negative response to what was a wrong understanding of the quotation.

The first phrase in the saying, "now the two are one," means that "when we speak to each other in truth . . . there is one soul in two bodies with no hypocrisy" (12.3). In other words, believers should relate to others with honesty and integrity. The unity should be manifested in agreement with others. He has already expressed the importance of "loving one another" (4.3). Intercommunal relationships are what this oneness is all about.

The second phrase, "the outside is like the inside," refers to the inner soul and the outer body. "Therefore, just as your body is visible, so let your soul be evident by your good deeds" (12.4). As the outward body can be seen, so the inner soul should manifest itself in good deeds.

The artificiality of his exposition here is forced, but it shows no allegorizing or extreme spiritualizing. He could be guilty of forcing his own

---

125. Tuckett translation, 2 *Clement*, 227.

126. Tuckett translation, 2 *Clement*, 227.

127. Donfried, *Setting*, 76–77; Baarda, "2 Clement 12," 547; Tuckett, 2 *Clement*, 229–30.

ideas on the text.[128] "See 2.1; 11.2–4; 14.2–4, for possibly similar examples of texts having to be forced to make them fit with the author's argument."[129] Modern hermeneutical principles may not be of that great a concern to Clement and others of the fathers, for example, Barnabas. Whatever be his flaws, the interpretation is again in the realm of morals and behavior, not in the realms of ideas and spiritual analogies.

The third statement in the text, "the male with the female is neither male nor female," is interpreted as "when a brother sees a sister he should not think of her as a female, nor she of him as a male" (12.5). This interpretation is ethical and behavioral and has nothing to do with any removal of human sexual distinctions. The expression counsels someone against having sexual desires for another of the other gender. The meaning may be that when a brother sees a woman, he should not think of her as a female. "It is also possible that the preacher is calling attention to the unimportance of physical appearance. Such distractions should be ignored among believers, so that each recognizes in another only the more important reality, that of the soul, where oneness may be found. The soul is visible not in appearance, but in the behavior that signals its quality."[130]

An ascetic attitude (Encratism) about abstention from all sex has been discerned by some interpreters.[131] On the other hand, the condemning of adultery elsewhere (4.3; 6.4) and the lack of any explicit ascetic counsel elsewhere in the book implies that Clement's condemnation is of inappropriate sexual acts.[132] His counsel about "self-control," which he declares as the summary of his counsel in 15.1, should not be viewed in any ascetic sphere, but in the sphere of moral behavior.

Clement's interpretation of this saying appears to lie within a moral and ethical sphere. Nothing approaching the so-called gnostic despising of the flesh or encratitic asceticism emerges from his interpretation of the saying. Donfried says that Clement "de-gnosticizes" this text.[133] This is unnecessary since we are not sure that the saying reflects Gnosticism, even if later generations may have used it that way. What we do have here is a hermeneutic that moves within a moral and ethical orbit.

As was mentioned previously, the words of 12.6 were probably part of the original quotation, and not simply an addition by Clement. They do

---

128. Baarda, "2 Clement 12," 535–36.
129. Tuckett, *2 Clement*, 233n20.
130. Hogan, *No Longer Male and Female*, 74.
131. For example, Lindemann, *Clemensbriefe*, 166; Pratscher, *Apostolic Fathers*, 84.
132. Baarda, "2 Clement 12," 555–56; Tuckett, *2 Clement*, 234.
133. Donfried, *Setting*, 153.

serve his purpose, however, as a sort of conclusion and final application of the saying. The original problem raised was one of timing, that is, when the kingdom will come. This conclusion tells us plainly: "When you do these things, . . . the kingdom of my Father will come." "The preacher presents a model of behavior for the here and now—if we treat one another as if male and female no longer exist, then the kingdom will come—on earth, it seems."[134] Eschatological fulfillment is, therefore, tied to ethical behavior, although some have objected because the eschaton is tied to promise and not to behavior.[135] Perhaps, however, this reflects a sense, witnessed to in the NT, that no contradiction is involved in holding what to some may appear to be mutually contradictory attitudes. The coming of the kingdom can depend on a divinely decided time, or the coming of the kingdom can depend on proper moral behavior.

This approach to the coming of the kingdom eliminates any current phase of the kingdom. From this language, it apparently does. In other words, it is possible that the "not yet" of Clement's kingdom eschatology has severely restricted the "now" of kingdom life. Our author, while emphasizing the present demands of ethical behavior, seems not to have been a subscriber to what has been called a "realized eschatology."

Chapter 13

1. Therefore, brothers, let us at once repent. Let us exercise self-control for our good, for we are full of much foolishness and wickedness. Let us wipe off from ourselves our former sins and let us repent with all our soul so we may be saved. Let us not be people-pleasers, and let us not desire to please ourselves alone by our righteousness, but also those who are outside, so that the Name not be blasphemed because of us.

2. For the Lord says, "My name is always blasphemed among all the Gentiles," and again, "Woe to him on whose account my name is blasphemed." Why is it blasphemed? Because you do not do what I desire.[136]

---

134. Hogan, *No Longer Male and Female*, 76.

135. Lindemann, *Clemensbriefe*, 237.

136. We have followed the reading represented by S ("you"/ ὑμᾶς) rather than the reading in A ("we"/ ἡμᾶς). Codex A ends at 12.5 and thus is not available at this point. Ehrman chooses ὑμᾶς (*Apostolic Fathers*, I, 184), while Holmes prefers ἡμᾶς (*Apostolic Fathers*, 154). Internal evidence of the author's style leans toward the first person pronoun, consistent with his often employed editorial *we*.

3. For the Gentiles, when they hear from our mouth the sayings of God, they are amazed at their beauty and greatness. Then, when they find out that our deeds are not worthy of the words we speak, they turn from then on to blasphemy, saying that it is a myth and a delusion.

4. For when they hear from us that God says: "It is no credit to you if you love those who love you, but it is a credit to you if you love your enemies and those who hate you." When they hear these things, they are amazed at such extraordinary goodness. But whenever they see that we not only do not love those who hate us but do not even love those who love us, they laugh scornfully at us, and thus the Name is blasphemed.

Literary Structure

The chapter opens with an intense series of five hortatory subjunctives, three expressed positively and two expressed negatively (13.1a). Two other subjunctive verbs express the desired result of the hortatory subjunctives (13.1b). The following verses (13.2–4a) provide three reasons for these exhortations, each introduced by the causal conjunction γάρ. The chapter concludes with two temporal clauses that expand and apply the previous exhortations (13.4b).

Commentary

The subject of the exhortations in 13.1, repentance, is familiar to the reader, while other themes appear for the first time and lead into the central theme of the chapter, namely the blasphemy of the Name, which is expounded in 13.2–4. The necessity of repentance has been mentioned before (8.1-3; 9.8) and will be mentioned again (15.1; 16.1; 17.1; 19.1). What is added at this point is the urgency of that repentance, which should be done "at once." This expression appropriately follows the previous chapter with its eschatological urgency.

The second command is, "Let us exercise self-control for our good."[137] The literal meaning of the verb is "to be sober" but its metaphorical meaning of general "self-control" is used often in the NT, as it is here, in eschatological contexts (for example, 1 Thess 5:6, 8; 1 Pet 1:13; 4:7).[138] Another noun

---

137. This is the translation of the expression suggested by Danker (BDAG, s.v. νήφω, 672).

138. The verb is only used figuratively in the NT but describes the athlete's self-control in Ign. *Pol.* 2.3.

meaning "self-control" (ἐγκράτεια) describes the author's main subject in 15.1. The reason for this self-control arises because "we are full of much foolishness and wickedness." (The noun ἄνοια can also be translated as "stupidity."[139]) Donfried argues that just as ἄνοια describes false teachers in 2 Tim 3:8–9, so ἄνοια also describes such teachers in 2 Clem. 13. The author's clear use of the Pastorals, however, is scant to nonexistent, and other types of "foolishness" here are probably in mind. Because the noun is paired with "wickedness," some sort of moral foolishness or stupidity is more probably held in mind. This moral meaning would also be closely tied to the lack of self-control being previously addressed.

Repentance is conveyed by another figurative exhortation to "wipe off from ourselves our former sins." While the verb is used of the wiping away of sins by initial repentance in Acts 3:19, the sins here are postconversion, or since one's baptism. This usage agrees with Hermas's stricter attitude about repentance following baptism. This wiping away of sins is synonymous with repentance, which again is to be "with all our soul," echoing an earlier description (12.3–4). The result clause "that we may be saved" refers to eschatological salvation.

For the first time in 2 Clement, a warning about not being "people-pleasers" appears, which signifies a turn in the subject toward what will become the main concern, namely, how we relate to others on the outside.[140] The sequel to this admonition, however, Tuckett calls "strange."[141] Clement then says that we should please ourselves, and the train of thought leads to actually trying to please outsiders so as not to bring shame on the name of the Lord. Therefore, it is not clear who are the people we should not seek to please. Perhaps the logic of all this was obvious to the author, although it may appear to be missing to us. The overall meaning, however, becomes clear in the end. We should be very concerned that our behavior toward the "outsiders" is circumspect "so that the Name not be blasphemed because of us." By the end of 13.1, therefore, this central theme of 2 Clem. chapter 13 emerges and will be his concern in 13.4.[142]

139. Holmes, ed., *Apostolic Fathers*, 155.

140. The noun is ἀνθρωπάρεσκοι, only here in the Apostolic Fathers, but the verb is in Ign. *Rom.* 2.1 and in the NT in 1 Thess 2:4.

141. Tuckett, *2 Clement*, 240.

142. Donfried's explanation of the following passage is excellent, and we are indebted to him in the following comments. He also credits van Unnik for informing his own remarks. See van Unnik, "Die Rücksicht auf die Reaktion der Nicht-Christen als Motiv in der altchristlichen Paränese." Tuckett also refers to van Unnik's chapter as a "valuable discussion of the theme" of this chapter (*2 Clement*, 240n14).

The reference to "those who are outside" (13.1) is new with Clement, but it can be found in the NT in such places as 1 Thess 4:11–12 and Col 4:5, with similar ideas expressed in 1 Cor 10:32 and Phil 2:15. Concern for what outsiders to the faith thought was an important concern in early Christian exhortation. The blasphemy of the Name is referred to again in 13.4. What is that "Name," and how can it be blasphemed? The context of 2 Clement suggests that the "name" refers to Jesus Christ. A major concern of the book is that the person of Jesus not be underestimated nor blasphemed, emerging in the opening statement that we ought not to think of him as other than God nor undervalue him. In 3.1 we are urged not to deny knowledge about Jesus Christ but instead to acknowledge him by doing what he says and obeying his commands (3.4). This is the very problem he raises at the end of chapter 13, namely, the dichotomy between deeds and words. Because our actions do not coincide with our confession, we can blaspheme that Name, namely, Jesus Christ.[143]

The use of the single word "name" is unusual, although it does appear in a sermonic context in Acts 5:41, as well as in Ign. *Eph.* 3.1. A reference to the rich blaspheming the name of Jesus appears in Jas 2:7. The citation in 2 Clem. 13.2 is from Isa 52:5 in the LXX, and commentators agree on this.[144] The expression is something "the Lord says," a citation formula that referred to Jesus' words in 2 Clem. 5.2 and 8.5. Although benefiting from Donfried's analysis, at this point I defer from his extended explanation of the supposed parallels at this point with the Gospel of Truth.[145] Such parallels are doubtful because there appear so many references to the name of the Lord and/or Jesus in early Christianity that it is unnecessary to posit a gnostic background for this language.

If the blasphemy of the "name" is referring to the name of Jesus, then how may this be done? Clement answers by a series of statements in 13.2–4. First, "because you do not do what I desire" (13.2). Second, "when they" (the Gentile outsiders) "find out that our deeds are not worthy of the words we speak" (13.3). Third, "whenever they see that we not only do not love those who hate us but do not even love those who love us" (13.4). The result of each of these actions is called "blasphemy." One can discern from the language used in 13.4 that the chief concern could be summed up as an inconsistency between what we "confess" and what we actually "do." Clement's concern is for the behavior of the believer. While he emphasizes accurate belief (for

---

143. Donfried, *Setting*, 155.

144. The quotation agrees more with the LXX of Isa 52:5 than to its allusion by Paul in Rom 2:24. With this agrees Donfried, *Setting*, 53; Tuckett, *2 Clement*, 237; Lindemann, *Clemensbriefe*, 238.

145. Donfried, *Setting*, 155–58.

example, 1.1), it is by our inconsistent behavior that we bring shame on the Lord and "thus the Name is blasphemed." The second quotation in 13.2, "Woe to him on whose account my name is blasphemed," cannot be traced to any preexisting source. The sentiment does appear in other patristic sources such as Ign. *Trall.* 8.2 and Pol. *Phil.* 19.3. It may, therefore, be a saying that was attached to Isa 52:5 and utilized as a comment on the text.

The reference to Gentiles hearing "from our mouth the sayings (or "oracles") of God" in 13.3 utilizes a word (λόγια) that can refer to Jewish scripture (Rom 3:2; Heb 5:12). It was also utilized for the sayings of Jesus, such as the famous *Logia* of Papias. An example of such a *logion* is found in 13.4, soon to be examined. The implication that to Clement the sayings of Jesus are equated with the sayings of the OT Yahweh should be evident to his readers. The lesson is that while outsiders may marvel at these sayings that they hear from us, our behavior may turn these sayings into a "delusion" (13.3). What they first viewed as a "marvel" (θαυμάζει) turns to a "myth" (μῦθόν). The validity of a moral philosopher's teaching, even among the Gentile pagans, was viewed as justified by whether the philosopher lived according to his moral teachings. If this was expected by those "outsiders," how much more was the seriousness of what they observed among these believers.[146]

Another citation of a Jesus saying appears in 13.4, apparently adapted from Luke 6:27 and 32, although resembling Matt 5:44 and 46. What is remarkable is that it is introduced by the formula "God says." What Jesus has said has been so encapsulated as part of the "oracles of God" that it can be taken as God saying it. The statement is an implication rather than a declaration that Jesus is to be thought of as God (1.1). The fact that Jesus could be viewed as blasphemed assumes his divine identity, although our author does not speculate on how the "persons" of God and Jesus fit into that existence. "The point is that they mock us, viz, Christians, and therefore scoff at the name, viz., Jesus Christ. This verse also strongly supports the interpretation given that the 'Name' refers to Jesus Christ."[147] First Clement 47.6–7 also provides an interesting parallel which should not be overlooked.

> It is disgraceful, dear friends, yes, *utterly disgraceful and unworthy of your conduct* in Christ, that it should be reported that the well-established and ancient church of the Corinthians, because of one or two persons, is rebelling against its presbyters. And this report has reached not only us, but also those who differ from us, with the result that you heap *blasphemies upon the*

---

146. See, e.g., Epictetus, *Diatr.* 3.7.17, as well as Matt 23:3.
147. Donfried, *Setting*, 158.

name of the Lord because of your *stupidity* and create danger for yourselves as well.¹⁴⁸

The parallels with 2 Clem. 13 are obvious. The bad behavior of the Corinthians is noted, as is that behavior being observed by the outsiders. Their behavior was foolish or stupid, and the result is that the "Name" was blasphemed. Donfried cannot resist making an application of this, one that is not affirmed by all interpreters. "It is worth raising the question whether both 1 and 2 Clement might be referring to the same situation in which the revolt against the presbyters in Corinth caused the Name to be blasphemed."¹⁴⁹ Whether the events are the same or not, the language is very clear about the serious nature of the offenses addressed in both documents.

The serious nature of these offenses parallels the teaching of Jesus that others will take notice of the reality of our confessions by our familial love (John 13:34; also 1 John 3:11-15). The command of Jesus, however, is not only that we love one another but that we love those who hate us (2 Clem. 13.4b, citing Luke/Matthew). This is the stinging observation by Clement that concludes the chapter. "But whenever they see that we not only do not love those who hate us but do not even love those who love us, they laugh scornfully at us, and thus the Name is blasphemed" (13.4b). Does this serious condemnation actually reflect a set of real circumstances facing the congregation from outsiders? It is difficult to be dogmatic. Second Clement says little about the relationship of believers to those who were outsiders to this community. Perhaps the language is rhetorical and is intended to address conflicts within the community caused by congregants' not loving one another, a responsibility stated plainly in 4.3 and 9.6. Using this language may be one attempt of Clement's to help form a social identity within the community vis-à-vis proverbial "outsiders." "The language here suggests that this is not just a general platitude but reflects a real concern about the internal relations within the author's community."¹⁵⁰

The Church as the Body of Christ 14.1-5

Chapter 14

1. So then, brothers, if we do the will of God our Father, we will belong to the first church, the spiritual one which was created before the sun

---

148. Quoted in Holmes, ed., *Apostolic Fathers*, 109 (italics added).
149. Donfried, *Setting*, 159.
150. Tuckett, *2 Clement*, 244.

and moon. But if we do not obey the will of the Lord, we will be among those of whom the scripture says, "My house has become a den of bandits." So let us choose, therefore, to belong to the church of life, so that we may be saved.

2. Now I do not imagine that you are ignorant that the living church is the body of Christ. For the scripture says, "God made mankind male and female." The male is Christ, the female is the church. Also the scrolls and the apostles say that the church belongs not to the present, but has existed from the beginning. For she was spiritual, as was also our Jesus, but he was manifested in the last days so that he might save us.

3. And the church, which is spiritual, was manifested in the flesh of Christ, showing us that if any of us guard her in the flesh without corruption, he will receive her back again in the Holy Spirit. For this flesh is a copy of the Spirit. Therefore no one who has corrupted the copy will partake in the original. So, then, he means this, brothers: guard the flesh, so that you may partake of the Spirit.

4. And if we say that the flesh is the church and the Spirit is Christ, then the one who abused the flesh has abused the church. Such a person, therefore, will not partake of the Spirit, who is Christ.

5. So great is the life and immortality this flesh is able to partake of, if the Holy Spirit is joined with it, that no one is able to express or to speak of the things "which the Lord has prepared" for his chosen ones.

Literary Structure

The structure of chapter 14 differs from other chapters in 2 Clement. Most chapters studied thus far open with an exhortation, usually in the form of a hortatory subjunctive verb (3.1; 4.1; 5.1; 7.1; 8.1; 9.1; 10.1; 11.1; 12.1; 13.1). This exhortation is then followed by a citation from an authoritative source to support the exhortation (3.2; 4.2; 5.2; 7.6; 8.2, 5; 9.11; 11.2; 12.2; 13.2).[151] In this chapter the protasis of a conditional clause (14.1a) leads to an apodosis that explains the theme of the following verses. A supporting text (14.1b) then leads to another hortatory subjunctive that is a call to become a part of the announced theme, the spiritual church. Another supporting text (14.2) elaborates this theme that follows through the rest of the chapter with a

---

151. The chapter divisions were not original to the author, but this repetition of exhortation and supporting text offered a pattern to those who later divided the book into chapters.

series of affirmations (14.2–5). This point is punctuated by the only other command in the chapter, an imperative to guard the flesh (14.3b) and is concluded by a possible scriptural allusion (14.5b).

Commentary

Second Clement 14 offers some unique problems and challenges to the reader and commentator. It is also the most theological section of the book. Its theological reflection, however, offers some real problems to solve, and not all have been impressed with the author's theological expertise. "The preacher is no theologian, as his efforts in chapters 9 and 14 make clear."[152] Others bemoan the density of the thoughts being expressed. "Ch. 14 is probably the most problematic section of the whole of the text of *2 Clement*. Further, the author's argument is at times very difficult to follow, and many have commented on the obscurity (and indeed questioned the sense) of what is said."[153] While examining the language in 14.4, one commentator observed that "the confusion of thought here is very great."[154] In his comments on 14.4, Lightfoot also observes that "It is almost impossible however to trace the connexion of thought in so loose a writer."[155]

Apart from his discussion in 2.1–3, the author also introduces some terms and ideas that are not found elsewhere in the book. Despite the different character of the discussion, however, his motive emerges to press upon the hearers and readers the important ethical behavior that must be part of a believer's life.

Lightfoot's summary of the chapter is a place to begin the analysis.

> If we do God's will, we shall be members of the eternal, spiritual Church; if not, we shall belong to that house which is a den of thieves. The living Church is Christ's body. God made male and female, saith the Scripture. The male is Christ, the female the Church. The Bible and the Apostles teach us that the Church existed from eternity. Just as Jesus was manifested in the flesh, so also was the Church. If therefore we desire to partake of the spiritual archetype, we must preserve the fleshly copy in its purity. This flesh is capable of life and immortality, if it be united

---

152. Grant and Graham, *First and Second Clement*, 109.
153. Tuckett, *2 Clement*, 246.
154. "Die Verwirrung im Denken hier ist sehr gross" (Knopf, *Zwei Clemensbriefe*, 175).
155. Lightfoot, trans., *Apostolic Fathers*, I.2, 248.

to the Spirit, that is to Christ. And the blessings which await His elect are greater than tongue can tell."[156]

The theme of doing the will of the Father and of Christ (14.1) has been prominent (5.1; 6.7; 8.4; 9.11; 10.1). Each time, as also here, the goal is salvation ("that we may be saved") in an eschatological sense. This may be an attempt to combat the idea of an overly realized salvation that divorces a person from any real obligation to obey. Against this idea, 14.1a states that if we obey that divine will, "we *will* belong to the first church."

Clement's concept of a spiritual church as the body of Christ has many resonances with NT teaching, especially Eph 4:4 and 5:23–32 where the church is his body or his flesh, and where the account of Adam and Eve also typifies Christ and the church.[157] The idea of "corrupting" the church (14.3) has a parallel in 2 Cor 11:2–3 and the Jerusalem "now" and "above" resonates with Gal 4:25–26. While Clement may have been aware of these Pauline themes, he takes the discussion in a more imaginative direction than this. He sees the church as the continuation of the preexistent bride of the Lord. He sees Christ and the church as the great realities of which the male and the female (14.2) are the shadows.[158]

He performs this imaginative piece of exegesis neither as an end in itself nor to impress others with his hermeneutical skill.[159] This recognition of the spirituality of Christ and the church serves his paraenetic purpose, which is that we "guard the flesh, so that you may receive the Spirit" (14.3), because "the one who abuses the flesh has abused the church" (14.4). To buttress his exhortation, he cites what appears to be a statement from Jer 7:11, quoted by Jesus in Matt 21:13. If we do not obey that divine will, we will be like that den of bandits so strongly condemned. On the contrary, we must belong to the church of life, for only then can we be saved, again in an eschatological sense (14.1). To Clement, the church preexisted, but not before God, because "it was created before the sun and moon" and was

156. Lightfoot, trans., *Apostolic Fathers*, I.2, 243.

157. For a persuasive argument that Clement reflects a familiarity with the Letter to the Ephesians, see Muddiman, "Church in Ephesians."

158. Hermas, *Vis.* 3 is comprised of a number of visions regarding a lady who is a personification of the church. One passage says of the church that she is the first of all the creation, and that the world was made for her. While similarities with 2 Clement abound, the treatments are still very different. The allegory is obvious, but the ethical admonitions like those found in 2 Clement are lacking.

159. One is reminded of Barnabas's self-delight after he unveils to his readers the supposed numerological Christology embedded in the 318 servants of Abraham in Gen 14. "The one who placed within us the implanted gift of his covenant understands. No one has ever learned from me a more reliable word, but I know you are worthy of it" (Barn. 9.9). Translation from Holmes, ed., *Apostolic Fathers*, 409.

spiritual (14.1). Its description as the "first church" is strange because no explanation is given of a "second church," one of the many unanswered conundrums in this passage.

It is possible that Clement is taking up a debate with Valentinian Gnosticism. Some authors, such as Donfried, base much of their analysis on this proposal.[160] "However, the author here gives no hint that he disapproves in any way of the sentiments or claims being made about the church. Indeed he seems happy to affirm them all fully and positively without any qualms."[161] As has been mentioned a number of times, the proposed parallels with Gnosticism, either approvingly or disparagingly, have been overdrawn, at least from this commentator's perspective.

Clement elaborates this analogy between the church and Christ in 14.2-4. The structure and text of 14.2 raise some textual and translation issues. First of all, at least two textual matters deserve attention. (1) Lightfoot, Ehrman, and Holmes adopt ὅτι ("that"), the reading of H instead of ἔτι ("moreover"), the reading of S, before "the scrolls and the apostles" in 14.2d.[162] Lake prefers ἔτι.[163] The reading ὅτι parallels the use of the conjunction earlier and supports the later proposal about the translation and meaning of the entire verse. (2) All scholars recognize the need to supply an understood word like "they say" (λέγουσιν) to makes sense of the sentence.[164] The resultant statement would thus be, "And that the scrolls and the apostles say . . ."

Assuming the presence of the ὅτι as mentioned above, my proposal is that the opening statement, "Now I do not imagine that you are ignorant," is followed by two main clauses: (1) "that the living church is the body of Christ"; and (2) "and that the scrolls and the apostles say that the church belongs not to the present, but has existed from the beginning." These two ὅτι clauses are thus the objects of the original statement concerning the author's confidence about their lack of ignorance. Clement employs a double negating expression of an idea which implies an affirmation of the opposite idea. In other words, the statement that he does not suppose that they do not know something means that he supposes that they do. He is confident

---

160. Donfried, *Setting*, 160-66.

161. Tuckett, *2 Clement*, 249.

162. Lightfoot, trans., *Apostolic Fathers*, I.1, 144; I.2, 245; Ehrman, ed., *Apostolic Fathers*, I, 186; Holmes, ed., *Apostolic Fathers*, 156.

163. Lake, *Apostolic Fathers*, I, 150.

164. Most suggest that the emendation be λέγουσιν δῆλον. Ehrman does not emend his Greek text but uses the word "indicate" as an understood action in his translation (*Apostolic Fathers*, I, 187).

that they are familiar with both of the ideas, about both the church's identity with Christ and the church's preexistence with Christ.[165]

The expression "the scrolls and the apostles" (τὰ βιβλία καὶ οἱ ἀπόστολοι) is the only occurrence of both these words in 2 Clement. That "the scrolls" has a wider reference than just the Prophets is evidenced by the fact that Jeremiah and Genesis have just been cited.[166] "The apostles" most probably refers to writings by the apostles, some of which have already been cited. Parallel expressions in 1 Clem. 42–43 support this suggestion. In the immediate context of 2 Clem. 14, the allusions to Ephesians and Colossians in 14.2-4 and possibly to 1 Corinthians in 14.5 support the idea that the writings of the apostles are intended by the expression.[167] A safe way of expressing the intention of Clement is to describe those authoritative texts that he is using.[168] While not denying that "apostles" may include the apostolic epistles, the focus here, especially because of his many citations of Jesus *logia*, is primarily to the Gospels. Tuckett calls attention to Justin Martyr's description of "the memoirs of the Apostles" being read in the church's services.[169] While it would be too confident to assume a full canonical list at this stage, it is interesting that this is probably the earliest expression used by a Christian to convey what eventually would be called the Old and New Testaments.

The meaning of every detail in these densely argued verses is beyond the scope of this commentary. The following sentence in 14.3, however, does deserve attention. "For this flesh is a copy of the Spirit. Therefore no one who has corrupted the copy will partake in the original." The word "copy" is what is often translated in theological discussions as "antitype" (ἀντίτυπος), while the word "original" (τό αὐθεντικόν) is that which is real or true. "The αὐθεντικόν is the eternal, spiritual archetype, the *original document*, as it

---

165. Muddiman argues from the speaker's confidence that his hearers know about this subject as evidence of his and his hearers' acquaintance with a book like Ephesians (Muddiman, "Church in Ephesians," 113–16). Kelhoffer suggests that Ephesians informed Clement's ecclesiology, and that 2 Clement may be correcting its soteriology. "Instead of a predestined elect already raised with Christ (Eph 1:3–5; 2:6), the writer of 2 Clement warns about the dangers of corrupting the flesh (14:3–5), hoping that his hearers will be prepared for the final judgment (cf. 17:3–7). Only those who keep the flesh pure belong to 'the first, spiritual church' (14:1) and will be reunited with Christ, with whom the church existed in the beginning (14:2)" (Kelhoffer, "Ecclesiology of 2 Clement 14").

166. This makes the unique addition in S of "the scrolls *of the prophets*" seriously problematic.

167. "This is a rough synonym [sic] for the Old and New Testaments respectively" (Lightfoot, trans. *Apostolic Fathers*, I.2, 245). See also Donfried, *Setting*, 95.

168. Lindemann, *Clemensbriefe*, 242.

169. Justin *1 Apol.* 66.3; *Dial.* 100–107; Tuckett, *2 Clement*, 254.

were, in God's own handwriting ... before it was corrupted by transcription. The ἀντίτυπον is the material, temporary manifestation, the imperfect and blurred *transcript* of the original."[170] At this point Clement may be borrowing from Neoplatonic categories of the present world of sense and the heavenly world of ideas.[171] Clement, however, is not interested in expounding on any of these philosophical categories, as much as modern readers would wish that he would! He immediately proceeds to end 14.3 by coming to his ethical point that one must guard the copy, which is "the flesh" (τὴν σάρκα), in order to partake in the original, which is "the Spirit" (τοῦ πνεύματος).

In 14.4 Clement again moves to the idea that abusing the "flesh" by improper behavior will abuse the church, which is the visible flesh of Christ. Thus one cannot hope to receive the Spirit, who is Christ. The equation between Spirit and Christ may be unexpected, but texts like 2 Cor 3:18 also utilize the same language to convey this apparent conundrum. "Altogether our preacher seems to be guilty of much confusion in his metaphor in this context; for here the relation of flesh to spirit represents the relation of the Church to Christ, whereas just above it has represented the relation of the earthly Church and Christ to the heavenly Church and Christ."[172] One should recall during this effort to unravel these words the earlier cited comment of Knopf that "the confusion of thought here is very great."[173] Perhaps, however, the confusion is more our problem of trying to measure these ancient sentiments by our modern categories of hermeneutics.

Rather than close the chapter with another hortatory command, 14.5 ends with an acknowledgment of wonder at what he has just described. "So great is the life and immortality this flesh is able to receive ... that no one is able to express or to speak of the things ..." He takes refuge in the fact that these wonderful things can only find their ultimate reality in the future. He has expressed this idea, found also in 1 Cor 2:9, earlier in 11.7. A parallel to this usage is in 1 Clem. 34.8, namely, that what lies ahead cannot be expressed in human words or conceived by the human mind. Without verbalizing a clear command, the implications of the future are clear and have already been confessed in a number of exhortations. Proper behavior now is essential to the enjoyment of the coming rewards. The language and images relayed in this, the most complex of chapters thus far, may perplex us, but the praxis in the message is clear: we must now "guard the flesh" (14.3) and thus not "abuse the church and Christ" (14.4).

170. Lightfoot, trans., *Apostolic Fathers*, I.2, 247.
171. Tuckett, *2 Clement*, 257.
172. Lightfoot, trans., *Apostolic Fathers*, I.2, 248.
173. Knopf, *Zwei Clemensbriefe*, 175.

Eschatological Section

(2 Clem. 15.1—20.5)

The Need for Urgency in Response to Christ 15.1—18.2

Appeal to Righteousness and Holiness 15.1-5

Chapter 15

1. Now I think that I have not given unimportant advice about self-control, which if anyone follows he will have no regret, but will save both himself and me, his advisor. For it is no small reward to turn to salvation a wandering and perishing soul.

2. For this is the return which we can pay back to God who created us: if the one who speaks and hears both speaks and hears with faith and love.

3. Let us, therefore, remain righteous and holy in our faith, that we may boldly ask God, who says, "While you are speaking, I will say, 'Behold, I am here.'"

4. For this saying is the sign of a great promise, for the Lord says that he is more ready to give than we are to ask.

5. Let us then share in such great kindness, and not begrudge ourselves the gaining of such good things, for as great is the pleasure that these words bring to those who do them so severe is the condemnation they bring to those who disobey.

Literary Structure

The structure of this chapter is different from most others, which begin with a hortatory command then followed by a citation from an authoritative source. Employing a litotes (a positive understatement made by negating the opposite quality) Clement makes a declaration about the nature of the work as a whole (15.1); this is followed by another affirmation what is expected from his hearers as a proper response (15.2). Then comes the hortatory subjunctive introduced by οὖν (15.3), supported by a scripture citation (15.3) and a scripture allusion (15.4). The chapter closes with another hortatory subjunctive introduced by οὖν and a reason given for the exhortation (15.5).

Commentary

The chapter opening sounds like Clement is concluding his discourse: "Now I think that I have not given unimportant advice about self-control . . ." (15.1a). More probably he is signaling a shift from what has been his main subject, self-control, to the final section of the discourse. While *ethos* will not be absent from his remaining points, there does seem to be a shift toward a greater emphasis on eschatological themes and their consequences. Note the emphasis on "the day of judgment" (16.3); "the day of his appearance" (17.4) and "day of judgment" (17.5); "the coming judgment" (18.2); "so we may be saved at the end" and "reap the immortal fruit of the resurrection" (19.3); and the closing emphasis on being crowned/awarded in the future (20.2–4).

Employing another litotes, as in 14.2, he understates by supposing that he has not given unimportant advice. In other words, "I have given important advice"! The verb οἴομαι, also used in 14.2, is defined as: "to consider something to be true but with a component of tentativeness, *think, suppose, expect.*"[1] This verb makes our author sound as if he is hesitant about his advice, but his use of this specific verb is part of his rhetorical understatement. He knows what he has done!

The differences between chapters 1–14 and 15–20 have not gone unnoticed by commentators. "There are some differences in vocabulary which are largely, but not entirely, related to differences in subject matter.

---

1. BDAG, s.v. οἴομαι, 701.

Chapters 1–14	Chapters 15–20
sarx (flesh); nineteen times	once (17.5); means "mankind"
pneuma (spirit); six times	once (20.4); means "person"
pneumatikos (spiritual) three times	not at all
psyche (soul)	
with body (5.4; 12.3–4)	body not mentioned
good or potentially so (6.2; 10.4; 13.1)	needs to be conquered (16.2)
	perishing (15.1; 17.1);
	indulgent (17.7)"[2]

Graham acknowledges that the differences do not imply two separate documents but point to the material in 15–20 being added to an earlier sermon, which was 1–14. Such conclusions are not necessary, since some of the semantic differences are a bit overdrawn. The shift in emphasis, as mentioned above, is enough to explain the differences of the words, not to mention that there is an expected difference between fourteen chapters and six chapters.

This is the first time that the author refers directly to himself (see also 18.2 and 19.1). He uses no official title here or elsewhere. Just as his message is described as "advice" (συμβουλία), so he is the "advisor" (τὸν συμβουλεύσαντα; substantival participle of the cognate verb συμβουλεύω). Neither word appears in the NT, although they are frequent in the LXX for "advisor" and "advice."[3] It is doubtful that this is a technical term for the genre of this discourse.[4] The word is intended to convey a summary of what has been said thus far. The author makes a deferential self-reference to being saved along with the reader who heeds his advice. Biblical references to such a humble attitude in the teacher/speaker can be cited (for example, 1 Tim 4:16 and Jas 5:19–20), and in 18.2 the author also indicates his own personal neediness (sinful and tempted). He employs another litotes ("no small reward") to describe the results of saving a needy soul who has wandered.

---

2. Grant and Graham, *First and Second Clement*, 127–28. Chart is reproduced as presented on p. 128.

3. The noun occurs nine times; the verb occurs thirty-three times.

4. See Tuckett's criticism of the word being used technically (*2 Clement*, 23, 260).

The subject of the advice is "self-control" or "self-restraint" (ἐγκράτεια).⁵ The adjective form of the word has already occurred in 4.3 as a way that we can acknowledge God by our actions. In the comments at that point we argued that there was no reason to think that the word was used in the technical sense as an Encratite, or as a word describing total sexual abstention. But how can it be used to sum up the message thus far?

In a seminal article on this chapter, C. L. de Wet explores the meaning of *enkrateia* in the ancient world and also in 2 Clement.⁶ What follows draws on his observations. The great difference between Christian self-control and that virtue in the Hellenistic world is that the latter was man-centered and featured masculinity as a major factor. No such masculinity was featured in the self-control of all believers. There was a similarity that must have appealed to the Greeks, but a difference as well that stood out.

According to 13.3–4 the pagans were observing the formation of virtue in believers. While virtue formation and *enkrateia* were factors in Greco-Roman ethical philosophy, the early believers were to develop their own version of it. Their performance of virtuosity was on display and in a sense proclaimed to outsiders. The legitimacy and validity of their Christianity was on display. Believers performing their own embodied virtue were a spectacle to the outsiders. Performance of this virtue of self-control would go farther even than the preaching of the message to them. "The virtuous body is constructed from a reimagined Hellenistic and Gnostic phraseology with the purpose of infiltration rather than confrontation."⁷ The appeal to the contest (7.1–4) relies on the virtue-centered voyeurism of the ancients central to civic life. As the athlete's flesh was scrutinized, so the flesh of Christians' "self-control" was scrutinized. Hence the appeal to guarding the flesh in 2 Clement. The performance of this virtue will continue into the eschaton and will be witnessed in the apocalyptic spectacle in which the wicked will be punished and the righteous will rejoice. De Wet has demonstrated that self-control was not an end in itself but was in a real sense a missional virtuosity empowered by the Father's provision and the Son's work of saving them.

This virtuous self-control is what leads to the believer's responsibility for a recompense to God in the terms of "payback" (15.2), which has been mentioned as one of the main aspects of the message of 2 Clement.⁸ "For

---

5. The last expression is preferred by Ehrman (*Apostolic Fathers*, I, 189).
6. De Wet, "No small counsel about self-control."
7. De Wet, "No small counsel about self-control," 10.
8. See the "Theology of 2 Clement" in the Introduction and the important role of this concept in the "Theological Praxis" of the book.

this is the return (ἀντιμισθία) which we can pay back to God who created us: if the one who speaks and hears both speaks and hears with faith and love" (15.2). Self-control motivated by the Christian virtues of faith and love is one of the ways we can offer that payback for his creation. This is the first and only appearance of the word for "faith" (πίστις) in the book. Rather than its general meaning of "trust," the focus here is probably more on "the faith" of the early believers as a whole.[9] Love has been mentioned (4.3; 9.6; 13.4) and is also an indication of the communal rather than individualistic character of the believing community. As 11.6 has mentioned, this payback includes another side of the coin, namely that as we pay God back, he will also pay us back according to our deeds.

The exhortation that follows in 15.3 is that we should remain righteous and holy in our faith as a consequence (οὖν) of our payback to God. Then follows a citation/allusion to the LXX wording of Isa 58:9, with an appropriate change from first person to third person as the speaker.[10] This promise is why "we may boldly ask God," and the reason is that he promises, "While you are speaking, I will say, 'Behold, I am here.'" In other words, whenever his people call out to him, he is present. "That 2 Clement has this chapter of Second Isaiah (58), as well as its larger context, in mind might possibly be suggested by the reference to the creator God (2 Clem. 15.2), and the remarks concerning the conversion of errant and perishing souls (15.1), both of which are important themes in Second Isaiah."[11]

"This saying is the sign of a great promise" (15.4a), and that promise is that the Lord is more ready to give than we are to ask (15.4b). While the speaker is not clearly mentioned as Jesus, the use of "Lord" in previous citations indicates that this should be viewed as another Jesus *logion*. Although not exact parallels, a saying like Matt 6:8 or 7:7 is the possible source. "It is possible that the saying attributed to Jesus and recorded in Acts 20:35 ('it is more blessed to give than to receive') may be in mind here, but again the parallel is not exact."[12]

The chapter closes with another dual exhortation: "Let us then share in such great kindness, and not begrudge ourselves the gaining of such good things" (15.5a). The exact meaning of the next clause in 15.5b ("and not begrudge ourselves the gaining of such good things") is not completely clear in the original language. Is the plural pronoun ἑαυτοῖς a true reflexive

---

9. Lindemann, *Clemensbriefe*, 246; Tuckett, *2 Clement*, 262.

10. 2 Clem. 15.3: ἔτι λαλοῦντός σου ἐρῶ ἰδοὺ πάρειμι; Isa 58:9: ἔτι λαλοῦντός σου ἐρεῖ ἰδοὺ πάρειμι.

11. Donfried, *Setting*, 169. For Isaianic references in this regard, see 42:5–6 and 45:22–23.

12. Tuckett, *2 Clement*, 263.

("ourselves")?[13] Is it an equivalent of the reciprocal ἀλλήλοις ("one another") as in 4.3?[14] In a well-argued article, van Unnik argues that the immediate context expects "we ourselves" but with an added irony.

> It is a very strong warning, with a touch of irony: who would be so stupid as to begrudge oneself the acquisition of the great blessing of God's presence? One may envy others, but not oneself, particularly in view of the choice between blessing and condemnation which are both contained in the same word of God. The begrudging consists in paying no heed to the word of God. Therefore, this admonition is a forceful argument to live righteous and holy lives in accordance with the Christian calling, one of the main themes of the homily.[15]

The concluding comment of 15.5b and the entire chapter is, "for as great is the pleasure that these words bring to those who do them so severe is the condemnation they bring to those who disobey" (15.5c). The word translated "pleasure" (ἡδονή) is surprising for a Christian writer. In the NT and in previous Jewish Greek literature, it is uniformly used in a negative sense.[16] Yet here in 2 Clement it is positive, as also in Hermas, Sim. 6, 5, 7. If the previous references to the lack of self-control could exemplify the negative aspects of ἡδονή, then true and genuine "pleasure" can be conveyed by what "these words bring to those who do them." There is, however, an equally strong "condemnation that they bring to those who disobey."

General Appeals for Repentance 16.1—18.2

Chapter 16

1. So, brothers, as we have received no small opportunity to repent, while we have time, let us turn to the God who calls us, while we still have the one who accepts us.

2. For if we renounce these pleasures and conquer our soul by not doing its evil desires, we will receive Jesus' mercy.

---

13. Lightfoot, trans., *Apostolic Fathers*, I.2, 249; Grant and Graham, *First and Second Clement*, 128; Lindemann, *Clemensbriefe*, 246.

14. Ehrman, ed., *Apostolic Fathers*, I, 191; Holmes, ed., *Apostolic Fathers*, 159; Brannan, *Apostolic Fathers*, 66.

15. Van Unnik, "Interpretation of 2 Clement 15,5," 34.

16. "Usu. in a bad sense," BDAG, s.v. ἡδονή, 434; for example, 4 Macc 5:23; Philo, *Agr*,. 83; Luke 8:14; Tit 3:3; Jas 4:1, 3; 2 Pet 2:13.

3. But you know that the day of judgment is already approaching like a burning oven, and some of the heavens will melt, and the whole earth will be like lead melting in a fire, and then both the hidden and the open deeds of people will be made visible.

4. Charitable giving is, therefore, as good as repentance from sin. Fasting is better than prayer, but charitable giving is better than both; and love "covers a multitude of sins," but prayer from a good conscience rescues from death. Blessed is everyone who is found to be full of these things, for charitable giving lightens the burden of sin.

Literary Structure

The chapter begins with the consequential "so, brothers" (ὥστε ἀδελφοί: 4.3; 7.1; 8.4; 10.1; 11.5; 14.1; 19.1; see also 7.3). This ties the following exhortation back to the eschatological argument of the previous chapter. As also in the previous appearances of this phrase, a hortatory subjunctive "let us turn" (ἐπιστρέψωμεν) then follows. Two temporal clauses, "while we have time ... while we still have the one who accepts us," remind the hearers of the urgency (16.1). A conditional sentence conveys the promise of mercy in the future if the conditional is fulfilled (16.2). An appeal to the hearers' knowledge about the future judgment of nature is coupled with a promise of judgment for individuals (16.3). The closing verse comprises two affirmations about charitable giving followed by a macarism for those who practice such charity and a concluding affirmation about the redemptive value of the virtue (16.4).

Commentary

The chapter opens with a thought that follows up 15.3–5 and largely repeats previous *paraenesis* in such verses as 8.1–2 and 9.7, namely, "while we have the opportunity, let us repent." What is added is the note of urgency, in keeping with the more intense eschatological context of the final chapters. What is new is the thought that we should turn to God, "while we still have the one who accepts us" (16.1b). This is the reading of the only surviving Greek text, Codex H, also called C. The Syriac version has the equivalent of "the Father who accepts us" and this is the reading adopted by Ehrman.[17]

17. Ehrman, ed., *Apostolic Fathers*, I, 158. The suggestion is that the participle παραδεχόμενον could have originally been a *nomen sacrum* πρα ("father") plus δεχόμενον ("receiving"). While this is a creative suggestion, it is probably best to follow Codex C,

From the following description of judgment, the sense of the expression is that now God the Father is a receiving figure, but in the future he will be a stern judge. Lightfoot calls attention to 2 Cor 6:2 where now is the time of acceptance, that is, the day of salvation.[18]

The conditional clause in 16.2 bases the future reception of Jesus' mercy as conditioned on our renouncing sinful pleasures and conquering our soul by not following its evil desires. The word translated "pleasures" (ἡδυπαθείαις) is found in all of early Christian literature only here and in 17.7. In earlier Greek literature, reflecting possible Stoic influence, it was a distasteful term.[19] See, for example, its only LXX use in 4 Macc 2:2, 4, where it refers to Joseph's sexual "desire." The warning agrees with the "self-control" previously commended in 15.1. The "soul" here is to be conquered and is the source of these evil desires (see also 17.7), although the soul is viewed positively in 5.4 and 6.2. The mercy of Jesus is a future experience here although a past experience in 3.1. Some still hold that Clement consistently reflects a future eschatology as here.[20] This apparent contradiction, observed often in the book, is more reflective of a "both/and" soteriology.[21]

This eschatological orientation comes to full fruition in 16.3 when the final judgment day will not only come but is "already approaching." The graphic description of that day with expressions like "a burning oven" and "heavens melting" and the earth like "lead melting in a fire" is almost certainly a citation from Mal 3:19 in the LXX (4:1 in the MT), even though no citation formula is expressed. The introductory "you know" (γινώσκετε) supports the reference being to Malachi.

While both surviving manuscripts agree, it has been difficult for some to imagine that "*some* of the heavens will melt." This is especially true since the biblical passages describe a universal conflagration. Lightfoot's oft-cited suggestion was that a textual corruption had taken place, and the reading was rather the "powers" of the heavens will be destroyed, in agreement with the LXX reading of Isa 34:4.[22] It is best, however, to remain with the reading in the sources and simply face its difficulty.[23] Another possible solution is

---

which is still "reasonably clear" (Tuckett, 2 *Clement*, 269). Lightfoot, trans., follows the Greek text (*Apostolic Fathers*, II, 250), as does Holmes, ed. (*Apostolic Fathers*, 158), and Brannan (*Apostolic Fathers*, 66).

18. Lightfoot, trans., *Apostolic Fathers*, I.2, 250.

19. BDAG, s.v. ἡδυπαθεία, "experience of a luxurious mode of life, *enjoyment, comfort*" (italics original); and Lightfoot, trans., *Apostolic Fathers*, I.2, 250.

20. Tuckett, 2 *Clement*, 270.

21. Lindemann, *Clemensbriefe*, 248, although not using that exact terminology.

22. Lightfoot, trans., *Apostolic Fathers*, I.2, 250.

23. Tuckett (2 *Clement*, 271n18) cites Lake's reference to the early belief of concentric

that the graphic saying may simply be a conflation and adaptation of the ideas expressed in 2 Pet 3:12: "destruction of the heavens by fire, and the elements will melt in the heat" (NIV). This last suggestion may help to explain the lack of a specific scripture citation.

Beyond these references in 2 Peter 3, the imagery of apocalyptic conflagration appears widely in early Christian eschatology (for example, 2 Thess 1:8-9; Jude 7; Rev 21:1).[24] As in all these texts, what accompanies these warnings is the fervent paraenetic impact that "both the hidden and the open deeds of people will be made visible." These eschatological references to the future age strengthen the behavioral exhortations in the present age.

The remainder of the comments in this chapter will focus on the significance of the reference to "almsgiving" in 16.4: "*Charitable giving* (ἐλεημοσύνη) is therefore as good as repentance from sin. Fasting is better than prayer, but *charitable giving* is better than both; and love 'covers a multitude of sins,' but prayer from a good conscience rescues from death. Blessed is every man who is found to be full of these things, for *charitable giving* lightens the burden of sin." The italicized translation is only one way to render this noun, but the variety of renderings does not reflect disagreement but rather the semantic richness of the word.[25]

David Downs has given thorough attention to the role of "almsgiving" in 2 Clement and early Christianity. His explanations and conclusions have greatly influenced the following comments.[26] The sudden introduction of this discussion of "almsgiving" (the English term we will use) has led some commentators to posit a corruption in the text.[27] Others have commented that the passage is simply confusing.[28] A more thorough context of almsgiving, especially in Jewish tradition, is needed for clarification of the intended message in 16.4.

---

heavens but concludes with Lindemann's pessimistic but honest comment that the saying "must remain unintelligible to us" (Lindemann, *Clemensbriefe*, 248).

24. See also Justin, *1 Apol* 20. 1-2; Tertullian, *Spect.* 30.

25. Lightfoot uses the old term "almsgiving" (*Fathers*, II, 251), as does Lake (*Fathers*, 155); Tuckett prefers "charity" (*2 Clement*, 115), as does Ehrman (*Apostolic Fathers*, I, 191); while Holmes prefers "charitable giving" (*Apostolic Fathers*, 159), as also Brannan (*Apostolic Fathers*, 67).

26. See Downs, "'Love Covers a Multitude of Sins,'" 489-514; Downs, "Redemptive Almsgiving and Economic Stratification in 2 Clement," 493-517; and Downs, *Alms*.

27. Lightfoot, trans., *Apostolic Fathers*, I.2, 251.

28. See references in Tuckett, *2 Clement*, 272, whose comment is that "the logic seems strained at best."

It is important to note the Jewish antecedents to what can be called "redemptive almsgiving."²⁹ The Theodotian Greek text of Dan 4:24 reads, "Therefore, O king, let my counsel be acceptable to you and atone for your sins with *alms* and for iniquities with compassion to the needy" (NETS). The word translated "alms" is the same word used in Clement (the plural ἐλεημοσύναις). This exact phrasing does not appear in the Aramaic text of Daniel, which reads, "Therefore, Your Majesty, be pleased to accept my advice: Renounce your sins by doing what is right, and your wickedness by being kind to the oppressed" (Dan 4:27 NIV). Some have thought that Clement is drawing on Tob 12:8-9: "Prayer is good with fasting and almsgiving and righteousness. A little with righteousness is better than much with injustice. It is better to give alms than to store up gold. For almsgiving delivers from death, and it will purge away every sin. Those who practice almsgiving and righteousness will have fullness of life" (NETS).

Clement, however, goes beyond Tobit in affirming that almsgiving is better than fasting and prayer. These three practices are often grouped together by Jewish writers. That is why it is difficult to understand one writer's statement that the reference here in 2 Clement "is the only combination of the terms charity, fasting and prayer in the New Testament or the Apostolic Fathers."³⁰ It is difficult because that is exactly the situation in Matt 6:1-18, although nothing is mentioned there about the redemptive role of any of the three practices.

The Jewish Christian document known as the Didache also portrays a "redemptive" function of almsgiving in 4.5-8:

> Do not be someone who stretches out the hands to receive but withdraws them when it comes to giving. If you earn something by working with your hands, you shall give a ransom for your sins. You shall not hesitate to give, nor shall you grumble when giving, for you will know who is the *good* paymaster of the reward. You shall not turn away from someone in need, but shall share everything with your brother or sister, and do not claim that anything is your own. For if you are sharers in what is imperishable, how much more so in perishable things!³¹

---

29. Downs, "Redemptive Almsgiving," 493.
30. Donfried, *Setting*, 170.
31. Holmes, ed., *Apostolic Fathers*, 350-51. The Didache utilizes patronage/reciprocity words in 4:7 that are echoed in 2 Clement, such as μισθός (see 2 Clem. 1.3; 3.3; 9.7; 15.1-2) and the semantically similar ἀνταποδότης (see 2 Clem. 1.3, 5; 9.7; 11.6; 15.2).

What is unique in our passage, however, is the introduction of a clear citation from 1 Pet 4:8 in addition to echoing sentiments from earlier literature such as Tobit. Clement also adds, "and love covers a multitude of sins." Not only is almsgiving better than fasting and prayer, but like love, almsgiving "lightens the burden of sin." Downs states that "the author constructs a hierarchy of praxis" and illustrates it as follows:

> almsgiving (as repentance for sin)
>
> fasting
>
> prayer

"If almsgiving is depicted as a means or sign of repentance in 16.4a, it may be ranked above fasting and prayer simply because almsgiving most clearly demonstrates the one thing that the preacher desires most from his audience, namely, repentance (8.1–3; 9.8; 13.1; 15.1; 17.1; 19.1)."[32]

Clement's reference to 1 Pet 4:8 is significant:

> With an emphasis on the eschatological context of ethics similar to that found in 1 Peter 4, the author of 2 Clement interprets this saying from 1 Pet 4:8 as an indication that the human love demonstrated through the giving of alms signifies one's repentance and covers a multitude of sins for the giving of alms. All those who hear this sermon are commissioned as agents in this mutual assistance, for all are called to repentance.[33]

For modern readers, particularly those in the Reformation heritage, such "redemptive almsgiving" still may be problematic for their theology of grace. Second Clement 16.4, however, is not intended to be read apart from the rest of the discourse, which references the mercy by which we were saved as well as Christ's action in saving those who were perishing (1.7; 2.3–4). "Scripture" says that Christ came to save sinners (2.4). Salvation thus only comes through the gracious and merciful work of Christ.

> That the document focuses so much on a call to repentance and the transformation of the moral life should be seen as part of the rhetorical purpose of the sermon and not as a theological deficiency. In this sense any tension between 2 Clem. and 1 Pet may be minimal. The author of 2 Clement holds together (1) the confession that salvation comes through the suffering of Jesus and (2) the affirmation that giving of alms both covers and lightens the burden of sin. Again, unless we are prepared to accept

---

32. Downs, "'Love Covers a Multitude,'" 503–4.
33. Downs, "'Love Covers a Multitude,'" 504.

the conclusion that only the "rich" have access to the forgiveness of sin mediated through almsgiving, we should assume that all in the community of faith are called to embody the practice of providing material assistance for those in need: "Blessed is everyone who is found full of these things, for almsgiving lightens the burden of sin" (2 Clem. 16.4).[34]

No criticism is implied by these words of prayer and fasting. The final *macarism* is a blessing for the one who is "full of [all] these things," namely, almsgiving, fasting, and prayer. Each of the three virtues, to borrow from the consistent thought of Paul, is a manifestation of love. The concluding thought that almsgiving "lightens the load" of sin may appear a bit unusual, but the message at the end of the chapter is evident. Sin is not lightened by just being given less weight; it is radically removed.

Clement has taken up a Jewish tradition pioneered in Daniel and Tobit and elaborated in the Didache and then adapted it by adding 1 Pet 4:8 while exploiting the whole to further his argument.[35] That argument is for a thoroughgoing repentance that manifests itself in all areas of life, even in the sphere of one's eleemosynary habits.

Chapter 17

1. Therefore, let us repent with our whole heart, so that none of us perish. For since we have commands that we should do this, to tear men away from idols and to instruct them, how much more must we save from perishing a soul who already knows God?

2. Let us then help one another, and restore those who are weak in goodness, so that we may all be saved, and turn each other around and admonish each other.

3. And let us not only appear to believe and pay attention now, while we are being admonished by the elders; but also when we have returned home, let us remember the commandments of the Lord, and let us not be dragged off by worldly desires. Rather by coming here more frequently, let us attempt to progress in the commands of the Lord, so that we may all think the same way and be gathered together for life.

---

34. Downs, "Redemptive Almsgiving," 516–17.

35. Pol. *Phil.* 10.2 seems to use Tobit (4:10, 12:9) and may also relate it to redemptive almsgiving.

4. For the Lord said, "I am coming to gather together all the nations, tribes, and languages." Now by this he means the day of his appearance, when he will come and rescue us, each one according to his deeds.

5. And the unbelievers will see his glory and power, and they will be astonished when they see the sovereignty of the world given to Jesus; and they will say, "Woe unto us, because it was you, and we did not know it or believe it, and we did not obey the elders who proclaimed to us about our salvation." "And their worm will not die, and their fire will not be quenched, and they will be a spectacle for all flesh."

6. He means the day of judgment, when they will see those who were ungodly among us and who perverted the commands of Jesus Christ.

7. But the righteous who have done good, who endured torture, and who hated the pleasures of the soul, when they see those who have gone astray and denied Jesus by words or deeds punished with terrible torment in unquenchable fire, will give glory to their God, saying that there will be hope for the one who served God from his whole heart.

Literary Structure

The chapter develops in two clearly distinguishable movements. The first section (17.1–3) is composed of at least six hortatory subjunctives augmented by purpose subjunctives and infinitive complements that further expand the exhortations. The second section (17.4–7) begins with a scripture citation giving the reason for the exhortations. In this section emerges a clear shift to eschatological reasons to justify the exhortations. Therefore, there is a shift to the future tense throughout this section. The focus on the judgment of "unbelievers" (the ungodly) in 17.4–6 gives way to a description of the reward for the "believers" (the godly) in 17.7. Chapter 17 is the longest chapter in 2 Clement, consisting of 265 Greek words, followed by chapter 14 with 236 Greek words. The brief following chapter (that is, chapter 18), consisting of only fifty Greek words, closes this part of the commentary.

Commentary

The intense hortatory nature of the chapter's opening connects with the final exhortation in 16:4, the turn toward an eschatological frame of reference in 17.4–7. This theme continues the eschatological focus of 16.1–3 that characterizes the conclusion of the book (chapters 15–20).

"[Second] Clement proceeds (that is, in this chapter) to define even more closely what will happen at the last judgment."[36] To avoid perishing at that judgment, we should repent, again "from the whole heart" (17.1; see also 8.2–3; 19.1). This renewed emphasis on the "whole heart" is an allusion to the Shema and its citation by Jesus in Matt 22:37 (see 2 Clem. 3.4; 17.7). The first person inclusion of the speaker among those who need to repent is a rhetorical effort to identify with his hearers, which comes to fruition in 18.2 with his self-description as a sinner. This repentance is not limited to evident unbelievers, described as idolaters in 17.1b, but extends to saving from perishing a soul who already knows God in 17.1c. This missional activity balances a concern for those within the Christian community, those who already "know God." "Clearly too, the author believes that the profession of the Christian faith in itself provides no guarantee of final salvation."[37] Modern theological discussion of the loss of salvation or the falling away of only professing believers does not enter the author's discussion. He is concerned about the seriousness of a continued repentance as an evidence that they will be saved from "perishing."

The language in 17.2 reflects this communal concern in helping "one another" and restoring and admonishing "each other."[38] This ministry is to be done with the goal "that we may all be saved." The "one who already knows God" (17.1) may need "help" so that "we all may be saved" (17.2). While the "weak ones" in Pauline usage are the overly scrupulous in regard to dietary laws (Rom 14:1–3), here they are those who are "weak in goodness." The language of communal exhortation and help moves the responsibility from any sort of priestly or ministerial responsibility to mutual ministry between and among believers.

This mutual ministry then leads to the first self-description of the immediate context of the speaker and those who hear this "advice" or "counsel" (15.2). Hearers should heed Clement's instructions, not only when the elders are admonishing them, but when they return to their homes! The speaker may be one of these "elders," although that is not clear. The inclusion of the first person may imply that he is an elder or this may be the general person and number used in rhetorical exhortations. Notice the description in Justin, 1 Apol. 67.4: "when the reader finishes, the leader verbally instructs, and admonishes to imitate these good things" (author's translation). What is

36. Donfried, *Setting*, 172. Donfried discerns this important eschatological theme and will be a guide for the explanation of the latter part of this chapter.
37. Tuckett, *2 Clement*, 280.
38. There seems to be no semantic difference in the reflexive pronoun ἑαυτοῖς and the reciprocal pronoun ἀλλήλους, both of which are used in these expressions. See BDAG, s.v. ἀλλήλων, 46, citing 1 Pet 4:8.

delivered is "admonishment" (νουθεσίαν), the noun form of the verb used in 2 Clement (νουθετεῖσθαι). The arrival at home should produce (1) a positive result to "remember the commandments of the Lord," and (2) a negative result that we "not be dragged aside by worldly desires." This happens "by coming here more frequently," words that echo the exhortation in Did. 16.2: "Gather together frequently" (the simple adverb πυκνῶς, while 2 Clement uses the comparative πυκνότερον), "seeking the things that benefit your souls." In this way we "attempt to progress in the commands of the Lord, so that we may all think the same way and be gathered together for life" (17.3). The expression "to think the same way" (τὸ αὐτὸ φρονοῦντες) is the same expression used by Paul in Phil 2:2 and may be a conscious allusion since such unity is commended by this language often in Paul (Rom 12:16; 2 Cor 13:11; Phil 4:2).[39] The goal of all this commended behavior again, as always, is eschatological. It is "to be gathered together for life," that is, eternal life.

One theme that emerges from 17.1–3 is the necessary obedience to the "commands" of the Lord (17.1; 2[2]).[40] The use of "the Lord" as the author of these commands indicates that the author did not reserve a title for the Father as distinct from the Son. We "have" these commands (1); we are to "remember" these commandments (3a); and we are to "progress" in these commands (3b). The word will also appear a fourth time in 17.6 in a different context to describe the awful fate of those "who perverted the commands (ἐντολάς) of Jesus Christ."

The positive description of the believers' goals in 17.1–3 has only one negative warning, which anticipates the serious dangers that are the subject of 17.4–7. While remembering the Lord's commandments, we should "not be dragged off by worldly desires" (17.3). While this echoes a description of these inner desires in Tit 2:12, the colorful verb is a *hapax legomenon* in all of known Greek literature.[41] This description of desires that can pervert their way (17.3) is similar to earlier warnings in 5.6 and 16.2.

An elaboration of the "perishing" that was mentioned in 17.1 is described in 17.4–7. Serious attention is now turned to the inevitable

---

39. Lake (*Apostolic Fathers*, 157) places the words "all have the same mind" in quotation marks, although subsequent versions have hesitated to follow suit. Richardson (*Apostolic Fathers*, 200) does provide quotation marks, although Lindemann (*Clemensbriefe*, 249) does not. Tuckett says that a quotation is "doubtful" (*2 Clement*, 282n22).

40. Two different Greek words are used for this substantive. In 17.1 and 17.3b it is the plurals ἐντολάς and ἐντολαῖς. In 17.3a the word is the plural ἐνταλμάτων. Although there is no clear semantic distinction between these words, especially since both are from "the Lord," I have translated the first and third occurrences as "commands" and the second as "commandments" to preserve the distinction.

41. BDAG, 90 s.v. ἀντιπαρέλκω, *let oneself be dragged over to the opposite side*. The verb ἕλκω does appear in the NT (for example, John 21:6; Jas 2:6).

judgment that awaits not only the pagans but also the disobedient soul who already knows God (17.1). The section opens with a quotation of Isa 66:18 as something that "the Lord said." The reference to gathering all nations, tribes, and languages is immediately applied to the second coming of Jesus (17.4). Lightfoot affirms that "Lord" here means "Christ" and employs Harnack for support, referring to chapter 3 "where Isa xxix. 13 seems to be put into the mouth of our Lord."[42] This takes us back to the very beginning of the book where Christ is described as "judge of the living and the dead" (1.1). This judgment will take place to "rescue us" as we are judged according to our deeds (17.4). This last standard appears in both the OT and NT (for example, Ps 61:33; Prov 24:12; Matt 16:27; Rom 2:6; 2 Cor 5:10).

The judged speak out in 17.5 by a "woe cry" as they see the governance of the world turned over to Jesus. They will bemoan the fact that "we did not obey the elders who proclaimed to us about our salvation" (17.5). The salvation which the elders proclaimed has a future dimension, but some in the congregation "recognized only a realized eschatology which had as its result a libertinistic attitude."[43] The judgment emerges in 17.6 as the condemnation of "the ungodly among us and [those] who perverted the commands of Jesus Christ." Rather than suggesting that blatant or even incipient Gnosticism is plaguing the church, in this second book Clement best describes the problem facing his hearers as behavioral laxity.[44]

The awful judgment awaiting these unbelievers is supported by another citation in 17.5 from Isa 66, this time in the exact words of Isa 66:24. This text has already been cited in 7.6 and was referred to by Jesus in Mark 9:44, 46, 48. These graphic words about worms not dying in an unquenchable fire describe the fate of those who do not respond now while time remains. It is obvious that this message had the goal of warning unbelievers, but the intended effect for the faithful was to fortify them against outsiders "who perverted the commands of Jesus Christ" (17.6). If believers felt threatened by them, they now can know that these libertines who offer "freedom" from restrictions on their behavior offer only illusory answers. One final observation about false teachers is that the way they are portrayed in 2 Clement focuses not on theological or ontological denials

---

42. Lightfoot, trans., *Apostolic Fathers*, I.2, 254.

43. Donfried, *Setting*, 172.

44. The reference to disobeying the elders may support the idea this address was a response by those elders because of their reinstatement after the letter called First Clement had a positive effect on the Corinthian congregation. Rejection of elders was the primary problem addressed in that letter. Refer to the earlier discussion for occasion and setting of this address. Donfried builds a strong case for this approach (*Setting*, 1–15).

but on behavioral deficiencies. This laxness in their actions echoes warnings in the NT about false teachers (2 Tim 3:1–7; Jude 11–16). The idea that believers will "see" the ungodly could be their visual evidence at the great assize, but perhaps it simply means that the unbelievers will be seen as receiving their just punishment.

The blessings for those who have been obedient are taken up in 17.7. Donfried's observations on the author's method in this verse are helpful.

> A number of key words used in 2 Clement are taken up again and put in this eschatological framework. (The verb) ὑπομένω is not only used here, but also in 11.5. What is there urged, "Rather must we patiently hold out in hope so that we may gain our reward," is here fulfilled. The tortures which the upright have patiently endured (17.7) are the same which Jesus endured (1.2). The righteous will see those who have "denied Jesus in word and act" (17.7) punished. Here again a theme which was discussed at the beginning of the ethical section (3.1) is taken up again and put in an eschatological context. It is now said that those persons who deny Jesus will be punished with "dreadful torments and undying fire . . . ." And the last sentence of 2 Clement 17, "there is hope for him who δεδουλευκότι θεῷ ἐξ ὅλης καρδίας," takes up themes which have also occurred before, namely, δουλεύω (6.1; 11.1) and ἐξ ὅλης καρδίας (3.4; 8.2; 17.1). We see, then, how 2 Clement takes up previous themes and puts them into an eschatological context, adding the specific sanctions of blessings and curses to what has been said earlier.[45]

The words of the righteous in 17.7 may seem strange with their shift from plural to singular ("saying" about "the one who served"). Some have suggested that this is a quotation from another context."[46] What the exact quotation is cannot be said apart from some general OT texts like Isa 54:17. It could be our author is expressing his opinion based on his general knowledge of his authoritative sources. The bluntness of the solemn ending in chapter 17 almost demands a final conclusion. That will be seen in a brief chapter which could be viewed as the conclusion of this one.

Chapter 18

1. Let us then also be among those who give thanks, who have served God, and not among the ungodly, who are judged.

---

45. Donfried, *Setting*, 173.
46. See, for example, Lindemann, *Clemensbriefe*, 253.

2. For I myself am also completely sinful, and I have not yet fled from temptation, but while still in the midst of the devil's tools, I am endeavoring to pursue righteousness, so that I may have the strength at least to come near to it, while in fear of the coming judgment.

Literary Structure

The structure of the shortest chapter in 2 Clement is simple. A hortatory subjunctive verb anchors an exhortation for thanksgiving in 18.1. The long sentence that follows in 18.2 is composed of a compound causal clause, followed by a temporal participial clause, followed by a purpose clause. It concludes with another temporal participial clause.

Commentary

While the form of the exhortation in 18.1 is a familiar beginning to many of the chapters in 2 Clement (for example, chs 4, 5, 7, 8, 9, 10, 11, 12, 13, 16, 17), the specific exhortation is new to the book, and the chapter contains a number of words and features that appear for the first time. Therefore, while a seamless transition is made from the previous chapter because of the mention of eschatological judgment (18.1b), it would be wrong to view these two verses simply as a summary of that chapter.

The first new feature is the exhortation for the hearers to "be among those who give thanks" (τῶν εὐχαριστούντων). This is the only occurrence of this verb (εὐχαριστέω), and its cognate noun (εὐχαριστία) is also absent. The description of thankful people as those who have served God (δεδουλευκότων τῷ θεῷ) echoes an expression in 17.7 which may be part of a quotation. What is familiar, however, is the warning of the eschatological judgment in which we should not be found (18.1c). This judgment theme, never far from the author's purpose, forms an *inclusio* with the final sentiment about judgment at the end of 18.2. Despite some commentators who separate the final two chapters from the first eighteen, the eschatological judgment theme will appear again in 19.3 and 20.4.

The second new feature in the chapter is the intense self-description of the speaker as also being one who is "completely sinful" (18.2a). The word (πανθαμαρτωλός) is a *hapax legomenon* in Greek literature that survives from this period.[47] While often using the first person plural rhetorically to

---

47. Tuckett calls attention to the similar adjective πανθαμάρτητος in Did. 5.2 and Barn. 20.2 (2 *Clement*, 289n3). In those contexts that word describes people who are

identify with his hearers, this is only the second time the speaker refers to himself in a specific way. He has briefly mentioned himself in 15.1 and later will describe what he is doing in 19.1. Grant sees this reference as "reminiscent of Phil 3:12" where Paul refers to his humble efforts toward pursuing Christ.[48] Clement, however, is being harder on himself than Paul, because he adds that he also has "not yet fled from temptation." The purpose of the two writers is different. While the word (πειρασμόν) may contain a reference to the "future trial," as it does in Matt 6.13, it more likely refers to his present failure to completely conquer every "temptation" to sin. In any case, it is a remarkable attempt at self-deprecation, which is significant because of the harsh exhortation to others that he has been delivering.

This "new" effort to associate himself with his hearers is followed by the vivid expression that he is "still in the midst of the devil's tools." The word for "tool" is ὀργάνον and is used literally as "tool" or "instrument, machine."[49] The word appears often in Philo (139x) and the LXX (27x). Because of 2 Macc. 12.27, the metaphor may be a military one, and this is the approach taken by Lightfoot. "The devil's tools are the various devices used by the opponents of the presbyter against him. The preacher finds himself ἐν ἀμφιβόλῳ, the enemy having environed him with his engines of war."[50] While the word does not appear in the NT, 1 Tim 3:7 and 2 Tim 2:26 refer to the devil's trap (παγίς). The noun is used for instruments of torture in 4 Macc 6:5; 9.20, 26. The author of *Mart. Pol.* 3.1 uses it to describe the wood for the martyr's fire, while Ign. *Rom.* 4.2 uses it of the animals he will face in the arena. These last three references inform the meaning of the word in Clement in a better way than a military metaphor. It is tempting to speculate on the specifics of this "confession," but it is best to take it as a vivid way of admitting that, like even Clement's more righteous hearers, he had not reached behavioral perfection either. It is also significant to note that no appeal is made, not only here but throughout the book, to any sort of authority or power adhering to whatever "office" he bore.

Despite his self-perceived failure, Clement is still seeking "to pursue righteousness." This use of the verb (διώκω) resonates more with its Pauline usage in Phil 3:12–14. Clement still desires, despite his following short of the goal, "at least to come near to it." This possible athletic metaphor, as also in Phil 3:14, recalls the effort of the athletes to come in as high as they can even if they do not achieve the "first place" finish (see 7.1–3). Thus, hope still remains

---

following the "way of death."

48. Grant, *Apostolic Fathers*, 2, 130.
49. BDAG, 720, s.v. ὀργάνον; Lampe, 969, s.v. ὀργάνον, for extensive patristic uses.
50. Lightfoot, trans., *Apostolic Fathers*, I.2, 256.

for those who fail if they try to succeed with their best effort. The strong ethical perfection that Clement has asked for over and over is tempered by the fact that he is a realist about the frailty of human behavior.

This humble and positive approach is still balanced at the end with a statement that includes the eschatological motivation of fearing the coming judgment. The singular participle that introduces the self-description (φοβούμενος), not only describes the one reading this discourse, but by implication exhorts the hearers (note the verb in the paraenesis of 4.4; 5.1, 4). Perhaps the concept of biblical "fear" that motivates the righteous soul is more at work here than the craven fear of simply escaping the judgment. Clement does look forward to the future with hope.

Summary and Conclusions

19.1—20.5

Chapter 19

1. So then brothers and sisters, following the God of Truth, I am reading you an appeal to pay attention to what is written, so that you may both save yourselves and the one who is the reader among you. For as a compensation I ask you to repent from all your heart, giving yourselves salvation and life. For when we do this, we will set a goal for all the younger ones who wish to devote themselves to piety and the goodness of God.

2. And we should not be displeased or be indignant in our foolishness when anyone admonishes us and attempts to turn us away from unrighteousness to righteousness. For sometimes, when we do evil, we do not realize it because of the double-mindedness and faithlessness that is in our breasts, and we are darkened in our understanding by useless desires.

3. Let us then do righteousness, so we may be saved at the end. Blessed are those who obey these instructions; although they may suffer evil for a short time in this world, they will reap the immortal fruit of the resurrection.

4. So then, the godly person should not grieve if he endures misery at this present time; a blessed time awaits him. He will live again with the fathers above and will rejoice in an age when there is no sorrow.

Literary Structure

The author utilizes the often repeated consequential conjunctions Ὥστε (19:1) and οὖν (19.3, 4) to mark out the three major sections of the chapter.[1] The first section (19.1–2) conveys a statement of purpose for the discourse with supporting causal clauses further amplifying the reasons and purposes of the reading. The second section (19.3) is an exhortation to practice righteousness with the added eschatological motivation. The final section (19.4) returns to an additional description of the positive future blessings despite the current miseries and sorrows.

Commentary

The issue regarding the integrity of these chapters as belonging to the original document or being added later was addressed in the Introduction under "The Structure of Second Clement." While this commentator affirms the original role of these chapters in the discourse, most of the comments on the contents of these chapters are not inordinately affected by that issue. If these two chapters were part of the original discourse, what role do they play? Before engaging in an analysis of these final chapters, it is necessary to explore the answer to that question that is offered by Karl Donfried. He proposes a threefold division of 2 Clement, composed of a theological section (1–2); an ethical section (3–14); and an eschatological section (15–18).[2] "What follows in chapters 19 and 20 is merely a summary, as is made clear by the words of the presbyter in 19.1 . . ."[3] Then follows the quotation of the words in that verse. This rather blunt statement, that the material in chapters 19 and 20 "is merely a summary," is not accurate because of some new material in these chapters. It appears, however, that Donfried recognizes that he has overstated this assertion because he then shows the significance of the chapters as more than a summary of previous themes. He offers a fascinating comparison of 2 Clement to the NT book of Hebrews, showing that the original "word of exhortation" in that book was composed of 1–12, with some interesting supporting passages to illustrate his comparison between the two. "Hebrews 13 would be a final paraenetic summary, similar to 2 Clement 19–20. Once again it is likely that we may have a hortatory discourse which was subsequently put into letter form

---

1. Ὥστε appears ten times in 2 Clement (19:1 is the last), while οὖν appears thirty-seven times.
2. Donfried, *Setting*, vii–viii; 42.
3. Donfried, *Setting*, 178.

and circulated, rather than having been originally composed as a letter."[4] Thus the threefold pattern was not unique, but even used with a degree of frequency in early Christianity. Although not entirely parallel, the example of the progression of thought in 2 Peter offers another similar pattern.[5] The overstatement by Donfried does imply, however, that eschatology is again employed in exhorting the believers in these two chapters. He fails to bring out, however, its unique function in being such a "summary." What are some of those unique features? The hearers are addressed, for the first time, as "brothers and sisters." Twelve earlier address references in the book mentioned only "brothers" (1.1; 4.3; 5.1, 5; 7.1; 8.4; 10.1; 11.5; 13.1; 14.1, 3; 16.1). The "sisters" will again appear in 20.2. This different address in 19.1 is probably the strongest reason to take this section as written at a different time and later added to the main text. But other possible echoes and resonances exist between 19–20 and 1–18 that should counsel care in too quickly concluding such a separate origin.[6]

Let us now examine further both the unique features of chapter 19 as well as some of those possible links with chapters 1–18. The phrase "following the God of Truth" (literally "after the God of Truth") uses a divine title that appeared in the LXX of Ps 30:6 as well as in the apocryphal 1 Esd. 4:40. The expression "Father of Truth" occurred in 3.2 and will appear again in 20.5. "The similarity in language with 3.1 represents one of the points of continuity (albeit not identity) between this section and the rest of 2 Clement."[7] Many commentators see the expression as a sort of ellipsis for a scripture reading that immediately preceded this address.[8] NT examples such as Luke 4:20–21 and Acts 13:15 reflect this order. The one delivering this address refers to his reading as an "appeal." The Introduction deals with the issue of whether this is a homily or sermon as normally understood, and reserve on this question was cautioned. See "The Genre of 2 Clement."[9] The word translated "appeal" (ἔντευξις) was also a self-description in 1 Clem. 63.2. Justin also uses it to describe his *First Apology* (1 *Apol*.1). While the NT could use it as a type of prayer (1 Tim 2:1; 4:5), in earlier Greek the word meant,

---

4. Donfried, *Setting*, 47.

5. Although not mentioning 2 Clement, Käsemann traced a similar pattern in 2 Peter. "Apologia for Primitive Christian Eschatology."

6. For the social identity implications of the address, "brothers and sisters," see Aasgaard, "Brothers and Sisters in the Faith."

7. Tuckett, *2 Clement*, 291.

8. Lightfoot, trans., *Apostolic Fathers*, I.2, 257; Lindemann, *Clemensbriefe*, 256; Tuckett, *2 Clement*, 291.

9. See Tugwell's suggestion about the role of a "reader" in the early Church and synagogue and the parallels in the Shepherd of Hermas. Tugwell, *Apostolic Fathers*, 136–37.

"a formal request put to a high official or official body, *petition, request.*"[10] The noun in later patristic literature rarely describes a sermon but is more a general appeal or discourse, as well as a type of prayer.[11] The purpose of this appeal in 19.1 is "to pay attention to what is written." The plural perfect participle (γεγραμμένοις) was used in earlier NT writings to describe scripture (Luke 18:31; 21:22; 24:44; John 12:16; 20:30; Acts 13:29; 2 Cor 4:13; Rev 1:3; 1 Clem. 13.1). While scripture has been appealed to quite often in chapters 1–18, because of this specific reference to what he is reading, the expression is best viewed as describing what is written in the present discourse. A number of commentators argue for this usage as well.[12]

The result, if Clement's hearers pay attention, is that they will save both themselves and the writer and reader of the manuscript. Clement had expressed himself in a similar way in 15.1 where, in another self-descriptive passage, he stated that if his hearer follows his "advice" then "he will save both himself and me, his advisor." It has been clear that it is Jesus in his mercy who "saved" his hearers (1.7). This current emphasis on actions saving them could be understood possibly as the "works" that must accompany a valid "faith."

His hoped-for success with this message will serve as his "compensation." This word (μισθός) again echoes what he hopes to receive for redirecting an errant sinner (15.10). The word conveys another of the shared themes in the sections 1–18 and 19–20. Their repentance must be "from all your heart," which again echoes a major theme in earlier passages such as 3.4; 8.2; 9.10; and 17.1. This will result in their experiencing a positive view of eschatology that is "salvation and life." For earlier references to salvation, see 1.1, 7 and 17.5. "Eternal life" appeared in 5.5; 8.4, 6; and 17.3. The earlier references to these ideas constitute another link between the sections.

Another new theme that concludes 19.1 is that the hoped-for obedience will set a goal for the younger hearer-readers. This is the first time another "group" appears within the larger group addressed. Their goal is to "devote themselves to piety and the goodness of God."[13] The language

10. BDAG, 339–40, s.v. ἔντευξις (italics original).

11. Lampe, 482, s.v. ἔντευξις.

12. See Tuckett, *2 Clement*, 292, and the commentators he cites in 292n10. Donfried's observation that the expression refers to the previous letter of 1 Clement seems a bit forced (*Setting*, 14–15). The purpose here is that the context differs from the context in 1 Clement, so the usage is different here from its usage in 1 Clement.

13. In two words in this context, the reading of the Syriac manuscript has been preferred over the scribal reading in Codex H, also called C. The Greek scribe wrote κοπόν ("work") but probably intended σκοπόν ("goal"). He also wrote φιλοσοφεῖν ("to philosophize") but probably intended φιλοπονεῖν ("to devote themselves") as the Syriac translates. See Lightfoot, trans., *Apostolic Fathers*, I.2, 206, for a vigorous defense of

probably refers to those younger in age rather than young in the faith. While the word translated "piety" (εὐσέβεια) is only here in 2 Clement, it is an evident theme in earlier Christian texts (1 Tim 2:2; 3:16; Tit 1:5; see also 1 Clem. 1:2; 32:4). Cognate words for "piety" will occur also in 19:4 and 20:4. God's "goodness" (χρηστότητα) has appeared in 15.4–5. Just as a common word between 1–18 and 19–20 cannot provide certainty about common authorship, the presence of new words does not necessarily indicate a different author.

Before our author moves on to a renewed exhortation in 19.3, he delivers in 19.2 a brief exhortation to those who might resent his entreaty.[14] "On verse 2, compare Matt 18:15–20."[15] It is difficult to see how the Matthean passage about reconciling with a brother enlightens this verse, except it be the person admonished is rejecting the approach of an offended brother. Our author is concerned about his hearers possibly rejecting his advice and entreaty, but he blames it on their "double-mindedness and unbelief." The adjective for being "double-minded" (δίψυχος) made its initial appearance in Jas 1:7; 4:7, but the concept had a history in Israel's Scriptures (for example, Ps 119:113) and the plural substantive also was used in 1 Clem. 11.2. The substantive was used earlier in a quotation of unknown origin in 2 Clem. 11.2, and the verbal idea occurs in 11.5.[16] Accompanying this double-mindedness that hinders success is the "faithlessness (ἀπιστίαν) that is in our breasts." In 17.5 people who refused to obey the elders were described by the substantive "unbelievers" (ἄπιστοι). The spiritual maladies of double-mindedness and faithlessness are compounded by our being "darkened . . . [in understanding] by useless desires." The use of the first person plural in describing those suffering spiritual paralysis and blindness reflects the humble confession of our author's own frailty in 18.2.

In the final exhortation of this chapter (19.3–4), our author makes a positive turn toward the blessedness of the eschatological hope—that is, for those who "do righteousness." As was the case in its previous appearances (4.2; 11.7; 18.2; 19.2), the noun δικαιοσύνη does not carry the Pauline idea of a state of righteousness but rather the idea of righteous behavior. Most often it is the object of an active verb, as it is here. It is those who "do" righteousness who will be saved, and the focus is not salvation in the past (cf. 1.7), but in the "end" (εἰς τέλος). Without trying to make our author into

---

these corrections to the text of Codex H, also called C.

14. The extended treatment of 19.1 necessitates a more concise handling of the issues in 19.2–4.

15. Grant and Graham, *First and Second Clement*, 131.

16. As with many other common themes, the idea is used extensively in the Shepherd of Hermas (approximately twenty-four times).

a modern theologian, it would be appropriate in solving the conundrum of whether salvation in 2 Clement is a past or future experience to describe his view of salvation as both "now and not yet." This reference to final salvation is followed by one of the few macarisms, or beatitudes, in the book. "Blessed (μακάριοι) are those who obey these instructions . . ." A previous blessing was pronounced on charitable givers (16.4), while the adjective refers to a "blessed" or "happy" time in 19.4. That blessedness awaits those who have suffered evil in this world, and their reward will be "the immortal fruit of the resurrection." The language is rather unique but not inconsistent with the NT portrayal. "Fruit" may recall that Christ was the "firstfruits" of the resurrection, while the believer's resurrection will be the full harvest (compare 1 Cor 15:33).[17] The construction is a genitive of apposition, namely, the "fruit which consists of resurrection."[18] While the language is general, it does recognize a "two ages" scheme for the eschaton.[19] The future verb "reap" (τρυγήσουσιν) recalls the literal act of gathering grapes (Luke 6:44) but also the metaphorical reaping of grapes as judgment in the Apocalypse (Rev 14:18–19).

The final exhortation in the chapter (19.4) encourages those who suffer now to be encouraged by the fact that a blessed time awaits them when they will live again with the fathers above when sorrow will be replaced by rejoicing. The verb "to live again" (participle ἀναβιώσας) has no other known occurrence in early Christian literature.[20] It does appear in the famous account of the Maccabean martyrs (2 Macc 7:9) and in Josephus's description of the beliefs of the Pharisees (Ant. 18.14). The reference to the "fathers" may reflect a Jewish influence, but the term was also used by Christian authors (2 Pet 3:4; 1 Clem. 23.3; 30.7; and the earlier reference in 2 Clem. 11.2).[21] In any case, in this future age there will be "no sorrow," an echo of the scene in Rev 7:14–17 and 21:3–5.

Chapter 20

1. But neither let it disturb your mind that we see the unrighteous being wealthy and God's servants being oppressed.

---

17. Grant and Graham, *First and Second Clement*, 131.
18. Tuckett, *2 Clement*, 296n29.
19. Lindemann, *Clemensbriefe*, 257.
20. BDAG, s.v. ἀναβιόω, 59.
21. Lindemann's observation that the resurrection here is "completely individualistic" (*Clemensbriefe*, 257) is countered by the statement that it will be enjoyed "with the fathers."

2. Let us then have faith, brothers and sisters. We are competing in the contest of the living God and being trained in the present life, so that we may be crowned in the coming one.

3. None of the righteous has received fruit quickly but waits for it.

4. For if God paid the wages of the righteous quickly, we would immediately be engaged in commerce and not in godliness, for we would appear to be righteous when we were pursuing not piety but gain. And because of this, divine judgment punishes a spirit that is not righteous and burdens it with chains.

5. To the only invisible God, the Father of Truth, who sent forth to us the Savior and Founder of immortality, through whom he revealed to us the truth and the heavenly life, to him be the glory forever and ever. Amen.

Literary Structure

Chapter 20 is the only one that begins with the strong adversative conjunction Ἀλλά although the conjunction does occur twenty-one other times in the book. This conjunction ties the contents here to the previous chapter, although in an adversative manner. The connection is the following imperative verb ταρασσέτω ("be disturbed") in 20.1, which also connects semantically with the verbs in 19.2 that we should not be "displeased" or "indignant." The two chapters also share the word "mind" (διάνοια) in 20.1 and 19.2, which is where we are disturbed or displeased.

The command is followed in 20.2 by a hortatory subjunctive clause introduced by the consequential conjunction οὖν. The command is to have faith because of the contest in which we are engaged for which we will be awarded in 20.3. A conditional clause in 20.4 offers a motive for pursuing righteousness. A separate doxology ends the chapter and the book in 20.5.

Commentary

The theme of possible discouragement in the Christian walk continues from the previous chapter.[22] What is new here is a reference to the "problem" of the

---

22. The issue of the integrity of chapters 19–20 was addressed in the Introductory chapters in the section, "The Integrity and Structure of 2 Clement." At that point the originality of these chapters as part of the original document was defended. Kelhoffer concludes that despite philological differences, there are also many similarities between

unrighteous experiencing material prosperity while the righteous continue to suffer. "Verse 1 expresses a common theme and problem of the Old Testament and of Jewish piety which comes to classical expression in Psalm 73 and is often reflected in the New Testament—for example, in the canticles in Luke or James 5."[23] The focus in this regard is on the unequal distribution of wealth. No immediate answer is offered, but this theme is renewed in 20.3–4 with the emphasis there on waiting for the final "wages."[24]

The subject of wages/rewards for the believer's faithfulness is expressed in 20.2 by returning to the metaphor so employed in 7.1–5, namely, the athletic competitions and the crowning of the victor(s). This is another link between the two sections of 2 Clement although the presence of links between the sections is not by itself a convincing argument for the book's unity. No mention is made here of the possibility of many winners or about commendation for those who may not win but still come close (cf. 7.3). What enables the contestant to finish well is the vital role of "faith." In this regard there appears to be at least a thematic identity of 2 Clem. 20 with the so-called faith chapter, Heb 11, which is followed by the exhortation to run well in Heb 12:1–2. The concept that our race on earth in the "present life" will result in our being crowned in the "coming one" is new in this chapter (20.2).

Therefore, 20.3 could be viewed also as a summary of Heb 11. The "fathers" in Hebrews (cf. 2 Clem. 19.4) looked forward in faith without receiving the reward of their faith in this life. They waited, so we must wait (patiently) for it. These ideas echo the same theme in such passages as Jas 5:7, which also share the common words "fruit" and "waits." The reference to "fruit" recalls the "fruit of the resurrection" in 19.3. "Unlike in 19.3, the author here seems to want to impress on his hearers the possibility, if not certainty, of an ongoing period in this life which will *not* necessarily be

---

2 Clem. 19–20, on the one hand, and both 1 Clement and 2 Clement, on the other hand. Those similarities suggest a compositional strategy underlying 19.1—20.5 that entailed the *imitation* of both Clementine writings in order to make the secondary addition appear authentic. Chapters 19–20 are thus significant for their reception of both 1 and 2 Clement and for their correction of some distinctive theological positions in 2 Clem. 1–18. As a correction of 2 Clem. 1–18, the addition of 19.1—20.5 may also have contributed to 2 Clement's preservation in the tradition alongside 1 Clement (Kelhoffer, "How Did Second Clement Originally End?"). This commentary will deal with the chapters as part of the composite document.

23. Grant and Graham, *First and Second Clement*, 132.

24. "This passage is quoted loosely and with some omissions in the *Sacr. Parall.* (ms Rupef.), which bear the name of Joannes Damascenus, *Op.* ii. p. 783 (Le Quien) . . . It will be seen that in the quotation the original words are altered, so as to conform to well-known scriptural passages; e.g. μὴ ταρασσέτω τὴν καρδίαν ὑμῶν is substituted for μηδὲ ἐκεῖνο τὴν διάνοιαν ὑμῶν ταρασσέτω, after John xiv. 1, 27; and εὐσέβειαν is substituted for θεοσέβειαν, after 1 Tim vi. 5" (Lightfoot, trans., *Apostolic Fathers*, I.2, 259).

short-lived, but which will still be followed by a time of blessedness."²⁵ The passing of generations has tempered the imminence so often expressed by some NT authors.

The formal ending of the book in 20.4 (verse 5 comprising a closing doxology) returns to a problem remedied by another appeal to eschatology. Building on the reward/fruit images of the previous verses, our author utilizes the metaphor of wages for a job performed, which in this context is the task of the Christian life. If the righteous were rewarded quickly (that is, in this life), then the metaphor is taken too literally. The divine/human relationship is not a commercial one. The righteous will still be "paid," and the language used (μισθός) reflects the metaphor of wages paid for work finished. The difference is that we will not be paid for doing our "job" until the eschaton, just as the "fathers" looked forward to their reward in another "heavenly country" (Heb 11:16). The issue involved is immediacy versus delay. Clement's conclusion is simple and is one not expressed exactly in this manner in other early literature. Any other method in paying would mean that "we were pursuing not piety but gain" (20.4). Perhaps the implication, although not stated, is that getting paid early might allow us to check out early in our obedience.

Post-Reformation theologians may perceive some soteriological problems with the way in which 2 Clement frames these issues.²⁶ As has often been mentioned, the stress on divine mercy and grace has been clear in the book (see, for example, 1.2–8). The concept of "payback" in the book has been explored by authors such as Kelhoffer.²⁷ There may be criticism that the author's stress on "works" calls into question his view on salvation by grace. I am convinced, however, that he did not see his emphasis as inconsistent with the salvific grace he so clearly described in chapter 1. A real danger emerges when modern interpreters wrongly read these ancient texts through post-Reformation glasses.²⁸ "The homilist has a deep sense of what Christ has done for his people (1.4–8). To approach such a text with notions of works-righteousness derived from much later debates would be

---

25. Tuckett, 2 Clement, 300.

26. This doctrinal issue was raised by such an author as Torrance (*Doctrine of Grace in the Apostolic Fathers*), whose view was discussed in the Introduction.

27. The issues raised by Kelhoffer ("Reciprocity as Salvation") were also addressed in the Introduction section called the "Theology of Second Clement."

28. This is a point clearly made by Tuckett (*2 Clement*, 301). See also Lindemann (*Clemensbriefe*, 259) for an even stronger affirmation of the author's evangelical theology, despite the language of earning one's wages.

to miss the whole point of it. It would be to miss precisely what made it, in that world, Good News."[29]

The last clause in 20.4, however, is rather obscure and takes a negative turn from these positive affirmations.[30] "And because of this, divine judgment punishes a spirit that is not righteous and burdens it with chains." Does the aorist tense of the verb "punishes" (ἔβλαψεν) express past action and suggest some past judgment? Translators have recognized the verbal aspect of the aorist tense form as reflecting a gnomic sense and not insisted on a past tense action.[31] The verb only appears twice in the NT (Mark 16:18 [disputed reading] and Luke 4:35), and neither refers to a divine punishment.[32] The references to punishing a "spirit" raise other issues, since a reference to a possible judgment on an individual known to the readers probably would not be referred to as a spirit. A reference to the judgment on angelic spirits (Gen 6:1-4; 2 Pet 2:4; Jude 6) might be supported by the later reference to the punished one as being "burdened with chains." Satan being bound by a chain in Rev 20:2 would certainly qualify as a spirit and would associate the author with a passage emphasized by chiliasts (who would later be called premillennialists). Some authors admit ignorance on the specific meaning of this expression.[33] It is best to view the statement as a very general one describing in vivid and apocalyptic terms the judgment on any person who as a spirit is now separated from the body by death.

While some might wish that the book had closed with the positive and hopeful note of the previous verses in the chapter, a stirring doxology remains (20.5). God is ascribed with three attributes and credited with two deeds. First, he is the "only" God, which evidently was not viewed as inconsistent with the initial observation that we should also think of Christ as God (1.1). Second, he is "invisible." Both of these attributes are quite similar to the "only invisible God" in 1 Tim 1:17. Third, he is the "Father of Truth," echoing the same expression in 3.1 and offering still another link to the first section of the book. Two divine events are then mentioned. First, God

29. Parvis, "2 Clement," 41.

30. Tuckett actually refers to the statement as "a notorious crux" (2 Clement, 301).

31. Lake, *Apostolic Fathers*, I, 163; Ehrman, ed., *Apostolic Fathers*, I, 199; Holmes, ed., *Apostolic Fathers*, 165.

32. "The word βλάπτειν is used especially of Divine vengeance surprising its victim, checking and maiming him in his mid-career; e.g. Hom. *Od.* i. 195 . . . Xen. *Symp.* viii. 45 . . . Plut. *Vit. Caes.* 45 . . . Trag. In Lycurg. *c. Leocr.* p. 159. . . and so frequently. Sordid motives bring their own punishment in a judicial blindness (βλάπτει πνεῦμα). The aorist here has its common *gnomic* sense, and is the most appropriate tense" (Lightfoot, trans., *Apostolic Fathers*, I.2, 260).

33. For example, Tuckett, *2 Clement*, 301.

sent Jesus as the "Savior" and the "Founder of immortality."[34] Since Jesus is the one who actively "saves," the initiatory idea of his being the "Founder" who makes immortality possible is the best translation. Although this is the first occurrence of the word "Savior" (σωτῆρα), Jesus was the subject of earlier cognate verbals in 2.7 and 9.5 (σῶσαι; σώσας). This emphasis is another evidence of the author's balancing emphases concerning our being saved by Jesus but also saving ourselves through obedience. Jesus is also the "Founder" or "Pioneer" or "Leader" (ἀρχηγόν) of immortality.[35] The use of this last word resonates with the application of that title to Jesus in Acts 3:15; 5:31; and especially in Heb 2:10 and 12:2. First Clement made extensive use of Hebrews—for example, utilizing this same title for Jesus from 2 Clem. 20.5.[36] The short book of 2 Clement, associated in the ancient church with the longer book of 1 Clement, also made use of the NT "word of exhortation" (Heb 13:22).

The second divine act is that God revealed "the truth and the heavenly life" through that same Jesus, the latter being the antecedent of the relative pronoun in the expression "through whom."

This life was described as "eternal" in 5.5 and 8.4 and simply as "life" in 14.5 and 17.3. Tuckett thinks that the "language tends to redundancy and wordiness."[37] This seems a harsh and modern judgment on language that possibly echoes the fulsome words of another benediction in Hebrews 13:20–21. I prefer calling it an example of iconic reinforcement for an intended effect. This reinforcement continues in the final clause, "to him be the glory forever and ever." This clause is found also at the end of such texts as Phil 4:20 and 2 Tim 4:18, as well as in that older sister, 1 Clem. 50.7. To this all hearing and reading these words could express their agreement in what became a liturgical practice of affirming "Amen."

Conclusion

As was mentioned in the Introduction, Bart Ehrman expressed regret that 2 Clement "is probably the most overlooked and least appreciated of the writings of the Apostolic Fathers." He regretted this widely held attitude "because it is in some ways a historically significant work."[38] I would affirm

---

34. The presence of one article before both these descriptors indicates that the two are the same person (Wallace, *Greek Grammar Beyond the Basics*, 270–90).

35. BDAG, 138–39, s.v. ἀρχηγός.

36. Hagner, *Use of the Old and New Testaments*, 179–95.

37. Tuckett, *2 Clement*, 303.

38. Ehrman, ed., *Apostolic Fathers*, I, 154.

Ehrman's assessment but also add that the book has far more than historical significance. Its rich use of earlier "sacred tradition" and its fervent appeal to live a godly life as a "payback" for divine grace also makes it, if not unique, at least an illustration of the passionate appeal to life and godliness that must have characterized the church of the early second century.

A quotation from Paul Parvis was also utilized earlier about 2 Clement's "sermonic character," although not all affirm that it was a homily. In considering how to summarize my own thoughts about this book after spending years analyzing it, I turn again to Parvis, who expresses an opinion which I now can heartily affirm.

> Second Clement is not a profound theological text, and it is, as critics from Photius on have not failed to observe, neither well written nor well organized. But what it is struggling to give expression to is the idea that it is precisely in the nitty-gritty of everyday life that we can see the Gospel at work. It spoke to the men and women of the second century of new possibilities for the transformation of human life, and that is what made it, for them, something worth reading and rereading, copying and recopying, and preserving for us.[39]

---

39. Parvis, "2 Clement," 41.

Bibliography

Aasgaard, Reidar. "Brothers and Sisters in the Faith: Christian Siblingship as an Ecclesiological Mirror in the First Two Centuries." In *The Formation of the Early Church*, edited by Jostein Adna, 285–316. WUNT 183. Tubingen: Mohr/Siebeck, 2005.

Baarda, Tjitze. "2 Clement 12 and Sayings of Jesus." In *Logia: Les Paroles de Jesus—The Sayings of Jesus*, edited by Joël Delobel, 529–56. BETL 59. Leuven: Peeters, 1982.

Baasland, Ernst. "Der 2.Klemensbrief and fruhchristliche Rhetorik: 'Die erste christliche Predigt' im Lichte der neueren Forschung." In *ANRW* 2.27.1 (1993) 78–157.

Barclay, John M. G. *Paul and the Gift*. Grand Rapids: Eerdmans, 2015.

Bartlet, J. Vernon. "The Origin and Date of 2 Clement." *ZNW* 7 (1906) 123–35.

Bartlet, J. Vernon et al., eds. *The New Testament in the Apostolic Fathers*. Oxford: Clarendon, 1905.

Batovici, Dan. "The Apostolic Fathers in Codex Sinaiticus and Codex Alexandrinus." *Bib* 97 (2016) 581–605.

Bauckham, Richard. *God Crucified: Monotheism and Christology in the New Testament*. Grand Rapids: Eerdmans, 1998.

Benecke, P. V. M. "II Clement." In *The New Testament in the Apostolic Fathers*, edited by J. Vernon Bartlet, et al., 124–36. Oxford: Clarendon, 1905

Bensly, R. L. *The Epistles of S. Clement to the Corinthians in Syriac*. Cambridge: Cambridge University Press, 1899.

Berding, Kenneth. "'Gifts' and Ministries in the Apostolic Fathers." *WTJ* 78 (2016) 135–58.

Bingham, D. Jeffrey. "Senses of Scripture in the Second Century: Irenaeus, Scripture, and Noncanonical Christian Texts." *JR* 97 (2017) 26–55

Borchardt, C. F. A. "The Spirituality of the Apostolic Fathers." *Studia historiae ecclesiasticae* 25 (1999) 132–52.

Bounds, Christopher Todd. "The Doctrine of Christian Perfection in the Apostolic Fathers." *WesTJ* 42 (2007) 7–27.

———. "The Understanding of Grace in Selected Apostolic Fathers." StPatr 48 (2013) 351–59.

Boyarin, Daniel. *The Jewish Gospels: The Story of the Jewish Christ*. New York: New Press, 2012.

Brakke, David. *The Gnostics: Myth, Ritual, and Diversity in Early Christianity*. Cambridge: Harvard University Press, 2010.

Brannan, Rick. *The Apostolic Fathers: A New Translation*. Lexham Classics. Bellingham, WA: Lexham, 2017.

———. *Greek Apocryphal Gospels, Fragments, and Agrapha*. Bellingham, WA: Lexham, 2014.

Brummel, Lincoln H., and Thomas A. Wayment, eds. *Christian Oxyrhynchus: Texts, Documents, and Sources*. Waco, TX: Baylor University Press, 2015.

Bultmann, Rudolf. *The Theology of the New Testament*. 2 vols. Translated by Kendrick Grobel. New York: Scribner, 1951–1955.

Burke, Jonathan. "Satan and Demons in the Apostolic Fathers: A Minority Report." *SEÅ* 81 (2016) 127–68.

Cotelier, J. B., SS. *Patrum qui temporibus apostolicis floruerunt; Barnabae, Clementis, Hermae, Ignatii, Polycarpi: opera edita et inedita, vera et suppositicia* . . . Paris: Petri Le Petit, 1672.

Crafer, T. W. *The Second Epistle of Clement to the Corinthians*. Texts for Students 22. London: SPCK, 1921.

Crowe, Brandon D. "Like Father, Like Son: Unraveling the Proto-Trinitarian Approach of 2 Clement." *WTJ* 77 (2015) 251–64.

Cullmann, Oscar. *Immortality of the Soul or Resurrection of the Dead?* London: Epworth, 1962.

deSilva, David A. "Patronage and Reciprocity: The Context of Grace in the New Testament." *AST* 31 (1999) 32–84.

De Wet, C. L. "'No Small Counsel about Self-control': *Enkrateia* and the Virtuous Body as a Missional Performance in 2 Clement." *HTS Teologiese Studies/Theological Studies* 69 (2012) 1–10.

Donfried, Karl P. "The Theology of Second Clement." *HTR* 66 (1973) 487–501.

———. *The Setting of Second Clement in Early Christianity*. NovTSup 38. Leiden: Brill, 1974.

Downs, David J. *Alms: Charity, Reward, and Atonement in Early Christianity*. Waco, TX: Baylor University Press, 2016.

———. "'Love Covers a Multitude of Sins': Redemptive Almsgiving in 1 Peter 4:8 and Its Early Christian Reception." *JTS* 65 (2014) 489–514.

———. "Redemptive Almsgiving and Economic Stratification in 2 Clement." *JECS* 19 (2011) 493–517.

Drobner, Hubertus. *The Fathers of the Church: A Comprehensive Introduction*. Peabody, MA: Hendrickson, 2007.

Dunn, James D. G. *Neither Jew nor Greek: A Contested Idea*. Christianity in the Making 3. Grand Rapids: Eerdmans, 2015.

Ehrman, Bart D., ed. *The Apostolic Fathers*. Vol. 1. 2 vols. LCL. Cambridge: Harvard University Press, 2003.

———. "Textual Traditions Compared: The New Testament and Apostolic Fathers." In *The Reception of the New Testament in the Apostolic Fathers*, edited by Andrew F. Gregory and Christopher M. Tuckett, 9–27. NTAF. Oxford: Oxford University Press, 2005.

Eusebius, Pamphilius. *The Ecclesiastical History: English Translation*. Vol. 1. Translated by Kirsopp Lake. LCL. Cambridge: Harvard University Press, 1926.

Evans, Robert. *Reception History, Tradition, and Biblical Interpretation: Gadamer and Jauss in Current Practice*. LNTS 510. Scriptural Traces 4. London: Bloomsbury, 2014.

Farrar, Thomas J. "Satanology and Demonology in the Apostolic Fathers: A Response to Jonathan Burke." *SEÅ* 83 (2018) 156–91.

Fischer, Joseph A. *Die ältesten Ausgaben der Patres Apostolici: ein Beitrag zu Begriff und Begrenzung der Apostolischen Väter*. Munich: Alber, 1974.
Foster, Paul. "The Absence of Paul in 2 Clement." In *The Apostolic Fathers and Paul*, edited by Todd D. Still and David E. Wilhite, 61–78. London: Bloomsbury T. & T. Clark, 2017.
———. Preface. In *The Writings of the Apostolic Fathers*, edited by Paul Foster, vii–xiii. T. & T. Clark Biblical Studies. London: T. & T. Clark, 2007.
Freese, J. H. *The Library of Photius*. Vol. 1. London: SPCK, 1920.
Frend, W. H. C. *The Rise of Christianity*. Philadelphia: Fortress, 1984.
Gallagher, Edmon L., and John D. Meade. *The Biblical Canon Lists from Early Christianity: Texts and Analysis*. Oxford: Oxford University Press, 2017.
Gallandi, Andreas. *Bibliotheca veterum partum antiquorumque scriptorium ecclesiasticorum*. Venice: Albritii, 1765.
Gathercole, Simon. *The Gospel of Thomas: Introduction and Commentary*. Texts and Editions for New Testament Study 11. Boston: Brill, 2014.
Goodspeed, Edgar J. *A History of Early Christian Literature*. Revised by Robert M. Grant. Chicago: University of Chicago Press, 1966.
———. *Index Patristicus: Clavis Patrum Apostolicorum Operum*. 1907. Reprint, Ancient Language Resources. Eugene, OR: Wipf & Stock, 2003.
———. *The Apostolic Fathers*. New York: Harper, 1950.
Grant, Robert M. "The Apostolic Fathers' First Thousand Years." *CH* 31 (1962) 421–29.
Grant, Robert M., and Holt H. Graham. *First and Second Clement*. AF 2. New York: Nelson, 1965.
Gregory, Andrew F., and Christopher M. Tuckett, eds. *The Reception of the New Testament in the Apostolic Fathers*. NTAF. Oxford: Oxford University Press, 2005.
———. "2 Clement and the Writings that Later Formed the New Testament." In *The Reception of the New Testament in the Apostolic Fathers*, edited by Andrew F. Gregory and Christopher M. Tuckett, 251–92. NTAF. Oxford: Oxford University Press, 2005.
Gruen, Erich S. "Christians as a 'Third Race': Is Ethnicity at Issue?" In *Christianity in the Second Century: Themes and Development*, edited by James Carleton Paget and Judith Lieu, 235–49. Cambridge: Cambridge University Press, 2017.
Hagner, Donald A. *The Use of the Old and New Testaments in Clement of Rome*. NovTSup 34. Leiden: Brill, 1979.
Harnack, Adolf. "Über den sogenannten zweiten Brief des Clemens an die Korinther." *ZKG* 1 (1873) 264–83, 329–64.
———. "Zum Ursprung des sog. 2. Clemensbriefs." *ZNW* 6 (1905) 67–71.
Harris, J. Rendel. "The Authorship of the So-Called Second Epistle of Clement." *ZNW* 23 (1924) 193–200.
Hartog, Paul A. "1 Corinthians 2:9 in the Apostolic Fathers." In *Intertextuality in the Second Century*, edited by D. Jeffrey Bingham and Clayton N. Jefford, 98–125. BibAC 11. Leiden: Brill, 2016.
———. "A Multifaceted Jewel: English Episcopacy, Ignatian Authenticity, and the Rise of Critical Patristic Scholarship." In *Defending the Faith: John Jewel and the Elizabethan Church*, edited by Angela Ranson et al., 263–83. Early Modern Studies Series. University Park: Pennsylvania State University Press, 2018.
———. "The Opponents in Polycarp, *Philippians*, and 1 John." In *Trajectories through the New Testament and the Apostolic Fathers*, edited by Andrew F. Gregory and Christopher M. Tuckett, 375–91. Oxford: Oxford University Press, 2005.

Hogan, Pauline Nigh. *No Longer Male and Female: Interpreting Galatians 3:28 in Early Christianity*. LNTS 380. London: T. & T. Clark, 2008.

Holmberg, Bengt, ed. *Exploring Early Christian Identity*. WUNT 226. Mohr/Siebeck, 2008.

Holmes, Michael W., ed. *The Apostolic Fathers: Greek Texts and English Translations*. 3rd ed. Grand Rapids: Baker Academic, 2007.

Hurtado, Larry W. *God in New Testament Theology*. Nashville: Abingdon, 2010.

———. *Lord Jesus Christ: Devotion to Jesus in Early Christianity*. Grand Rapids: Eerdmans, 2005.

Ittig, Thomas. *Bibliotheca Patrum Apostolicorum Graeco-Latina*. Leipzig: Richter, 1699.

Jeremias, Joachim. *Unknown Sayings of Jesus*. New York: Macmillan, 1957.

Jefford, Clayton N. *The Apostolic Fathers: An Essential Guide*. Abingdon Essential Guides. Nashville: Abingdon, 2005.

———. *The Apostolic Fathers and the New Testament*. Peabody, MA: Hendrickson, 2006.

———. "Prophecy and Prophetism in the Apostolic Fathers." In *Prophets and Prophecy in Jewish and Early Christian Literature*, edited by Joseph Verheyden, 295–316. WUNT 2/286. Tübingen: Mohr/Siebeck, 2010.

———. *Reading the Apostolic Fathers: A Student's Introduction*. 2nd ed. Grand Rapids: Baker Academic: 2012.

Johnson, Luke T. *The Letter of James*. AB 37A. New York: Doubleday, 1995.

Käsemann, Ernst. "An Apologia for Primitive Christian Eschatology." In *New Testament Questions of Today*, 169–95. Philadelphia: Fortress, 1982.

Kelhoffer, James A. "How Did Second Clement Originally End? A Study of 2 Clement 19–20 and the Imitation of Both First and Second Clement." *Early Christianity* 9 (2018) 432–83.

———. "'How Soon a Book' Revisited: EUAGGELION as a Reference to 'Gospel' Materials in the First Half of the Second Century." In *Conceptions of "Gospel" and Legitimacy in Early Christianity*, 39–75. WUNT 324. Tübingen: Mohr/Siebeck, 2014.

———. "If Second Clement Really Were a 'Sermon,' How Would We Know, and Why Would We Care? Prolegomena to Analyses of the Writing's Genre and Community." In *Early Christian Communities between Ideal and Reality*, edited by Mark Grundeken and Joseph Verheyden, 83–108. WUNT 342. Tübingen: Mohr/Siebeck, 2015.

———. "Pigeonholing a Prooftexter? The Citations in 2 Clement 2 and Their Allegedly Gnostic Background." *ZNW* 107 (2016) 266–95.

———. "Reciprocity as Salvation: Christ as Salvation Patron and the Corresponding 'Payback' Expected of Christ's Earthly Clients according to the Second Epistle of Clement." *NTS* 59 (2013) 433–56.

———. "*Second Clement* and Gnosticism: The *status quaestionis*." *Early Christianity* 8 (2017) 124–49.

———. "The Ecclesiology of 2 Clement 14: Ephesians, Pauline Reception, and the Church's Preexistence: The Person of Paul and His Writings Through the Eyes of His Early Interpreters." In *Receptions of Paul in Early Christianity*, vol. 2, edited by Chris L. Keith, et al., 377–408. BZNW 240. Berlin: de Gruyter, 2018.

Kenyon, Frederick G. *The Codex Alexandrinus (Royal MS I D V–VIII) in Reduced Photographic Facsimile*. London: British Museum, 1909.

Khomych, Taras. "Diversity of the Notion of Apostolicity in the Apostolic Fathers." In *Heiligkeit und Apostolizität der Kirche*, edited by Theresia Hainthaler et al., 63–81. Pro Oriente 35. Innsbruck: Tyrolia, 2010.

King, Karen L. *What Is Gnosticism?* Cambridge: Harvard University Press, 2003.

Klauck, Hans-Josef, with the collaboration of Daniel P. Bailey. *Ancient Letters and the New Testament: A Guide to Context and Exegesis*. Waco, TX: Baylor University Press, 2006.

Knopf, Rudolf. *Die Lehre der zwölf Apostel: Die zwei Clemensbriefe*. AV 1. Tübingen: Mohr/Siebeck, 1920.

Koester, Helmut. "The Apostolic Fathers and the Struggle for Christian Identity." In *Writings of the Apostolic Fathers*, edited by Paul Foster, 1–12, T. & T. Clark Biblical Studies. London: T. & T. Clark, 2007.

———. *Introduction to the New Testament*. Vol. 2, *History and Literature of Early Christianity*. Philadelphia: Fortress, 1982.

———. *Synoptische Überlieferung bei den Apostolischen Vätern*. TU 65. Berlin: Akademie, 1957.

Krüger, Gustav. "Bemerkungen zum zweiten Klemensbrief." In *Studies in Early Christianity*, edited by Shirley Jackson Case, 419–38. New York: Century, 1928.

Kruger, Michael J. *Christianity at the Crossroads: How the Second Century Shaped the Future of the Church*. London: SPCK, 2017.

Lake, Kirsopp, trans. *The Apostolic Fathers I*. LCL 24. Cambridge: Harvard University Press, 1965.

Lampe, G. W. H. *The Seal of the Spirit*. London: SPCK, 1967.

Lanfranchi, Pierluigi. "Attitudes to the Sabbath in Three Apostolic Fathers: *Didache*, Ignatius, and *Barnabas*." In *Jesus, Paul, and Early Christianity*, edited by Rieuwerd Buitenwerf et al., 243–59. NovTSup 130. Leiden: Brill, 2008.

Lawson, John. *A Theological and Historical Introduction to the Apostolic Fathers*. New York: Macmillan, 1961.

Lieu, Judith M. *Christian Identity in the Jewish and Graeco-Roman World*. Oxford: Oxford University Press, 2004.

———. "Modelling the Second Century as the Age of the Laboratory." In *Christianity in the Second Century: Themes and Developments*, edited by James Carleton Paget and Judith Lieu, 294–308. Cambridge: Cambridge University Press, 2017.

———. *Neither Jew nor Greek? Constructing Early Christianity*. 2nd ed. Cornerstones. London: Bloomsbury T. & T. Clark: 2016.

Lightfoot, Joseph B., trans. *The Apostolic Fathers*. Part 1, *S. Clement of Rome*. 2 vols. London: Macmillan, 1890.

Lightfoot, J. B., and Harmer, J. R., trans. *The Apostolic Fathers*. Grand Rapids: Baker, 1984.

Lincicum, David. "The Paratextual Invention of the Term 'Apostolic Fathers'." *JTS* 66 (2015) 139–48.

Lindemann, Andreas. "The Apostolic Fathers and the Synoptic Problem." In *New Studies in the Synoptic Problem: Oxford Conference, April 2008 ; Essays in Honour of Christopher M. Tuckett*, edited by Paul Foster et al., 689–719. BETL 239. Leuven: Peeters, 2011.

———. *Die Clemensbriefe*. HNT 17. Tübingen: Mohr/Siebeck, 1992.

Longenecker, Richard N. *Biblical Exegesis in the Apostolic Period*. Grand Rapids: Eerdmans, 1999.

Lookadoo, Jonathon. "Polycarp, Paul, and the Letters to Timothy." *NovT* 59 (2017) 366–83.
Lührmann, Dieter, and P. J. Parsons, "4009, Gospel of Peter?" In *The Oxyrhynchus Papyri LX*, edited by R. A. Coles, et al., 1–5. London: Egypt Exploration Society, 1994.
Marshall, I. Howard. "The Holy Spirit in the Apostolic Fathers." In *The Holy Spirit and Christian Origins*, edited by Graham N. Stanton et al., 257–69. Grand Rapids: Eerdmans, 2004.
Martin, E. G. "Eldad and Modad." In *The Old Testament Pseudepigrapha*, edited by James H. Charlesworth, 2:463–66. 2 vols. Garden City, NJ: Doubleday, 1985.
McGuckin, John A. "Christ: The Apostolic Fathers to the Third Century." in *The Routledge Companion to Early Christian Thought*, edited by D. Jeffrey Bingham, 256–70. Routledge Companions. London: Routledge, 2010.
Moreschini, Claudio, and Enrico Norelli. *Early Christian Greek and Latin Literature: A Literary History*. Vol. 1. 2 vols. Translated by Matthew J. O'Connell. Peabody, MA: Hendrickson, 2005.
Moss, Candida R. "On the Dating of Polycarp: Rethinking the Place of the *Martyrdom of Polycarp* in the History of Christianity." *EC* 1 (2010) 539–74.
Muddiman, John. "The Church in Ephesians, *2 Clement*, and *The Shepherd of Hermas*." In *Trajectories through the New Testament and the Apostolic Fathers*, edited by Andrew F. Gregory and Christopher M. Tuckett, 107–21. NTAF. Oxford: Oxford University Press, 2005.
Norris, Richard A. "The Apostolic and Sub-Apostolic Writings: The New Testament and the Apostolic Fathers." In *The Cambridge History of Early Christian Literature*, edited by Frances M. Young et al., 11–14. Cambridge: Cambridge University Press, 2004.
Paget, James Carleton, and Judith Lieu, eds. *Christianity in the Second Century: Themes and Development*. Cambridge: Cambridge University Press, 2017.
Parvis, Paul. "*2 Clement* and the Meaning of the Christian Homily." In *The Writings of the Apostolic Fathers*, edited by Paul Foster, 32–41. London: T. & T. Clark, 2007.
Perrin, Nicholas. *Thomas, the Other Gospel*. Louisville: Westminster John Knox, 2007.
Petersen, William L. "Patristic Biblical Quotations and Method: Four Changes to Lightfoot's Edition of *2 Clement*." *VC* 60 (2006) 389–419.
———. "Textual Traditions Examined: What the Text of the Apostolic Fathers Tells Us About the Text of the New Testament in the Second Century." In *The Reception of the New Testament in the Apostolic Fathers*, edited by Andrew F. Gregory and Christopher M. Tuckett, 29–46. NTAF. Oxford: Oxford University Press, 2005.
Porter, Stanley E. *Sacred Tradition in the New Testament: Tracing Old Testament Themes in the Gospels and Epistles*. Grand Rapids: Baker Academic, 2016.
Porter, Stanley E., and Sean A. Adams, eds. *Paul and the Ancient Letter Form*. PAST 6. Leiden: Brill, 2010.
Pratscher, Wilhelm, ed. *The Apostolic Fathers: An Introduction*. Waco, TX: Baylor University Press, 2010.
———. "The Corpus of the Apostolic Fathers." In *The Apostolic Fathers: An Introduction*, edited by Wilhelm Pratscher, 1–6. Waco, TX: Baylor University Press, 2010.
———. "The Motivations of Ethos in 2 Clement." In *Identity, Ethics, and Ethos in the New Testament*, edited by Jan G. van der Watt, 597–610. BZNW 141. Berlin: de Gruyter 2006.

———. "Die Rezeption des Neuen Testament bei den Apostolischen Vätern." *TLZ* 137 (2012) 139–52.

Richardson, Cyril. *Early Christian Fathers*. LCC 1. London: SCM, 1953.

Robinson, Thomas A. *Ignatius of Antioch and the Parting of the Ways: Early Jewish-Christian Relations*. Peabody, MA: Hendrickson, 2009.

Rothschild, Clare K. "'Belittling' or 'Undervaluing' in 2 Clem. 1:1–2?" In *New Essays on the Apostolic Fathers*, 111–24. WUNT 375. Tübingen: Mohr/Siebeck, 2017.

———. *New Essays on the Apostolic Fathers*. WUNT 375. Tübingen: Mohr/Siebeck, 2017.

———. "On the Invention of *Patres Apostolici*." In *New Essays on the Apostolic Fathers*, 7–34. WUNT 375. Tübingen: Mohr/Siebeck, 2017.

———. "Sailing Past the Competition: Euergetism in 2 Clement 7." In *New Essays on the Apostolic Fathers*, 143–57. WUNT 375. Tübingen: Mohr/Siebeck, 2017.

———. "Two *dispositiones* in 2 Clement 2." In *New Essays on the Apostolic Fathers*, 125–42. WUNT 375. Tübingen: Mohr/Siebeck, 2017.

Rudolph, Kurt. *Gnosis: The Nature and History of Gnosticism*. Translation edited by Robert McLachlan Wilson. San Francisco: Harper & Row, 1983.

Seitz, Oscar J. F. "Antecedents and Signification of the Term ΔΙΨΥΧΟΣ." *JBL* 66 (1947) 211–19.

Skarsaune, Oskar. "Ethic Discourse in Early Christianity." In *Christianity in the Second Century: Themes and Development*, edited by James Carleton Paget and Judith Lieu, 250–64. Cambridge: Cambridge University Press, 2017.

Stanton, Graham R. "2 Clement VII and the Origin of the Document." *Classica et Mediaevalia* 28 (1967) 314–20.

Stark, Alonzo Rosecrans. *The Christology in the Apostolic Fathers*. Chicago: University of Chicago Press, 1912.

Starr, James, and Troels Engberg-Pedersen, eds. *Early Christian Paraenesis in Context*. BZNW 125. Berlin: de Gruyter, 2004.

Steenberg, M. C. "Irenaeus on Scripture, *Graphe*, and the Status of *Hermas*." *SVTQ* 53 (2009) 29–66.

Stegemann, Christa. "Herkunft und Entstehung des sogenannten zweiten Klemensbriefes." PhD diss., University of Bonn, 1974.

Stewart-Sykes, Alistair. *From Prophecy to Preaching: A Search for the Origin of the Christian Homily*. VCSup 59. Leiden: Brill, 2001.

Still, Todd D., and David E. Wilhite, eds. *The Apostolic Fathers and Paul*. Pauline and Patristic Scholars in Debate 2. London: Bloomsbury T. & T. Clark, 2017.

Stowers, Stanley K. *Letter Writing in Greco-Roman Antiquity*. LEC. Philadelphia: Westminster, 1986.

Streeter, Burnett H. *The Primitive Church*. London: Macmillan, 1929.

Stroker, William D. "Agrapha." In *ABD* 1:92–95.

———. *Extracanonical Sayings of Jesus*. Sources for Biblical Study 18. Atlanta: Society of Biblical Literature, 1989.

Taylor, C. "The Homily of Pseudo-Clement." *Journal of Philology* 28 (1903) 195–208.

Thiselton, Anthony C. *The Holy Spirit in Biblical Teaching, through the Centuries, and Today*. Grand Rapids: Eerdmans, 2013.

Torrance, Thomas F. *The Doctrine of Grace in the Apostolic Fathers*. London: Oliver & Boyd, 1948.

Trevett, Christine. *Christian Women and the Time of the Apostolic Fathers (AD c 80–160): Corinth, Rome and Asia Minor*. Cardiff: University of Wales Press, 2006.

Trigg, Joseph W. "The Apostolic Fathers and Apologists," in *A History of Biblical Interpretation*, edited by Alan J. Hauser and Duane Frederick Watson 1:304–33. 3 vols. Grand Rapids: Eerdmans, 2003.

Tuckett, Christopher M. *2 Clement: Introduction, Text, and Commentary*. Oxford Apostolic Fathers. Oxford: Oxford University Press, 2012.

———. "2 Clement and the New Testament." In *Intertextuality in the Second Century*, edited by D. Jeffrey Bingham and Clayton N. Jefford, 24–36. BibAC 11. Leiden: Brill, 2016.

———. "Lightfoot's Text of *2 Clement*: A Response to W. L. Petersen." *VC* 64 (2010) 501–19.

Tugwell, Simon. *The Apostolic Fathers*. Outstanding Christian Thinkers. Harrisburg, PA: Morehouse, 1989.

———. *The Apostolic Fathers*. Outstanding Christian Thinkers. London: Continuum 2002.

Unnik, Willem C. van. "Die Rucksicht auf die Reaktion der Night-Christen als Motiv in der altchristlichen Paranese." In *Judentum, Urchristentum, Kirche: Festschrift für Joachim Jeremias*, edited by Walther Eltester, 221–34. BZNW 26. Berlin: Töpelmann, 1960.

———. "The Interpretation of 2 Clement 15, 5." *VC* 27 (1973) 29–34.

Varner, William. *The Way of the Didache: The First Christian Handbook*. Lanham, MD: University Press of America, 2007.

Vries, Johannes de, and Martin Karrer, eds. *Textual History and the Reception of Scripture in Early Christianity*. Septuagint and Cognate Studies 60. Atlanta: Society of Biblical Literature, 2013.

Wake, William. *The Genuine Epistles of the Apostolical Fathers: S. Barnabas, S. Ignatius, S. Clement, S. Polycarp, the Shepherd of Hermas, and the Martyrdoms of Ignatius and St. Polycarp*. London: Ric. Sare, 1693.

Wallace, Daniel B. *Greek Grammar beyond the Basics*. Grand Rapids: Zondervan, 1996.

Wallace, Daniel B., et al., eds. *A Reader's Lexicon of the Apostolic Fathers*. Grand Rapids: Kregel Academic, 2013.

Warns, Rüdiger. "Untersuchungen zum 2. Clemensbrief." PhD diss., University of Marburg, 1989.

Weima, Jeffrey A. D. *Paul the Ancient Letter Writer: An Introduction to Epistolary Analysis*. Grand Rapids: Baker Academic, 2016.

White, James L. *Light from Ancient Letters*. Foundations and Facets. Philadelphia: Fortress, 1986.

Whitenton, Michael R. "After ΠΙΣΤΙΣ ΧΡΙΣΤΟΥ: Neglected Evidence from the Apostolic Fathers." *JTS* 61 (2010) 82–109.

Wilhite, Shawn J. *The Didache: A Commentary*. AFCS. Eugene, OR: Cascade, 2019.

Williams, Michael Allen. *Rethinking "Gnosticism": An Argument for Dismantling a Dubious Category*. Princeton: Princeton University Press, 1996.

Yonge, C. D., ed. *Works of Philo*. New updated ed. Peabody, MA: Hendrickson, 1991.

Young, Stephen E. *Jesus Tradition in the Apostolic Fathers: Their Explicit Appeals to the Words of Jesus in Light of Orality Studies*. WUNT 2/311. Tübingen: Mohr/Siebeck, 2011

Zahn, Theodore. *Ignatius von Antiochien*. Gotha: Perthes, 1873.

Zetterholm, Magnus, and Samuel Byrskog, eds. *The Making of Christianity: Conflicts, Contacts, and Constructions; Essays in Honor of Bengt Holmberg*. ConBNT 47. Winona Lake, IN: Eisenbrauns, 2012.

Author Index

Aasgaard, Reidar, 144n6, 155

Baarda, Tjitze, 107n121, 107n123, 108n127, 109n128, 109n132, 155
Baasland, Ernst, 26, 26n14, 27, 155
Barclay, J. M. G., 43n23, 155
Bartlet, J. Vernon, 33n13, 33n14, 104n16, 155
Batovici, Dan, ixn5, 155
Bauckham, Richard, 37n6, 155
Benecke, P. V. M., 55, 55n18, 104n116, 155
Bensly, R. L., 155
Bingham, D. Jeffrey, xn6, 155
Bounds, Christopher Todd, xiin29, 155
Boyarin, Daniel, 39n10, 155
Brakke, David, 23, 23n97, 23n99, 23n100, 23n101, 24n106, 155
Brannan, Rick, 7n19, 51n4, 55n19, 67n16, 67n17, 75n35, 127n14, 129n17, 130n25, 155
Brummel, Lincoln H., 7n19, 156
Bultmann, Rudolf, 42, 42n18, 43, 45n33, 101n104, 156
Byrskog, Samuel, 46n38, 162

Crafer, T. W., 8n28, 156
Crowe, Brandon D., 106n119, 156
Cullmann, Oscar, 91, 91n77, 156

De Wet, C. L., 125, 125n6, 125n7, 156
deSilva, David A., 43n23, 156
De Vries, Johannes, 29n5, 162
Donfried, Karl P., 4, 4n12, 5n13, 14, 14n50, 15, 16, 16n54, 16n56, 17, 17n57, 20, 20n78, 22n89, 22n91, 22n92, 22n93, 27, 27n116, 27n117, 29, 29n2, 32, 32n11, 33n12, 34n18, 35, 35n21, 35n22, 36n4, 41n14, 53n12, 54, 54n13, 54n14, 59n26, 62n2, 66, 66n12, 67n13, 69n22, 69n24, 73n29, 73n32, 75, 75n36, 77, 77n38, 80n43, 84n59, 87, 87n65, 89n69, 92, 92n78, 92n79, 95, 95n85, 98, 98n99, 99, 99n100, 101n106, 107n121, 107n123, 108n127, 109, 109n133, 112, 112n142, 113, 113n143, 113n144, 113n145, 114n147, 115, 115n149, 119, 119n160, 120n167, 126n11, 131n30, 135n36, 137n43, 137n44, 138, 138n45, 143, 143n2, 143n3, 144, 144n4, 145n12, 156
Downs, David J., 41n15, 130, 130n26, 131n29, 132, 132n32, 132n33, 133n34, 156
Drobner, Hubertus, 4n4, 156
Dunn, James D. G., 45n32, 156

AUTHOR INDEX

Ehrman, Bart D., x, xi, xin16, 3n1, 3n3, 4, 4n6, 7, 7n24, 8, 8n26, 8n27, 12n43, 16n55, 17n60, 18n65, 36n3, 51n4, 53n10, 63n4, 67, 67n16, 67n17, 75n34, 82n47, 89n71, 90, 90n72, 93n80, 94n82, 104n116, 107n123, 110n136, 119, 119n162, 119n164, 125n5, 127n14, 128, 128n17, 130n25, 151n31, 152, 152n38, 153, 156
Engberg-Pedersen, Troels, 21n86, 161
Eusebius, Pamphilius, xx, 9, 9n33, 10, 11, 17, 156
Evans, Robert, 29n5, 30n7, 35, 35n20, 156

Foster, Paul, ixn3, 32n10, 157
Freese, J. H., 10n37, 157
Frend, W. H. C., 12n43, 157

Gallagher, Edmon L., 10n35, 157
Gathercole, Simon, 77n37, 157
Goodspeed, Edgar J., 11n41, 38n8, 157
Graham, Holt H., 4, 4n10, 36n2, 55n21, 65n9, 80n45, 88n66, 99n102, 107n121, 117n152, 124, 124n2, 127n13, 146n15, 147n17, 149n23, 157
Grant, Robert M., ixn4, 4, 4n10, 36n2, 55n21, 65n9, 80n45, 88n66, 99n102, 107n121, 117n152, 124n2, 127n13, 140, 140n48, 146n15, 147n17, 149n23, 157
Gregory, Andrew F., xiin22, 8n29, 33, 33n15, 55n18, 107n121, 156, 157, 160

Hagner, Donald A., 101, 102n107, 152n36, 157
Harnack, Adolph von, 11, 11n41, 137, 157
Harris, J. Rendell, 12, 12n442, 69, 69n23, 157
Hartog, Paul A., xn15, xiin24, 105n117, 157

Hogan, Pauline Nigh, 109n130, 110n134, 158
Holmberg, Bengt, 46n38, 158
Holmes, Michael W., xi, xin16, 3n3, 4n4, 8, 8n25, 12n43, 16n55, 18n65, 50, 50n1, 51n5, 53n10, 63n4, 67, 67n15, 67n17, 68n19, 75n35, 78, 82n47, 87n64, 89n71, 93n80, 94n82, 104n116, 107n123, 110n136, 112n139, 115n148, 118n159, 119, 119n162, 127n14, 129n17, 130n25, 131n31, 151n31, 158
Hurtado, Larry W., 37n6, 39, 39n11, 158

Jeremias, Joachim, 107n122, 158, 162
Jefford, Clayton N., ixn1, ixn2, xn12, xn14, xin16, xin19, xin21, xiin22, 11n38, 17n60, 18n66, 27, 27n118, 28n119, 157, 158, 162
Johnson, Luke Timothy, 21, 21n86, 158

Käsemann, Ernst, 144n5, 158
Kelhoffer, James A., vii, xvi, xvii, 5, 20, 20n76, 20n77, 20n79, 21n80, 21n81, 24, 24n105, 24n108, 26, 26n113, 35, 35n19, 42, 42n20, 43, 43n21, 43n22, 44, 44n27, 44n28, 44n29, 44n30, 44n31, 51, 51n6, 58, 58n24, 59n25, 59n28, 62, 63n3, 83, 83n55, 91, 91n76, 93, 93n81, 99, 99n101, 120n165, 148n22, 149n22, 150, 150n27, 158
Kenyon, Frederick G., 159
King, Karen L., 159
Klauck, Hans-Josef, 18n62, 159
Knopf, D. Rudolph, 84n58, 117n154, 121, 121n173, 159
Koester, Helmut, xin21, 22n89, 159
Krüger, Gustav, 159
Kruger, Michael J., 39n12, 159

AUTHOR INDEX

Lake, Kirsopp, 51n4, 66n11, 89, 90n72, 93n80, 119, 119n163, 130n25, 136n39, 151n31, 156
Lampe, G. W. H., xxii, 41n15, 84, 84n60, 94n83, 140n49, 145n11, 159
Lieu, Judith M., 46n37, 46n38, 157, 159, 160, 161
Lightfoot, Joseph B., x, xn15, xi, 4, 4n9, 6n14, 6n15, 6n16, 7, 7n18, 7n20, 7n21, 7n23, 8, 8n31, 10n36, 12n46, 13, 13n46, 14, 14n47, 14n49, 15n53, 18n64, 18n65, 25, 31, 34n18, 36n1, 43, 43n24, 53n10, 63n4, 64, 64n8, 67n14, 70n26, 72, 72n28, 73, 73n30, 82n47, 84n59, 93n80, 94n82, 97, 97n91, 102, 102n108, 102n109, 103n113, 107n123, 117, 117n155, 118n156, 119, 119n162, 120n167, 121n170, 121n172, 127n13, 129, 129n17, 129n18, 129n19, 129n22, 130n25, 130n27, 137, 137n42, 140, 140n50, 144n8, 145n13, 149n24, 151n32, 159
Lindemann, Andreas, xiin23, 4, 4n8, 12n45, 25n110, 26n112, 52n8, 57, 58n22, 59, 59n25, 59n27, 64n6, 67n14, 69n22, 73n30, 78n41, 80n44, 84n59, 88n67, 88n68, 97n92, 97n93, 102n107, 103n114, 104n116, 107n121, 107n123, 109n131, 110n135, 113n144, 120n168, 126n9, 127n13, 129n21, 130n23, 136n39, 138n46, 144n8, 147n19, 150n28, 159
Longenecker, Richard, 89n70, 159
Lookadoo, Jonathan, xiin24, 160
Lührmann, Dieter, 73, 73n31, 160

Martin, E. G., 102, 103n110, 160
McGuckin, John A., xiin27, 160
Meade, John D., 10n35, 157

Moreschini, Claudio, 26n114, 45n33, 160
Moss, Candida R., ixn1, 160
Muddiman, John, 118n157, 120n165, 160

Norelli, Enrico, 26n114, 45n33, 160
Norris, Richard A., xiin22, 160

Paget, James Carleton, 46n37, 157, 159, 160, 161
Parvis, Paul, 4n5, 18n64, 25n110, 36n4, 151n29, 153, 153n39, 160
Perrin, Nicholas, 77n37, 160
Petersen, William, 8, 8n29, 160, 162
Porter, Stanley E., 18n62, 29n1, 160
Pratscher, Wilhelm, xin17, xiin22, 4, 4n7, 12, 12n43, 16n55, 18, 18n63, 18n64, 22, 22n88, 22n90, 22n91, 22n94, 22n95, 23, 25, 25n109, 26n111, 27, 29, 29n4, 31n9, 36n1, 37, 37n5, 41n16, 45, 45n34, 45n35, 45n36, 63n5, 80n46, 109n131, 160

Richardson, Cyril C., 136n39, 161
Rothschild, Clare K., 15, 15n52, 51, 51n6, 51n7, 83, 83n51, 83n52, 83n53, 83n54, 83n56, 161
Rudolph, Kurt, 22, 22n96, 23n97, 161

Seitz, Oscar J. F., 161
Stanton, Graham R., 83n50, 160, 161
Stark, Alonzo Rosecrans, xiin27, 161
Starr, James, 21n86, 161
Stegemann, Christa, 17n59, 161
Stewart-Sykes, Alistair, 18n68, 161
Stowers, Stanley K., 18n62, 161
Streeter, B. H., 161
Stroker, William D., 107n22, 161

Taylor, C., 161
Thiselton, Anthony C., 38n7, 161
Torrance, Thomas F., xiin29, 42, 42n19, 45n33, 150n26, 161

Tuckett, Christopher M., xiin22, xvii, 4, 4n11, 7, 7n17, 7n22, 8, 8n29, 8n30, 8n31, 11, 11n39, 11n40, 12, 12n43, 12n44, 14n48, 17, 17n58, 17n60, 19, 19n70, 19n72, 20, 21, 21n87, 23, 24n103, 24n104, 26, 26n115, 27, 29, 29n3, 33, 33n15, 34, 34n16, 34n17, 34n18, 36n1, 38, 38n9, 39, 40n13, 41n17, 45n33, 50n2, 50n3, 53n10, 54n17, 55n18, 55n20, 58, 58n23, 59n25, 59n26, 60n30, 64n7, 65n10, 67n14, 68, 68n20, 69n21, 69n22, 69n24, 70, 70n25, 73n29, 74n33, 78, 78n40, 80n44, 82n48, 83n50, 84n58, 84n59, 88n67, 90n73, 91, 91n74, 94, 94n84, 97n90, 97n93, 98n97, 102, 102n107, 102n109, 103n111, 103n112, 104n116, 105, 105n118, 107, 107n120, 107n121, 107n124, 108n125, 108n126, 108n127, 109n129, 109n132, 112, 112n141, 112n142, 113n144, 115n150, 117n153, 119n161, 120, 120n169, 121n171, 126n9, 126n12, 129n17, 129n20, 129n23, 130n25, 130n28, 135n37, 136n39, 139n47, 144n7, 144n8, 145n12, 147n18, 150n25, 150n28, 151n30, 151n33, 152, 152n37, 156, 157, 159, 160, 162

Tugwell, Simon, xin19, 18, 19n69, 20, 23, 23n102, 144n9, 162

Unnik, Willem C. van, 112n142, 127, 127n15, 162

Varner, William, xvi, xviin1, xviii, 162

Wallace, Daniel B., xiin25, xviii, 152n34, 162
Warns, Rüdiger, 22n89, 162
Wayment, Thomas A., 7n19, 156
Weima, Jeffrey A. D., 18n62, 162
White, James L., 18n62, 162
Whitenton, Michael R., xiin29, 162
Wilhite, Shawn J., xiin23, xiii, 3n3, 30, 30n6, 162
Williams, Michael Allen, 23, 23n98, 24n106, 162

Yonge, C. D., 162
Young, Stephen E., xiin23, 162

Zetterholm, Magnus, 46n38, 162

www.ingramcontent.com/pod-product-compliance
Lightning Source LLC
Chambersburg PA
CBHW031429150426
43191CB00006B/453